To

———————————————————

From

———————————————————

Date

———————————————————

Visit Christian Art Gifts website at www.christianartgifts.com.

Daily Hope for a Woman's Heart

Published by Christian Art Gifts, Inc.

Daily Hope for a Woman's Heart © 2021 by Sarah Beth Marr. All rights reserved.

Designed by Alyssa Montalto

Cover and interior images used under license from Shutterstock.com.

ISBN 978-1-64272-848-4
     978-1-64272-652-7

Printed in China

28 27 26 25 24 23
12 11 10 9 8 7 6 5 4 3

DAILY HOPE
—FOR A—

Woman's Heart

BACK PORCH REFLECTIONS
ON GOD'S WORD

SARAH BETH MARR

January

GOD SEES ALL THE
PAGES OF YOUR LIFE

All the days ordained for me were written in
Your book before one of them came to be.

Psalm 139:16, NIV

God sees all the pages of your beautiful life. He has written your marvelous story, and day by day He unfolds a new page. Day by day He draws you close to His heart with His unfailing love. Day by day He leads your footsteps, whispering to your heart, *This is the way, walk in it* (Isaiah 30:21). Day by day and sunrise to sunset He relishes your company and holds your hand.

I know that sometimes you yearn to see the whole story. You wonder how all the chapters will fit together and sometimes you feel unclear if you're even walking in the right direction. Rest assured that God understands how you feel. Know today that He delights in helping you navigate your life. He will use all the ups and downs to draw you close to His heart and to shape you into all He created you to be. Trust Him with your story and believe that you are divinely led by Him. When you feel a little unsure on your journey, come back to the truth that every one of your days was written in God's book before one of them came to be. Instead of stressing over the details, focus on enjoying the One Who leads you. He has more good than you can imagine in store for you. He sees all the pages of your life, and He lovingly leads you.

Lord, help me to trust You with each page, each chapter, and each
season of my life and story. Thank You that You lead me day by day.

Today may you trust God in a new way with your beautiful life.
May you look to Him to guide you, and may you live with
expectancy and joy as you lean on Him and watch Him work.

A YEAR OF GRACE

But He gives more grace.
James 4:6

The beginning of January is a time we typically like to evaluate our lives, to check in with our hearts, and to really think about how we are investing our time. It's a time to press the restart button on our lives and a chance to do things differently. But sometimes setting New Year's resolutions overwhelms us because there are so many things we want to do better. I wonder if we put too much pressure on ourselves to change or to improve ourselves. What if this year, instead of striving so hard to change, we instead challenge ourselves to embrace who we already are? What if instead of strict goals and impossible standards, we set ourselves up for a year of grace? Maybe we can focus on the little things that make a big difference in our overall sense of well-being.

Here's what my list of little things might look like:

- I need to exercise in a way that's fun for me and gentle on my body. Exercise simply needs to be something I enjoy, not something that punishes my body.
- I need to take long breaks from screens and the internet for my soul to have room to breathe.
- I need to slow my pace and take time to enjoy the day instead of just plowing through it.
- And most importantly, I need to hang out with Jesus. I need to read His Word so that it is the strongest influence in my life. I need to go on long walks and sit on the back porch so I can hear His voice.

What if we took the pressure off of ourselves to become better and instead celebrated who we already are and how far God has already brought us? What if this was a year of grace?

Lord, today I trade in the pressure to be better for the grace to
just be who I already am. Thank You for Your sweet grace.

*Have a date with God. Talk to Him about your
year of grace and celebrate who you already are.*

TRUST THAT GOD IS WITH YOU

Have I not commanded you? Be strong and courageous.
Do not be frightened, and do not be dismayed,
for the Lord your God is with you wherever you go.

Joshua 1:9

Just as the Lord spoke to Joshua, the Lord speaks to you. Just as the Lord was in control of Joshua's circumstances in the Old Testament, God is in control of your life. The Lord is leading you day by day. He is constantly at work in your heart and in your life. And that is why you can have hope even on the darkest days. Know that the Lord is moving in your midst, providing for you and guiding you, even though it doesn't feel like it sometimes.

God calls us to be strong and courageous, to trust Him as He works in our lives and in our circumstances.

Today, hold on to these truths:

- God still speaks today.
- God encourages us to not fear, but instead be courageous.
- God always provides, even when we can't see it.
- God is always with us.

Today, listen for God's still, quiet voice. Choose faith over fear, gratitude over discouragement, strength over unbelief, and prayer over worry. Notice how God is providing for you today, and know that He is personally watching over and guiding you through every detail of your life.

Lord, help me to trust that You are with me in this day.
Help me to be strong and courageous as I lean on Your presence.

Today may you feel God's presence in a fresh way
as you trust that He is with you wherever you go.

LIVING WITH JOY
AND PURPOSE

I'm trying my best to walk in the way of integrity,
especially in my own home. But I need Your help!

Psalm 101:2, TPT

You are a woman who loves God and desires to walk with Him. You want to lead a life of purpose. You want your life to reflect the love of God to others. You want God to shine through you.

And He does—He shines brightly through you! But some days you don't feel it, you can't see it, and you don't know it. A lot of days, you're just struggling to stay focused on the things that need to get done. You feel like you're being carried by the wind of the pace of life. You're running through your days on autopilot, but you feel like you are lacking purpose, aim, or meaning.

Maybe self-doubt, perfectionism, distraction, insecurity, comparison, or fear have a hold on your heart. They're steering the boat; they're in the front seat. Joy, peace, faith, steadfastness, hope, and grace got lost somewhere in the back seat of your heart. But it doesn't have to be that way.

David was a man after God's own heart, but he was also flawed, imperfect, remorseful, and at times really frustrated with himself. He strove to follow God, but often he went back and forth between following God with all his heart and following his own sinful desires. The Psalms contain David's anthems of crying out to the Lord, praising the One Who showered him with grace, and renewing his desire to walk with the Lord.

If even David needed God's help to keep his desires in line with God's will, how much more do we need it? We need God's help to live with joy, peace, faith, steadfastness, hope, and grace. We need God's help to rise above self-doubt, perfectionism, distraction, insecurity, comparison, or fear.

Tell God about your desire to live a life that pleases Him. Ask for His help. And know that He's already shining through you, regardless of your mess-ups or hang-ups.

Lord, remind me today that You live in me and are shining
through me even on the days when I feel like I'm stumbling.

May you feel a fresh wave of God's grace today as you bring
before God your desire to walk in faith with Him day by day.

GRACE FOR YOUR CURRENT SEASON

The Lord reigns; He is robed in majesty … Yes, the world
is established; it shall never be moved. Your throne is
established from of old; You are from everlasting.

Psalm 93:1-2

Remember today that the Lord reigns. He is always on His throne, no matter what storm you are walking through. The world He created is established; it's in His hands. Like the old sweet song says, "He's got the whole world in His hands." Jesus is still on His throne, and He is here with you, in your world, moving in your circumstances. Jesus is King above all, in all, and through all—just like He always has been.

Jesus sees you. He hasn't left your side. He knows that sometimes you feel shaky. He knows you feel anxious and worried. But you are His beloved daughter. He's speaking to you throughout your day with whispers of grace, of love, of hope, of comfort. He will carry you through your current season. Let Him be your shelter and home for your heart.

1. **Choose God first.** Be gentle on your heart in this season, and give it the nourishment it needs for the day by fueling up on God's Word and promises before you do anything else. Let Him take the weight of your worry by bringing your heart to His.

2. **Choose prayer.** Jesus said, "Pray about everything" (Philippians 4:6, NLT). Prayer calms our hearts, soothes our worries, connects us with God, and moves the hand of God in our circumstances. Choose to bring Him everything.

3. **Choose soul care.** Be tender with your soul. Unplug from the news and the phone for a while each day. Get outside, take a bubble bath, fuel your body with good meals, hydrate your body with lots of water, and move your body with exercise. Read, rest, and recover from the busyness of life out on your back porch. Let yourself linger with God. Take a nap. Create something. Cook a meal with music on. Do what you need to do to take care of yourself.

Lord, thank You for Your grace for my everyday life. Thank You that
You hold the whole world and my life in Your hands. Help me to rest
in the truth that You are on the throne in every season of my life.

May you walk through this season with a deeper
awareness of God's grace and love and a deeper
security in your calling as His beloved daughter.

WHEN YOU NEED PEACE

He who dwells in the shelter of the Most High
will abide in the shadow of the Almighty.

Psalm 91:1

I'm settled out on my back porch, putting my fingertips to the keyboard. My puppy, Shaka, is lounging nearby, taking his third or fourth nap of the day. The birds are chirping, swooping from tree to tree, eagerly stockpiling their materials for nest-building. The squirrels are heartily leaping from one branch to the next. Our garden fountain melodically plays its tune of calming, flowing water, like a sound machine that soothes any uneasiness I feel in my heart. According to the birds and the squirrels, life is as happy as can be.

I know sometimes you feel angst and uneasiness rising up in your heart.

Remember today that God wants to be your shelter. He wants to carry you through your day. He wants to be the One you turn to. He wants to calm the angst in your heart. He wants to soothe the worry, mend your anxious thoughts, and refresh your tired soul. He desires for you to rest in the shelter of His presence.

Follow the example of the birds and the squirrels. Don't worry about the details of your life. God wants you to rest and let Him work out all the circumstances of your life for good. Like the garden fountain, He wants to keep His living water flowing through you as you look to Him daily for peace, provision, and guidance.

So today, when you feel the angst building, find your back porch and take a breath. Watch the birds. Look at nature. Listen for God's still, small voice. Listen for the One Who wants to be your shelter. Abide and live in the shelter of God's company.

⚜

Jesus, I look to You for the peace I crave. Help me to run to You for the shelter I need. Please wrap Your calming presence around my heart as I walk through my day. Thank You that You never leave me.

Today, may you experience God's peace deep in
your heart as you remember that He is sovereign
over your life and is taking care of every detail.

GUARD THAT SWEET HEART OF YOURS

Above all else, guard your heart,
for everything you do flows from it.

Proverbs 4:23, NIV

I know sometimes you look around and see gals doing big things for God. You wonder if you're doing enough. You wonder if you're spiritual enough. You wonder if what you do matters. You wonder if anyone sees you.

Or maybe you feel left out. Maybe you feel unnoticed. Maybe you feel alone. Maybe you feel out of the loop.

Today, I want to simply pour some truth into your heart in case you need a little glimpse of God's sweet grace and relentless love toward you.

You don't have to do or be enough. What you do matters—the big, the small, the in-between things, all of it.

God has adopted you as His daughter. He notices every little thought, every little nuance, every little thing about you. He sees you in the carpool line, He sees you on your messy-bun-and-no-makeup days, He sees you when you pray in your slippers, He sees you as you sip your coffee. He delights in you as you do the everyday things. Don't let the world tell you otherwise. Don't let the successes, victories, fame, fortune, glitz, and glamour of others steal your joy.

Operate from a place in your heart that says you are known, seen, and loved instead of from a place of wondering if you're enough. Operate from a place in your heart that is secure in God's love, content in His provision, and strong in His truth. Guard that precious heart of yours by keeping your eyes on your beautiful path.

Lord, help me to keep my heart focused on You instead of looking to the world for direction. Be my heart's true north. Thank You for the beautiful path that You have me on. Help me to savor and enjoy where You have me.

May you guard your heart by keeping focused on the Lord.
May you see your path as God-given and enjoy
the beauty of where God has you right now.

EXPERIENCE A MORE PEACEFUL MORNING

Let the morning bring me word of Your unfailing love, for I have put my trust in You. Show me the way I should go, for to You I entrust my life.

Psalm 143:8, NIV

When you wake up in the morning, does your mind swirl with dates, to-dos, and worries? Does the pull of your phone draw you away from a peaceful morning? Does your email inbox suck you in and disturb your sense of calm? I want to invite you to experience a more peaceful morning. This will be a gift to your soul, a relief to your weary heart, and a way to start your day with more peace and strength. Jesus wants to pour peace into your heart before the day begins so that you:

- Experience peace instead of anxiety.
- Hear His voice throughout the day instead of the noise of the world.
- Have a newfound trust in the Lord.
- Walk in faith from being rooted in His Word.

Here are a few tips to help you get God's Word into your heart before the busyness of the day begins:

Use the power of sticky notes. A little forethought goes a long way and will help you remember to choose quietness over the noise. Write something like "Word first," and stick it right on your coffee maker or on your nightstand so that you will see it first thing when you wake up.

Have your quiet time materials ready to go. Help your morning self out a bit by taking a few minutes the night before to set out your Bible, a journal, pens, a devotional book, or whatever you use for your quiet time. Have a blanket ready and set up a cozy spot that you'll look forward to sitting in. Make a plan for what you will read in the morning.

Keep the phone far, far away! This is important! The saying is so true—*out of sight, out of mind.* Let the phone spend the night in a desk drawer or on a charger in a room you will not go into first thing in the morning.

Ask God to give you the strength to choose Him. You don't have to do this in your own strength. As your feet hit the floor in the morning, whisper a simple prayer in your heart: *Lord, help me to choose You first.*

Choose quiet moments with God first thing in the morning, and trust that the rest of your busy day will fall into place.

Lord, give me strength to choose You first each morning.

May your back porch or your cozy living room chair be the first place you run to each day so that you can experience the fullest measure of God's peace every morning.

SLOWING DOWN IS MAGIC

Be still, and know that I am God.
Psalm 46:10

As we slow down and unplug from the distractions, not rushing through our time in the Word, the Word comes alive and fuels us for the day ahead.

But our week comes at us fast! There are places to be, people to see, errands to run, kiddos to carpool, jobs to tend to—not to mention emails to respond to, text messages to go through, and calendars to work through.

Breathe. Just breathe.

When you take a second to slow your pace, unplug from the world, and tune into God and His beautiful Word, time will slow. God will feel nearer.

Your heart will settle down. Your anxiety will ease. Your perspective will shift.

It's in the slowing down that we find God. It's in the unplugging that we hear His sacred voice. As we bring our hearts to His, the Word comes alive and He speaks just what we need through the pages of Scripture.

Slowing down is magic. Slowing down gives Jesus space to draw us back to Himself.

So today, take a cozy moment. Wherever you are—take a pause. Take a breath. Ponder the gift of God's company. And breathe in the gift of Jesus' presence. He's right here with you. Let His Word come alive to you as you soak in slow, unplugged, quiet moments with Him.

**Lord, remind me to take some moments of quietness and
stillness with You today. Help me to linger with You and
find jewels of truth to hang on to from Your beautiful Word.**

*May you feel the delight of God's presence as you slow
down and meet with Him in the quiet moments of your day.*

DEAR SISTER, HOLD ON TO HOPE

Rejoice in hope.

Romans 12:12

Sometimes God feels really far away. There are seasons in life where darkness paints a shadow over the light, and you wonder when the shadow will lift.

You wonder if God hears your prayers. You wonder if you can even pray. You wonder if God will come through. You wonder if your circumstances are too deep. You wonder if it's too late for a miracle.

I've been there at times. But even still, I know the darkness will lift. I know God hears our prayers. I know I can pray even when my heart feels dry. I know God always comes through. I know my circumstances aren't too much or too big for Him. I know, deep in my bones—although sometimes it's hard to believe—that it's never too late for a miracle.

Oftentimes, I have to *choose* to believe His truth for my life because I have a hard time feeling it. Whatever your current darkness is, dear sister, please hold on to hope even when it feels hopeless.

Hold on to God even when He feels far away. **Trust** in the One Who formed the world, the One Who formed you. **Believe** that God sees and cares about the details of your life. **Know** that God has not left you. **Wait** in expectation for the miracle you need. **Rest** as you wait, knowing He's got you completely covered. And **pray**. Never stop praying, because your prayers move the hand and heart of God.

Hold on, Trust, Believe, Know, Wait, Rest, Pray.

Lord, help me to keep preaching truth to my heart even when I'm having trouble believing it. Remind me to keep turning to You. Thank You that You never leave me—not once. Thank You that there is always hope because of You.

May you hold on to hope today as you look to the Lord.
May you feel the love of God in a fresh way and
sense His nearness and presence in your life.

A REMINDER THAT GOD IS IN CONTROL

But You, LORD my God, brought my life up from the pit.
Jonah 2:6, NIV

Sometimes a gal just needs a reminder that God is in control. She needs a reminder that God sees her, knows her, loves her, and is with her—always.

I pray that today you will know, deep in your heart, that God is faithfully guiding your path and tenderly steering your heart. Even when you can't see what's ahead. Even when things feel impossible. Even when you're unsure.

I pray today that you would know that God sees you. God knows you. God loves you. And God is with you.

Always. Every day. Even today, right this moment.

We all have those question marks in our heart where we wonder how God will move, we wonder how God will answer, and we wonder *if* God will answer. Doubts cloud our faith, fog up our focus on God, and stir up our anxiety.

But when we remember Who God is, our doubts lose their hold. Our God is the One Who rescued Daniel from the lions (Daniel 6:1-28). Our God is the One Who pulled Jonah out of the depths of the ocean (Jonah 1-2:10).

Daniel and Jonah continued to pray and praise God right in the middle of their difficult circumstances. What "pit" do you find yourself in this week? What prayers need answering? What doubts need reassuring?

To trust God is to discover the deepest peace in your soul.

*Jesus, clear the doubts in my mind and remind me that
You are always in control and always at work in my life.
Take this pit, this unanswered prayer, this question mark in
my heart, and do what only You can do. Move in this situation.
Calm my angst. Build my faith. Draw my heart close to You.
Thank You that no pit is too deep, no situation is
too difficult, and no concern is too small for You.*

*When the doubts creep in, keep praying and praising God.
Know that He is at work to deliver you, and He's never, ever left you.*

GOD NEVER STOPS PURSUING YOUR BEAUTIFUL HEART

The earth was without form and void, and darkness was over the face of the deep.
And the Spirit of God was hovering over the face of the waters.

Genesis 1:2

Jesus is pursuing you. He has *always* been pursuing your beautiful heart. When you came into this world as a newborn baby, His Spirit hovered over you and drew you in. When you were a little girl in pigtails swinging on your swing set, His Spirit hovered over you and drew you in. When you were a young gal, on the edge of adulthood, His Spirit hovered over you and drew you in. When you became a wife or a mama, His Spirit hovered over you and drew you in. When you couldn't sleep because you were worried, His Spirit hovered over you and drew you in. When you had to make a big decision that pulled your heart in a million directions, His Spirit hovered over you and drew you in. When you felt darkness creeping in because of the world we live in, His Spirit hovered over you and drew you in. When you felt wobbly in your faith, His Spirit hovered over you and drew you in. When you needed assurance that He is real, His Spirit hovered over you and drew you in.

When Jesus was on the cross, you were on His heart. When Jesus stayed on the cross instead of saving Himself, you were on His heart. When Jesus rose from the grave three days later, you were on His heart.

Every day, His Spirit hovers over you and draws you in. Every day, you are on His heart. He will never stop pursuing you. You will *always* be on His heart.

Jesus, thank You that You pursue me. Thank You that throughout
all of the seasons of my life, You have been drawing me close
to Your heart. As I go about my day today, help me to remember
that You are constantly pursuing me and always right by my side.

Today, may you remember that the God
of the universe has YOU on His heart.

WHAT DO WE DO WITH ANXIETY?

Do not be anxious about anything, but in everything by prayer and supplication with thanksgiving let your requests be made known to God. And the peace of God, which surpasses all understanding, will guard your hearts and your minds in Christ Jesus.

Philippians 4:6-7

We have a Counselor—the Holy Spirit—Who guides, leads, and teaches us. What we need is not so much a perfect answer to our anxiety, but to know we are not alone in it. There have been moments and seasons where I can't seem to shake off my worries or lay aside the heavy weight of anxiety. It's frustrating! Sometimes I try to exercise my way to peace, or dress my way to peace, or shop my way to peace, or distract my way to peace. Maybe you do that too.

In moments of anxiety, sometimes prayer isn't our go-to remedy. Instead, we dwell on our anxious thoughts or run to something else to calm the angst. So often I do everything but the very thing that God says leads to peace—pray (Philippians 4:6-7). I try all the other options first, then in desperation I finally pray. But the times when I go to God first are the times when my peace is the deepest.

God wants to know all that is going on in your heart. Yes, He already knows your thoughts and feelings, but He wants you to talk to Him just like you are Daddy and daughter sitting on a back porch swing together. God wants to hang out with you. He wants to hear from you, and He wants to speak to you. God longs to be the One Who comforts you, the One you turn to, the One Who lifts you up, and the One you delight in. He longs to care for you, speak to you, love you, and encourage you. God wants to do life with you. When you let God into every aspect of your life, He takes the weight off your anxiety.

Jesus, thank You that I am not alone in my anxiety. Thank You that You will gladly take the burdens I am carrying and help me navigate life as I trust in You. Remind me today to let any anxiety point me to You. Remind me to pray about everything and then turn each burden over to You.

Today may you find peace like a river as you turn any anxiety over to God.

A SECRET TO LIVING TRANSFORMED

Christ in you, the hope of glory.
Colossians 1:27

You may have spotted signs in your neighborhood that declare, *Drive like your kids live here.* You drive differently when you see that sign. You put the brakes on, you're more mindful of your surroundings, and you drive more delicately, watching out for little ones who may scamper into the street after a ball.

I think I need something similar on my bathroom mirror some days: *Live like Christ lives in you.* Not as a reminder to follow all the rules or to live holier-than-thou, but as a note each morning that I don't have to do the day on my own or tussle my battles on my own. Just like a driver is changed when they see that physical sign, perhaps we might be changed and live differently if we bear in mind that Christ lives in us.

Each day, Christ lives in you. Each day, you have the power of God functioning in and through you. Each day, you have the Helper, Counselor, Spirit of God, and Provider at your right hand to help, counsel, navigate, and provide for you. Each day, you have God with you, in you, around you, in front of you, and behind you. How might that viewpoint change your day? What would it look like to live each day like Christ lives in you?

This is not a call to live better, try harder, or be a better person. It's a call to *live loved.* It's a call to remember Who we belong to, to know how cherished we are, and to live like a little girl again—dancing through life with her heavenly Father. It's a call to welcome His invitation to walk with Him through life, relying on Him for the day-by-day, grace-by-grace steps. It's a call to believe in the Father's love despite our mess-ups, hang-ups, or struggles. It's a call to let our joy swell up because we've been given all we need for both eternal life and earthly life. It's a call to stay amazed at the wonder of it all. You carry, in a sense, an exquisite garden of life in you, blossoming with seeds of truth, promise, and constant hope.

Jesus, thank You that You live in me. Remind me today of Your constant love, grace, and presence.

Live like Christ lives in you.

ONE PRAYER THAT CAN CHANGE YOUR DAY

Strengthen me according to Your Word!
Psalm 119:28

We must always remember that there is an enemy working hard to get us down. He's strategically striving to pull our hearts away from hope. He's deceptively devising plans to pull our hearts away from grace. He's cunning and crafty and knows just the thing that gets us down. But we must always remember that we always have hope, and we always have God with us.

There is this battle going on for your sweet heart every day. And oftentimes the battle makes you weary. It's real. It's frustrating. But you know what? Sometimes I think it's a bit liberating to remember that there is a war going on for your heart because it's a reminder that Someone is fighting for you. God will never stop pulling you back into His grace and love and light. He will always steer you toward His truth. He will always rescue you from the darkness of the world, the pull of the enemy, or even the lure of your own negative thoughts. He loves to rescue you over and over and over again.

Perhaps you can't quite name the struggle you're experiencing today. Maybe you don't understand why you feel stuck, discouraged, or like you've lost a bit of that light in your beautiful eyes. Remember that there is a war going on for your heart every day, and the One Who has redeemed you eternally loves to redeem you daily.

Here's a simple prayer to pray when you feel that "stuckness" or discouragement creeping in: *Lord, strengthen me according to Your Word.*

When we cry out to God for strength, guidance, or anything at all, He comes running to meet our needs. And when we go to the Word of God, we find God Himself. Through His Word He restores the light to our hearts.

Lord, strengthen me according to Your Word. Take what feels stuck and move me toward hope. Take what feels hard and move me toward grace. Take what feels discouraging and remind me of Who You are and who I am to You—Your precious daughter. Lord, thank You for fighting for my heart every day.

May the Lord strengthen your precious heart with His Word.
May His presence and company be your fuel for the day.

BECOMING A WOMAN
WHO FLOURISHES

But I am like an olive tree flourishing *in the house of God;*
I trust in God's unfailing love forever and ever.

Psalm 52:8, NIV, emphasis added

We want to be women who are flourishing. But too often we're distracted, overly busy, and depleted. Sometimes it feels as if we are wilting rather than flourishing. What's distracting you from being focused on God, the Source of all flourishing? Is it the phone? The internet? The mirror? The to-do list? Keeping up with the latest trends? Scrolling through the newsfeed? What's keeping you from flourishing, sweet one?

God wants us to let go of the things that deplete our joy, busy our souls, or cause us inner turmoil. Some of those things are unavoidable, and that's okay. There is grace here. There is always grace. Some things we can let go of, even if it's hard. And when we do let go, we will find more of God.

In our day and age, it's easy to be so busy and full of stuff that we don't realize we are hungry for God. Sometimes we can't find Him because we are already full inside. God wants us to be full in a different way—full of His love and presence. He wants us to be so full of Him that we flourish. But flourishing takes space—space to know God, space to seek Him, space to hear Him, space to be with Him. And sometimes it's hard to make that space for God.

When you make space for God in your heart, you will flourish as His daughter. You will know the peace and joy He offers. You will be changed from the inside out. Today, try to view making space for God as an absolute delight and a pathway to true flourishing.

God, You know how busy and distracted I feel. Help me to set those things aside
and make space for You to fully invade my heart. I long to be a woman who is
flourishing because her heart is full of God. I choose You over all the things that
distract me from You. Help me to make space for You. Invade my heart completely.

Make space in your heart for God. Let the flourishing begin.

ALWAYS INVITED

I was a stranger and you invited me in.
Matthew 25:35, NIV

God invites us into eternal life and into abundant life on earth. He holds out an invitation to us to experience life in a deeper, sweeter, and more fulfilling way. He has no requirements, other than that we believe in Him. He invites us because He loves us.

We all have those people in life who make us feel: so invited. They make us feel welcome no matter who we are. They make us feel loved. I know you and I both want to be that kind of woman to others, the one who makes others feel loved and always invited to the table of God's family. We want to be the gal who reaches out, who pulls a friend in, who sits by the one who feels alone, who encourages the one who needs a lift.

God's love, His constant invitation of welcome, His grace, and His company stir in us a desire to do the same for others. So this week, when you see a gal who looks like she could use a friend, a smile, or a hug—follow the example of the One Who extends a welcoming invitation to you. Be the one to extend the invitation to talk. Be the one to ask how she's doing. Be the one to offer your presence and your company. Be a woman who invites others in simply because the One Who made you and loves you invites you in every day by His grace and love. You don't have to manufacture this character quality; you can lean on God's Spirit to help you. He will gladly help you become a woman who invites others in.

Lord, thank You for inviting me into Your family, not by anything
I did or do, but by Your grace and love. Make me a woman who invites
others in, who reaches out, who loves simply because. And may that all
come from You—not something I manufacture on my own. Make me a
woman who is inviting because she knows that she is always invited by You.

*Today may you discover the blessing of rich
fellowship as you aim to be a blessing to others.*

BECOMING A WOMAN OF GRACE

For sin will have no dominion over you,
since you are not under law, but under grace.

Romans 6:14

As we look to God to transform us into the women He wants us to be, we have to be careful that we aren't always in "improvement mode." In our good intentions to grow more into the women we long to be, we can slip into a constant state of wanting to be *more* and *better*. And when we feel like we are never quite hitting the mark or living up to the standards we've set for ourselves, a sense of despair and failure can set in. That can make a gal feel quite wobbly-hearted.

God saved us by grace. Not because of what we did, not because of what we accomplished, not because we cleaned up our act, not because we hit a certain mark. In His love and by His grace, He saved us. We have salvation—eternal life—because of His grace toward us. He adopts us as His children because He loves us, not because we earned it. He calls us *daughter* not because we live perfectly but because we are His. He loves us in our imperfect state. He pursues us because He just wants to be near us. He wants to help us navigate this life. He is the God of grace. And as we look to Him, He grows us into women of grace.

A woman of grace extends grace to others. She has a deep-down peace in her soul because she knows she's filled with the One Who extends grace to her every day. She gives herself grace when she feels like she has messed up. She keeps the wonder of grace in her heart. Transforming into the women we want to be doesn't have to look like a program or a set of rules—Jesus set us free from all that. Instead, we can walk in His grace and take one graceful step at a time through life.

God, thank You for Your grace. Thank You for Your saving grace
that granted me eternal life, and also for the loving grace You extend
to me for this earthly life. Help me to live in grace today, not by rules
and standards, but by Your Spirit. Make me a woman who exudes grace.

May you feel the grace of God extended to you today as
you let go of striving and live in the beauty of His grace.

A WILLING SPIRIT

Restore to me the joy of Your salvation and
grant me a willing spirit, to sustain me.

Psalm 51:12, NIV

Our default mode as busy women is to do our day in our own strength and might. We enter into "go" mode and often find ourselves weary from plowing through our day. Do you ever get to a place of feeling so busy *doing* that you miss the simple joy of *being*? God invites us to the simple joy and blessing of allowing Him to do our day *through* us. All it takes is a willingness to let Him. It's a willingness to look to God to order our day, lead our way, and guide us in all we do. Sometimes that can feel kind of elusive. We want to see the full, laid-out plan of the day and of our lives, but God asks us to walk by faith. He doesn't show us the whole plan. He asks us to walk with Him one moment at a time. And that's really hard to do sometimes, right?

But when we are willing to let Him lead, guide, direct, and order our days and our lives, what He shows us is that there is unexpected joy and delight in that God-paced, God-fueled perspective. When God is leading, we find the deepest joy. When God is leading, we find more peace. When God is leading, our time seems to multiply. When God is leading, we reflect God to a hurting world.

Being willing to let God have His way in us doesn't look like a formula, a program, or a particular routine. It looks and feels more like dancing, perhaps. It looks more like following the lead of His Spirit and less like following our own way. It can't fully be pinpointed down to a perfect structure or to-do list. But know this: being willing to let God lead each day brings the sweetest joy.

God, restore to me the joy of my salvation. Grant me a willing spirit to follow You,
to go where You lead, to let You guide my life and my heart day by day.
Make me a woman who is willing to lay down her plans for Your divine plans.

Surrender to God's lead. In the surrendering,
you will find a God-paced, God-directed life.

SPREADING GOD'S KINDNESS

Love is patient and kind.
1 Corinthians 13:4

Think of those people in your life who make you feel loved. The ones who make you feel at ease and like you can be yourself without having to try so hard. The ones who show nothing but grace toward you when you mess up and who bring out the best side of you. The ones who light up your day.

That type of kindness changes the atmosphere. It changes our day and lifts our mood. Kindness is like little love notes from heaven, delivered especially to our heart at just the right time. We all want to be the ones who make others feel loved and at ease like that. We want to make others feel like they can be themselves around us without having to try so hard. We want to be grace-givers. We want to bring out the best in others. We want to be the ones who check in just because, who encourage those who need a kind word. We want to light up someone's day. Deep down, we want to be carriers of kindness. And we can, because that type of kindness comes from God. It flows out from a heart that seeks God and knows His kindness.

God's love is kind—the kindest of all. He sees you when you feel unloved, unknown, and unseen. He pursues you when you feel like no else does. You are His daughter, and He wants to make sure you feel loved. So in ways that only He can, He expresses His kindness to you in the little moments. He sends you the encouragement you need at just the right time. He sends the provision, the boost of joy, the comfort, and the peace right when you need it most. His love is kind, and as we look to Him, He stirs up kindness in us. We don't have to try so hard to stir up kindness in ourselves. It will overflow from a heart that knows the kindness of God.

God, thank You for Your kindness. Make me a woman of kindness.
Make me a gal who brings encouragement, comfort, and joy to
those she crosses paths with each day. Let Your kindness bring
comfort to my heart each day so that I can turn around and bless
someone else. Thank You, Lord, for Your kindness toward me.

May you notice the kindness of God today, and in turn
spread His kindness to the people whose paths you cross.

BECOMING
A WOMAN OF WISDOM

She speaks with wisdom.
Proverbs 31:26, NIV

I think we would agree that we want to become women of wisdom. We want to travel through life from a place of knowing God, counting on His truth and promises, looking to Him for guidance and discernment. In short, we want to live life well, and a life well-lived begins with wisdom from God.

How do we gain wisdom for life? Wisdom comes from our relationship with God. It comes from knowing Him—spending time with Him, lingering with Him, inviting Him to lead us, and getting to know Him through His Word. God's Word is our source for true wisdom, and when we spend time in His Word, we become women of wisdom.

A woman of wisdom radiates life, encouragement, and truth. Maybe she doesn't say it out loud or speak it from a stage, but her life exudes a wisdom that comes from above. Each of us needs wisdom for life. Today, may we remember that the wisdom we long for comes from God Himself.

If you're feeling stuck, lost, or unsure today, seek the One Who gives you all the wisdom you need for life. You will gain God's wisdom for your life as you get to know God more and more. There's no perfect way to seek God. There's no right quiet time formula, or right number of verses to read per day. There's no right way to spend time with God. Simply open up your heart and life to Him. Invite Him into your day. Open His life-giving Word. Ask Him to lead you to wisdom, and then listen for His whispers over your life. His wisdom will help you navigate life.

Lord, thank You that Your Word is my guide, my light, my wisdom,
and all I need to navigate life. Help me to always keep Your Word and
my relationship with You as my number one priority so I can walk
through my life in wisdom. Make me a woman of wisdom as I seek You.

As you seek God, you will become a woman of wisdom.

GOD WANTS TO BE YOUR EVERYTHING

*And my God will supply every need of yours
according to His riches in glory in Christ Jesus.*

Philippians 4:19

The world will tell you that to be the woman you want to be, you need *more, better, the next big thing,* or *something different*. The world promises it can satisfy your heart's needs if you will just buy this one thing, move to a better place, or upgrade your status in life. But while some of those things are good things, most times, the things we think will fulfill us don't fully satisfy our hearts. When we fill up on what the world claims will fill our heart, we still feel like something's missing. So we try the next thing or something different. But we are left feeling the ache of our need, desperately wondering where to find the fulfillment and satisfaction we crave.

Sweet one, God delights in meeting all your needs. He delights in meeting your need for *more, better, the next big thing,* or *something different* because He is:

- The more you're looking for
- The best—better than anything else
- The biggest thing
- The something different you're longing for

God is *everything* you've ever been looking for. You can stop looking for *more, better, the next big thing,* or *something different* because He wants to be all of that for you. He wants to satisfy your heart. He wants to provide you with deep contentment. He wants to give you greater joy. He wants to be your everything. All you have to do is let Him be that for you. What would that look like practically for you today?

When we let Him be our everything, we find that we have everything we need.

Jesus, be the more I'm looking for. Be the best thing I need. Be the biggest thing. Be the something different I've been longing for. Help me to sense Your presence in a fresh way today as I look to You as my Everything.

Run to God today for every need.

GOD IS AT WORK IN THE DREAMS OF YOUR HEART

Before I formed you in the womb I knew you.
Jeremiah 1:5

God is at work in the dreams He places in our hearts. They manifest themselves in different ways: A **prayer request**, something we are believing God for. A **goal**, something we are collaborating with God for and trusting Him to lead the way in. A **change** we want to make in our lives, something personal that would help us live with joy and enthusiasm. A **step of surrender**, something we are turning over to God because we're just not sure what to do with a particular dream of our heart or where He's leading us. A **desire**, something we want to turn over to God to allow Him to shape. A **habit** we want to change, something we need His Holy Spirit to take over in our hearts. A **miracle** we are hoping for, something that feels over-the-top impossible, but we're believing God is still in the business of doing miracles.

The common theme of all the dreams we have in our hearts is that they involve a process of waiting on God's timing and trusting His ways. It's in this process that He cultivates our relationship with Him. Dreaming, then, becomes more about our relationship with the One Who formed us than about the dream itself. Today, remember that God knows, sees, and hears every prayer request of your heart, every grace-filled goal of your heart, every desire for change, every desire to live life well and in step with God, every step of surrender, every habit you want to change, and every hope for a miracle. God sees all of your heart, your life, and your daily steps of faith. And He wants you to remember that He is with you in all your dreaming steps. God is in the process. He is at work in your dreaming heart and in the dreams He has for your life. Don't give up, and don't lose heart.

Lord, thank You that You have specially formed and fashioned me.
When I feel discouraged in the waiting, remind me that You are always at work.

Since before you were born, God has known you.
He cares about all those dreams in your heart.

WHEN YOU LONG TO KNOW YOUR PURPOSE

… called according to His purpose.

Romans 8:28

Your life has purpose every single day and every single moment because you are called by God according to *His* purposes. You are part of God's story. He is using you as part of His great plan for redemption for all people. Sometimes your purpose may involve big, grand things—and that's beautiful. But most days your purpose is the everyday things. Purpose is strewn together by a lifetime of letting God lead. Purpose may feel mundane or routine, but it's in the everyday moments that we know God and grow closer to Him.

Every moment is important. Every season of your life matters. Your whole life is full of purpose. I know sometimes you wish God would more clearly lay out His purposes for you. I know sometimes you wish you could define your purpose. Know today, that you're already living a life of purpose because you are part of God's bigger purposes. He is using you, though you may not realize it.

You don't have to manufacture purpose all on your own; God gives you purpose. And even when it feels like no else sees you, He sees you. Your life with God is your purpose. Just dance it with Him. Dancing day to day with God gives your life purpose. Rest in that. Rest from striving to define and figure out your purpose. Purpose comes out of that place of keeping company with your Savior. Keep your heart close to His, and you will be living out your purpose beautifully.

❧

**Thank You, Lord, that You have called me according to Your purposes.
When I can't see or feel my purpose, help me to rest in the fact that life with
You gives my life purpose and meaning every single day, every single moment.**

*God will fill you with a sense of purpose
as you look to Him to guide your life.*

SOAK IN
YOUR SEASON

So teach us to number our days that we may get a heart of wisdom.
Psalm 90:12

I remember when my boys were babies and sweet older ladies in the grocery store would pat my back as I passed them in the grocery aisles with my little crew and say, "Enjoy those babies. Time flies." I remember in those moments kind of wishing time would fly a little faster so that my babies would sleep all night or I could have a bit more time to myself. But the ladies in the grocery store were right! Time does fly! My boys are turning into young men before my eyes, and of course that's what I want them to do. I want them to grow and become the young men God created them to be. But every so often I feel a burden in my heart and an urgency to soak my current season in a bit more. To not wish away the days. To not hurry the seasons.

My youngest son came home from school one day with an announcement. "Forty-five days!" he excitedly shouted when he plopped in the car after school. "Forty-five days till what?" I asked. "Till the last day of school!" He was counting and proud of it. I was thinking, *where had the time gone?*

In all my son's excitement, he decided it would be fun to make a chain out of construction paper to count down the days. So we sat outside on the back porch on a beautiful sunny day and cut forty-five slips of colored paper and stapled them together in loops. We hung the colorful chain on his bunk bed, and he assured me he would pull one chain off each day. It became a way for us to count down the days and a reminder for me to savor each one.

Whatever season of life you are in, I hope today you are encouraged to soak it all in. Soak in the season and enjoy the everyday moments. Number your days. See each one as bright and beautiful and colorful, all working together to form a beautiful tapestry of your beautiful life.

Lord, teach me to number my days and soak in the moments.
Thank You that You are weaving together the tapestry of my life, and that
I can live fully in the present moment while I trust You with the future.

*God has good things for you ahead, but don't forget
to enjoy the good things He has for you right now.*

THE YOU YOU'RE MEANT TO BE

I praise You, for I am fearfully and wonderfully made.
Psalm 139:14

What if we embraced the unique way God made us? What if we even celebrated the way God made, wired, and wove us together, unique from all other human beings? The thing about becoming the women we want to be is that sometimes we think that woman should look like someone else, someone we are not. But the truth is, the woman God wants you to be is YOU.

She's already beautiful. She's already amazing. She's already full of life, purpose, and passion. She's kindhearted and loving. She's just who He created her to be. She's just who He had in mind when He formed her. She's just who He wanted. She's already chosen. She's already loved. She's already the woman God wants her to be. Yes, she's growing still. Yes, she's still being transformed into His image. Yes, she's changing as she goes. She's becoming more herself as she looks to Christ. God wants her to be herself. Because when she's fully herself, she reflects God in her own unique and beautiful way.

When you think about becoming the woman God created you to be, don't look left, right, behind you, ahead of you, or at that gal over there who seems to have it all together. Look to the One Who formed you. You are fearfully and wonderfully made. God wants you to be uniquely *you*. He helps you find yourself as you look to Him.

Your version of unique is beautiful. Celebrate the way God made you. Don't worry about what the world will think. Don't let the pressure to conform squelch your joy and your personality. God dreamed you up in His heart before time began. He made you on purpose and for a purpose. Embrace the *you* you're meant to be and trust God to shape you more and more into His image.

God, help me to be fully myself. Help me to be the gal
you created me to be as I look to you. Help me to know
the joy and freedom of being ME by looking to YOU.

What makes you unique makes you beautiful.

WHEN YOU'RE RUNNING ON EMPTY

Jesus said to them, "I am the bread of life; whoever comes to Me shall not hunger, and whoever believes in Me shall never thirst."

John 6:35

To stay spurred on in life, we must find ways to be renewed and refreshed. We were made to need refueling. We were created to thirst and to find our soul's deepest thirst quenched with the presence of God. Maybe you have been feeling a bit dry, discouraged, or thirsty lately. Maybe you have tried running to things or the world for satisfaction, but you have come up empty again. I want to point you to the water of God's Word, His presence, and His love again. That is the only place where not only will you find food for your soul, comfort, and unconditional love, but joy will rise up in you. Peace will envelop you. Contentment with where you are and who you are and Whose you are will firmly plant your feet. Your heart will grow steady.

And when you lose your way again—we all do at one time or another—God will keep chasing after your heart. That's what He does. He draws us back to Himself. He waits with open arms for you to come to Him. When you collapse into His embrace, you truly find yourself and the life He made for you. So draw near to Him again and again. Take a U-turn from the world's enticements and find true and abundant life in Jesus. Keep your heart pointing toward His grace, for there you will find your heart steady again. And in Him, you will never run dry. He will keep refreshing and renewing you. He will keep you going. He will provide you with all that you need to do the things He has called you to do. He will keep your heart dancing with His joy as you run to Him for refreshment day by day. Keep walking in step with your Savior. Don't give up when you feel dried up. Instead, fill up by running to Him.

May your heart be reminded where to run when you feel dry. May your heart stay focused on the One Who loves to keep spurring you on.

Lord, thank You that I can run to You when I am running on empty in life.
Thank You that Your love, grace, and refreshment are unending and a constant
source of fuel for my heart and my life. Remind me to run to You for refreshment.

Jesus is your endless source of refreshment.

YOU'RE STRONGER THAN YOU THINK

The name of the LORD is a strong tower.
Proverbs 18:10

You are stronger than you think. You are becoming a woman of strength as God works in your heart and makes His home in your heart. You are strong because He lives in you. Life will throw obstacles at you. Your own emotions may tell you you're weak, overly sensitive, too emotional, or powerless. But Christ is in you, and He makes you strong in your weakness. His name is your strong tower.

When you feel weak, tired, or insignificant, remember Who lives in you. When you feel weak, you are strong because of Him. When you feel weary, you have His strength. When you feel powerless, you have His power. When you feel lost, you have Him as your light. When you feel alone, He's always with you.

The Holy Spirit in you makes you a strong woman of God. He gives you the power, strength, and fuel you need for everyday life. You are stronger than you think, sweet one.

Thank You for making me strong when I feel weak, Lord.
You in me—that's where my strength comes from. Help me
to lean on You for all the strength, power, light, and joy
I need from day to day. You are my strong tower, always.

Walk in His strength today.

YOU HAVE BEEN SET FREE

You have been set free from sin.
Romans 6:18, NIV

You have been set free from sin. The enemy wants you to think you'll never be free. The enemy wants you to think you will always be entangled and entrapped by sin. But God set you free once and for all through Jesus. And day by day, while sin still tries to pull you in, the Spirit helps you in your weakness. God walks you through your day, offering a way that leads to more life. So while sin always lingers, trying to convince you to take its route, God always offers His route of hope and life.

Don't believe the enemy's lies that you'll never be free. You are free. Jesus has set you free from sin. So while the enemy will still tempt you, you have a power inside you—God Himself—who helps you overcome. And when you do slip into sin, which we all do, God extends His grace over and over again. We acknowledge the sin, and He offers forgiveness over and over again. We never have to wallow in shame and guilt. We are always set free.

God, I praise You for Your grace, love, and forgiveness. Thank You for
making me right with You through Jesus, and thank You that I don't
battle sin on my own. You are always with me, for me, and in me. Remind
me that I'm set free from sin, and help me to walk in that freedom and grace.

You have been set free.
Don't let the enemy convince you otherwise.

A SENSE OF WELL-BEING

His soul shall abide in well-being.

Psalm 25:13

What I notice in life is that when my heart is happy and steady in God's promises— fully trusting in Him, fully believing He's constantly with me, firmly rooted in His love—I feel a sense of well-being. I feel strong, joyful, and purposeful. But when my heart loses its footing, I can't seem to find that beautiful sense of well-being.

When our hearts are unsteady, our confidence slips, our joy deflates, and our sense of purpose dissolves. A gal who feels unsteady in her heart needs the love of God to show up in a real, tangible way in her life so that she can live with joy, purpose, and steadiness of heart.

Sweet one, God will do that for you. He will gladly show up and get your heart back to a place of well-being. God's love for you never changes. He's not going anywhere. Every day when you wake up, you can know that God's love is your firm foundation. His love is not dependent on circumstances, the pace of culture, your emotions, or anything else. You are loved with the steadfast love of God. Let that be your sure footing and your steadiness of heart. As you look to Him, you will experience a sense of well-being.

Practically speaking, when you feel a little wobbly in your heart, head to the back porch with a cup of coffee and God's Word instead of flipping on the news. Go outside in the sun to take a walk and listen for God's whispers over your life instead of checking your phone. Take a pause in your day and pray about the things on your heart instead of stuffing your emotions. It's in the little choices of the day where you can find more of God. And when you fill your day with more of Him, you will find that you have a stronger sense of well-being all day long. God is always waiting to flood you with more of His peace and joy.

Lord, in those moments today where I find myself worrying or I am stuck on a problem and my soul feels a little wobbly, remind me to come to You. Remind me that You bring me the sweetest and greatest sense of well-being, joy, and peace. Help me to choose to seek You throughout my day today.

May you seek God throughout your day, and may you be sweetly surprised by the joy, peace, and well-being that fills your heart and soul.

HE TENDERLY STEERS YOUR HEART

*The LORD will guide you always; He will satisfy your needs in
a sun-scorched land and will strengthen your frame. You will be
like a well-watered garden, like a spring whose waters never fail.*

Isaiah 58:11, NIV

When a gal is searching for significance, she wants to know that her future matters. She wants to know that her days are purposeful and her life is impactful. She wants to know that she's living out God's specific plan for her. But often that search for significance can feel messy. She loses her confidence. She's not sure she's really making a difference. She's not sure what step to take next. Her heart feels a little wobbly and her faith feels a little weak.

Remember today that the Lord tenderly steers your heart. The God of your heart is the Shepherd of your heart and your life. And just as a shepherd of sheep tenderly steers, guides, and leads his flock, so God tenderly steers, guides, and leads you. I know it often doesn't feel like He's leading. Maybe you wish you could just know for sure where God is guiding your life. This is where faith comes in. Trusting God doesn't come naturally to our fickle hearts. Faith is more like a muscle that strengthens over time. It's not that we need to try harder to have a stronger faith. In my life, I've found that faith follows steps of faith. In other words, sometimes a step of faith builds our faith.

In our search for significance, we can easily begin to believe the lie that we're not good enough, we're not trying hard enough, and we're a mess. But our Shepherd and the steerer of our souls invites us to replace those lies with truth: *You are strong because He lives in you. You are chosen to be His daughter. You have a God-given purpose. You are loved by the God of the universe.* You can step out in faith today when you stand on the firm foundation of the truth about how God sees you and how He's steering your life. Let Him steer and guide your heart; He will never lead you astray.

**Lord, thank You that You faithfully steer my heart and
lead me into a life of purpose. Help me to look to You for
direction as I grow into the woman You're calling me to be.**

Trust God to guide your life.

February

AN INVITATION TO SOUL REST

He leads me beside still waters.

Psalm 23:2

God does not want you to live in a constant state of deep stress and anxiety. He has so much more peace and joy for you. He created you to live in the rhythms of His grace, right at His pace, in step with Him. Our culture urges us to keep moving, to hurry, to run, to go, and it makes us feel like stress is something we should just accept and deal with the best we can. God invites us to choose a better way: living with His help. He wants us to evaluate our lives, determine what's causing our stress, and choose His way—the way of peace and rest.

This choice to go deeper with God, to make space and time to linger with Him and to protect our hearts, souls, and minds from overload and stress is an invitation to the deep waters of God's refreshing company. It's an invitation to a more abundant life and to the deepest kind of soul rest. What's short-circuiting your peace and joy today? What's feeding your stress and unrest and causing you to miss out on real soul rest? Take some time and space today to take those things to the Lord and release your burdens to Him.

When we take the time to ask ourselves the hard questions, to sit with the tensions we're feeling and bring them to the One Who wants to take us deeper, we will find the refreshing waters of His peace and joy. *Still waters.* God does not want you to live with a heart that feels turbulent, stressed, and anxious. No matter what your stress, you can experience the deep-down soul rest that Jesus came to offer you by bringing every burden, anxiety, and stressful circumstance to Him in prayer. There you will find the peace of knowing that God has you and that He's ultimately in control of your life and all that concerns you.

Lord, lead me to the still waters of Your presence. Help me to bring every stress and burden to You. Thank You for carrying my burdens.

When you feel stress and anxiety overtaking your heart,
turn to the One Who offers soul rest and peace.

WHAT'S AROUND THE CORNER

*Surely Your goodness and love will follow me all the days of
my life, and I will dwell in the house of the Lord forever.*

Psalm 23:6, NIV

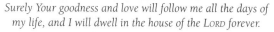

I believe God is excited about what He has around the corner for your life. While you can't see it or know it or dream it, He's got good things coming your way. That doesn't mean life is going to be easy or pain-free or like a frolic through a field of wildflowers, but it does mean that His goodness and love are chasing after you. He's pursuing your heart all your days.

Isn't it sweet that He never stops pursuing us? He's always drawing us in. He's always whispering, *I'm here*. He's always inviting us into His presence. He never stops pursuing us. I know He must be excited not only for the things He has in store for you in the coming months, but also to draw you closer and closer to Himself. So as you venture out into another day, remember that He's got good things ahead for you.

When life feels a bit mundane and your week feels like the same routine again and again, remember that God loves to surprise you. When it feels like there's nothing exciting ahead for your future, knock down that lie with the truth that because the Lord's goodness and love follow you all the days of your life, He's not finished surprising you with delights that are just for you. God can see what's around the corner. You can rest in this day knowing that the God who loves you has sweet and precious things planned for you.

**Lord, when the day ahead feels mundane, refresh my perspective by reminding
me that You have more for me around the corner than I can comprehend.
You have delights and joys and gifts and goodness in store because
You are my loving Father. Thank You for Your sweet grace.**

*May you walk into this day with expectancy, trusting God
to surprise You with little delights throughout your journey.*

GOD CAN USE YOU NOW

And we all, who with unveiled faces contemplate the Lord's glory,
are being transformed into His image with ever-increasing glory,
which comes from the Lord, who is the Spirit.

2 Corinthians 3:18, NIV

Whether you're 16, 42, 88, or 102, you're a light for Jesus right now. You are His disciple, His messenger, and His ambassador. You're on a journey of becoming who God created you to be—more like Christ. But in all your growing, changing, and becoming, you're already a light in this dark world. God is using you *today* to make a difference in the world around you. You are bringing kingdom light to people's hearts right now. Today. In whatever state you are—whether you're feeling like a mess, or like a puzzle that can't quite get all her pieces together, or like a beautiful painting one day and a splatter of paint the next—you are a light *right now*. God can use you *now*. The world can see God in you today. You are shining for Jesus!

You don't have to wait until the kids graduate, the house is remodeled, your dream job comes along, the laundry is folded, or anything else. God is using you in extraordinary ways in your ordinary days. No day is wasted. No moment is meaningless. God uses everyday moments to display His love, and you, my friend, are one of His instruments. Scripture tells us that we are "children of God without fault in a warped and crooked generation … [who] will shine among them like stars in the sky" (Philippians 2:15, NIV).

Thank You, Lord, for using me for Your Kingdom purposes. It's nearly too much for me to comprehend! I long to be a light for You. Thank You that You use me to be an instrument of Your love and grace, simply as I depend on You. Help me to trust You to shine Your light through me today as I lean on You.

Even as you're growing, learning, changing, and becoming,
God sees you as one of His shining lights today.

WHEN YOUR FAITH
FEELS WOBBLY

If you have faith as small as a mustard seed …
Luke 17:6, NIV

Whatever you're praying for, whatever you're going through, whatever you're unsure about, whatever direction you are seeking, whatever answer you are waiting for, God is with you. You are not alone on this journey. When we are going through something, feeling uncertain, and looking for direction and answers, it's easy to feel alone. It's easy to let doubts creep in and steal our faith. But know this: Even in the praying, the uncertainty, the seeking, and the waiting, God has you. You are not alone in your journey.

Sometimes we get a little wobbly in our hearts. Sometimes our faith feels foggy. Don't be hard on yourself. Faith in the God of the universe whom we cannot see with our physical eyes does not come naturally. It goes against every ounce of practicality and reality that's in us. It's okay if your faith in God feels hard sometimes. Or unnatural. Or even a little crazy! It's okay if you feel like you don't have enough faith. All it takes is a seed. *A mustard seed*, Jesus said.

Our faith is kind of like a muscle, and the more we exercise it, the stronger it becomes. Sometimes the way to exercise it is to preach the gospel to our own hearts. To remind ourselves of God's truth. The more we remember, the stronger our faith in the unseen God grows. So when you feel a little unsure, a little foggy in your faith, a little wobbly in your heart, give yourself the same grace God gives you. Don't beat yourself up for your doubts. Instead, replace your doubt with God's truth and let Him build up your faith.

Lord, help me to choose faith today instead of fear and worry.
Help me to trust You, Lord. Thank You for the joy of being in
a relationship with You. Sometimes my faith feels wobbly, but I thank
You that You know I am human and weak. Strengthen my faith day by day.

You have God in your corner, on your side, in you, around you,
before and behind you. God surrounds you completely.
So walk in faith today. Even just a little bit of
faith will make a huge difference in your day.

EVERY PART
OF YOUR STORY

But the plans of the Lord stand firm forever,
the purposes of His heart through all generations.

Psalm 33:11, NIV

Every part of your story matters to God. Every struggle you have wrestled through, every difficult season, your past, your present, your hopes, your dreams, your fears, the ups and downs—all of it matters to God because all of it is part of your story.

The hard parts of your story do not define you because what truly defines you is the love that comes from the Father. When He looks at your story, He sees you with eyes of grace, a heart of love, and a smile that lights up His face. He wants to use every nook and cranny of your story to shape a bigger story that He can use for His kingdom purposes. So instead of hiding your story, embrace it. Because the One Who created you has a story to tell through you.

God is writing your story—your dance through life—one step of grace at a time. You don't have to conjure it up. You don't have to make it happen. You don't have to strive to become all that He created you to be. Your job is simply to lean back and enjoy Him. Your job is to be with God, to know Him, and to enjoy Him. From that place of grace and rest, your light will shine for Him. From that place of intimacy with the Lord, He will use you. From that place of abiding in Him, He will graciously unfold His plans for you one day at a time. Enjoy knowing God. He will take care of everything else.

Lord, thank You for my story—the good, the hard,
and all the in-betweens. Remind me today that You use every
part of my story to grow me into the woman You created me to be.
You use every part of my story to make me more like You.

Your story is beautiful, and God will use
every chapter for your good and His glory.

BE GENTLE
ON YOURSELF

And God is able to make all grace abound to you, so that having all
sufficiency in all things at all times, you may abound in every good work.

2 Corinthians 9:8

My Bible study leader one year reminded me to be gentle on myself when I was in a particularly busy season of motherhood. She could have told me to pull myself together, try harder, and pull myself up by my bootstraps to be the best mom ever. But instead, her gentle encouragement felt like the sweetest invitation to trust God and to relax into my current season: *Be gentle on yourself.*

In that season, I learned that I didn't have to be a perfect mama. I learned that taking care of myself was vital if I wanted to take care of my three little ones. I learned that pushing, striving, and putting high expectations on myself only made me feel like I wasn't doing a good job. But when I remembered to be gentle on myself—to give myself grace just like God gives me grace every single day—I learned to depend more deeply on God as my strength and as the Shepherd of my life. I realized that I didn't have to wish away this trying season because God was leading me in it. I realized that I didn't have to do motherhood alone. I realized that I needed rest and grace. I realized that I didn't have to do everything perfectly. And in realizing all those things, I fell in love with that season. I learned to soak it in. I realized that being gentle on myself physically and mentally was a gift to my own heart.

In your current season, sweet one, remember to be gentle on yourself. Give yourself grace to mess up, grace to learn, grace to rest, grace to cease striving, grace to depend on God for the strength you need, grace to be imperfect, grace to start over, and grace to enjoy your current season. My little ones are so big now—they are 10, 12, and 15. And today I'm reminded again to be gentle on myself. It's a different season, but the need for grace hasn't changed. The need for rest, nourishment, contentment, peace about the future, and time with God will never change. Today, be gentle on yourself. Give yourself grace to be loved and tended by the God who sees you, knows you, loves you, and has you in His grasp.

Lord, remind me to be gentle on myself today. Remind me to lean
on You for strength. Thank You for Your beautiful and constant
grace in my life. May I show myself the same grace You show me.

May your day be fueled by grace.

LET GOD TEND YOUR STRESS

When I called, You answered me.
Psalm 138:3, NIV

What do you do to de-stress? We all experience stress in some way or another, and today, I want to encourage you to note what you need when you feel stressed, and then give yourself permission to do the things that help de-stress your heart from busyness, worry, or whatever else is weighing you down. We all need different things to de-stress. Some of us need to be alone, and some of us need to be with people. Some of us need to rest, and some of us need to move! Think about the unique ways you de-stress your soul. For me, a good way to de-stress is a long walk with my puppy, Shaka—coffee cup in hand. It's a time to think, to ponder, to pray, or even to not think. It's a time to refresh my soul in God's creation. Another way I de-stress is by taking pen to paper. Journaling my thoughts to God helps unravel my stress. Spending time in my garden or in the kitchen de-stresses my soul. Time with my people de-stresses me too—there's nothing like good conversation and company. But my favorite way to de-stress is good ole back porch sitting.

Tend to your stress. Notice when your heart, thoughts, or body are feeling stress. Notice when you're feeling overwhelmed, too busy, or too full of to-do lists, emails, or the news. Notice when you're on overload and pull over for a pause. Stress causes wear and tear on our physical bodies and our hearts, and while we cannot avoid all stress, we can make sure we're getting enough sleep, good food, rest, sunshine, water, time with God, and time with others. When your stress-o-meter feels like it's off the charts, do the things that help you unwind from stress. And remember, God uses those moments to minister to your heart. He can use His creation to restore your sense of His presence. He can use a walk around the block to whisper His love notes to your heart. He can use the company of a good friend to encourage your soul. He can use the time you draw close to Him on your back porch to refresh your soul. He can use the things you need to de-stress to minister to your soul.

Lord, help me to notice when stress is taking its toll on my mind
and body, and help me to take care of myself. Thank You that
I can bring my stress to You, and You so sweetly sort me out.

Today, remember to be kind to your soul.
Notice when stress is weighing you down.
Invite the Lord into your stress and let Him bring you
back to the calm center of knowing He's in control of your life.

DISCOVERING YOUR TRUE BEAUTY

Do not let your adorning be external—the braiding of hair and the putting on of gold jewelry, or the clothing you wear—but let your adorning be the hidden person of the heart with the imperishable beauty of a gentle and quiet spirit, which in God's sight is very precious.

1 Peter 3:3-4

In a world full of images and celebrities, a gal can easily feel the lies that say she's not quite enough—not put together enough, not beautiful enough, not thin enough, or just in general *not enough*. There is relief in embracing who God made you to be and how He so intricately designed and created you. I don't believe Peter is saying we shouldn't braid our hair (who doesn't love a cute side braid!) or wear gold jewelry (this girl loves the color gold!) or wear cute clothes (we all love cute clothes!), but he is saying that true beauty comes from deep within our hearts. True beauty comes from a place of knowing we are loved, seen, known, and created by the God of the universe. And true beauty from within never fades. In fact, I believe it only grows more beautiful with age. True beauty is more about your unique, sweet spirit than about the size or brand of your clothes.

True beauty is when a gal owns who she is. She's herself. She wears what makes her feel beautiful even if that looks different from the rest of the crowd. She exercises the way that's life-giving to her, and that, too, may look different from the rest of the crowd. She notices when she's believing a lie about herself and learns to take that thought to God. She remembers that she was made in God's image. And when she starts to feel the pressure to be better or look better, she takes a pause. She gives herself grace. She takes her eyes off the external and remembers that what's going on inside her heart is where her true glow and beauty will come from. Grace moment by grace moment, she learns to be kind to herself, to love the skin she's in, and to embrace the unique design that her Maker gave her. She doesn't do this perfectly. She's still learning. Still growing. Still stumbling on her way sometimes. But she's learning to keep her eyes on Jesus in a world that tells her she needs to be more than she is.

Lord, help me to embrace, enjoy, and love the way You made me.
Help me to keep in mind that true beauty comes from being
loved by You. Help me to let go of chasing perfection in my
appearance, and instead focus on my relationship with You.

You can let go of the chase to be more than you already are.
God made you. He wants you to embrace your uniqueness.
You shine from the inside out as you look to Jesus every day.

PRAY ABOUT ANYTHING AND EVERYTHING

Don't worry about anything; instead, pray about everything.
Tell God what you need, and thank Him for all He has done.

Philippians 4:6, NLT

We really can pray about anything and everything. Nothing is off-limits. I believe God wants to hear about all the details of your life, and He wants to help you with all of it. Here's the thing: our burdens, cares, hopes, and circumstances can cause anxiety in our hearts. And God doesn't want us to live in anxiety. He wants us to turn all of that anxiety over to Him because He cares so deeply for us. Over and over again, the Scriptures echo, peace be with you (John 20:21). Praying about anything and everything opens the pathway to living life with a deeply-rooted peace of knowing God has all our cares and prayers under control.

Have you noticed that at times anxiety can paralyze our hearts, making us feel like prayer won't work? Our circumstances or feelings can overwhelm us and cause us to think that bringing our cares to God won't solve the problem. But you know what? We can pray about that, too. We can ask the Lord to help us bring our anxiety, our cares, and our circumstances to Him in prayer. Even when we don't feel like praying, even when we're too overwhelmed and burdened to pray, and even when we lack faith to believe that God will come through. We can ask God to break through any wall that is keeping us from coming to Him.

So bring Him anything and everything. Nothing is too small. Nothing is too big. Nothing is too heavy. Nothing is too insignificant. Pray about everything, and you will know the deep peace of God. And when you feel that block in your heart that makes it difficult to turn to God in prayer, pray about that too. You are God's precious daughter, and He is happy to help you at any moment. He has the power to break through any barrier that is keeping you from Him. When you pray, you are also cultivating your relationship with God. Just as you would grow closer to a friend or family member by talking with them, you build intimacy with God by praying to Him.

Lord, I know I should pray about anything and everything,
but sometimes it's really hard to pray. Break through my
anxiety about praying. Break through my feelings of overwhelm.
Remind me over and over again to bring everything to You in prayer.

Ask God to break through any resistance you feel
in your heart about praying to the One Who cares
so deeply for you. Then watch Him do just that.

YOU CAN TRUST GOD TO ORCHESTRATE

*How much more will your Father in heaven
give good gifts to those who ask Him!*
Matthew 7:11, NIV

Maybe you're dreaming of a job, a role, a provision, or even a miracle. Whatever your dream, whether it's big, small, fancy, simple, impossible, or totally doable, today I want to encourage you that you can trust God to orchestrate it. You can trust that He is moving and working on your behalf behind the scenes of your dream. Sometimes we forget that we can let go of the dream we so desperately want and truly let God lead. We can let Him handle all the details. We can trust Him to orchestrate our dreams and our whole lives.

I imagine there are all these moving pieces behind the scenes of our dreams and lives, and God, as the orchestrator, is carefully working to move all the pieces together into a beautiful reality handmade for you. He's hard at work, tenderly moving on your behalf. He knows how much you care about this dream. In fact, He's moving in you, shaping your desires, and leading your dreaming heart. Like a father loves to give good gifts to his children, so our heavenly Father delights in giving us the dreams of our hearts. Not every dream will necessarily come into fruition. But even in that, God orchestrates. He is working all things together for our good (Romans 8:28). His plans and His heart for us are good.

So you can rest. Take the steps He's nudging you to take, but then rest, knowing He's got the rest. He's composing all the beauty of your wonderful dreams. You can let go. You can trust Him to take care of all of it. You can trust Him to orchestrate it all.

Lord, You know the dreams of my heart in this season
of my life. I turn them over to You. Thank You for
leading me day by day. Help me to trust You step by step.

*You don't have to orchestrate your dreams or your life.
God is happy to take the lead. In fact, He longs
to lead you. He longs for you to trust Him.*

KEEPING YOUR LIFE SPACIOUS FOR GOD

Draw near to God, and He will draw near to you.
James 4:8

One of the keys to living in step with God is to be in tune with Him. We have to guard and protect our relationship with Him. We must make room for Him and protect that time and space to meet with Him and dream with Him. Being in tune with God is tricky when we're busy, moving at a fast pace through life, and keeping up with responsibilities, emails, news, and everything else. Take some time today to slow down, to savor God, and to make space in your life for Him. In the slowing down and savoring, God's directing hand begins to lead your heart so that you experience His presence and know His peace. In the quiet spaces of time when you meet with Him, His presence begins to take over in your life and wraps you in a warmth and peace that you cannot find anywhere else.

Choose today to pull your heart up close to God. Maybe grab a journal and Bible instead of turning on the news. Maybe take a few minutes to soak in the sunset instead of checking your email inbox. Maybe set aside your to-do list for a few minutes, and simply be still and listen for God's whispers. Maybe tune out the newsfeed for a while and take some to time to dream with God about how He wants to use you for His purposes.

Our busyness isn't bad or wrong, but sometimes the busyness keeps us constantly on the go and pulls us away from the One Who wants to settle and establish our hearts. We will flourish as we tend our souls by giving ourselves space and time to draw close to God. Let today be a fresh start for you. A clean slate. A new beginning of slowing down and tuning more fully into the One Who has dreams for you and who delights in His relationship with you. Lean into your desire to start fresh, to slow your pace, and to experience more of God's presence in your life.

Help me to be fully in tune to You, Lord, so that I can know You more
and discover Your dreams for my life. Transform my heart to desire
a slower pace and a deeper awareness of You. Establish Your deep
peace in me so that I may live with satisfaction, joy, focus, and freedom.

*Keep your life spacious for God by
making space in your life for Him.*

GOD IS PARTING
WATERS FOR YOU

*For the LORD your God dried up the waters of the Jordan for you until you
passed over, as the LORD your God did to the Red Sea, which He dried up for
us until we passed over, so that all the peoples of the earth may know that
the hand of the LORD is mighty, that you may fear the LORD your God forever.*

Joshua 4:23-24

The God who parted waters in the Old Testament is *your* God. The God who led
Moses, Aaron, and Joshua is the same miracle-working God who is working in
your life. You can expect to be led. You can expect miracles. You can expect the supernatural movement of God in your life. God loves to surprise us with bursts of encouragement, joyful moments, heaven-sent glimpses of His grace and love, and answers to
our prayers. You can expect God to surprise you!

God is parting waters in your life. The same God who parted the Red Sea and
the Jordan River is parting obstacles, moving mountains, granting dreams that feel
blocked, and answering prayers that feel impossible. He's in control. That doesn't
mean He's going to part the waters in the exact ways we want them to be parted. But
if He's not parting a particular "water" in our lives, He must have good reason for it.
He's the God who tenderly cares for His daughters and knows just what is very best
for them. So we can trust His ways and know that if the water is meant to be parted,
it's going to part on His timetable.

Today, wherever you are, press into God's Word and prayer. And expect Him to
surprise you with jewels in His Word that delight your heart, refresh your hope, and
stir your joy. Record those revelations. Write them down so you can see God at work
in your life. Whatever obstacles, dreams, or prayer requests you are waiting on or
wondering about, know today that the God who parts waters is working behind the
scenes this very minute to do just that. Expect Him to surprise you! Rest in Him,
knowing that all your cares, burdens, and obstacles are in His care.

Lord, You know the "waters" in my life that need parting.
You know my impossible situations. You know my needs. You know
my desires. Thank You that I can bring all of that to You in prayer.
Keep my heart steady through the promises of Your beautiful Word
and give me faith to trust You to move the mountains in my life.

*Trust God with every circumstance.
He delights in amazing you!*

DON'T MISS THE GREATEST TREASURE

Do not lay up for yourselves treasures on earth, where moth and rust destroy and where thieves break in and steal, but lay up for yourselves treasures in heaven, where neither moth nor rust destroys and where thieves do not break in and steal. For where your treasure is, there your heart will be also.

Matthew 6:19-21

God knows all your desires and dreams. He knows every prayer that you have sent His way. He knows every concern. He knows every dilemma. He hears you as you bring Him everything that is on your heart. He loves to lead you, give you direction, and encourage your heart along the way. But don't miss the greatest treasure—God Himself. Sometimes I can get so busy bringing God all my concerns that I forget that He is the true treasure. Knowing Him and being in a relationship with Him is the best part of walking with God. Yes, I love that He gives me purpose, direction, clarity, and guidance. He helps me, shapes my heart, and empowers me with His Spirit. He blesses me with good things and wonderful gifts. But today, I'm reminding my heart that He is my greatest treasure. In a way, it takes the pressure off needing to know more about the direction He's leading me in because I already have the treasure. It takes the pressure off needing an answer right away because I know the One Who has the answer has me. It takes the pressure off needing more because He is everything I could ever need.

I can't get over the fact that God didn't just offer the gift of salvation and leave it at that. That would have been enough. But He went so much further by offering us the gift of relationship with Him. We never have to do life alone. We never have to handle troubles alone. We never have to be alone. He's with us every step of the way. When you know Jesus and believe in Him, you know the greatest treasure. Nothing in the world can give you joy, purpose, peace, and satisfaction like He can. When you know Jesus, you get to dance with Him for eternity, and you also have the best dance partner through this earthly life. He's always with you. He's always tuned into you. He's always watching over you. Know Him, and you've found the greatest treasure.

❧

Jesus, thank You for the gift of being in a relationship with You. May I never get over the wonder of You.

May you live this day with a new awareness of the treasure you hold inside—Jesus.

A FRESH, NEW DAY

*Because of the LORD's great love we are not consumed, for His compassions
never fail. They are new every morning; great is Your faithfulness.*
Lamentations 3:22-23, NIV

Every single day is a new day. Every single day is a fresh slate of grace. It's easy to get so stuck in the grind of the everyday that we miss the joy and grace of a new, fresh day! In the hustle and bustle of our morning routine in the Marr household, it often takes me a while to comprehend the joy and grace of a new day. Lunches packed, backpacks zipped, teeth brushed, hair combed, shoes tied, breakfast in tummies, doggie fed—we do this sometimes humorous dance of dashing out the door to beat the tardy bell, and after we make it, I breathe a sigh of relief and rush off to my day. I slip into "go" mode instead of taking some time to breathe in the grace of a new day. To breathe in the gift of God and His love and mercy. To breathe in His faithfulness. To recount the ways He's so generously lavished His love on me, both for eternity and for this earthly life.

You know, the enemy does not want us to enjoy the grace and joy of a new day. He wants to weigh us down with stress, anxiety, and whatever else he can distract us with so that we see each new day as a hustle instead of a joyful dance to be savored with the Lord. But we were made to dance through our day with joy and peace in the Lord. That doesn't mean that we won't have difficult days, but we always know we are not alone.

God is with you in this precious and glorious day. Don't worry about living this day perfectly, just dance it with Him. Enjoy the gift of *this* day. Don't miss the joy. Don't get caught up in the negative stuff. Be strong and courageous. And let His mercy and faithfulness fall fresh on you today as you live this day with an awareness of God's presence.

**Lord, thank You for Your faithfulness and Your new mercies for every morning.
Thank You for a fresh new day. May I savor it as a heavenly gift from You.**

*You have a fresh start today. Take a moment to ponder
the gift of having God with you in every moment.*

WHAT'S SQUELCHING YOUR JOY?

Yet I will rejoice in the LORD;
I will take joy in the God of my salvation.

Habakkuk 3:18

Daughter of Christ, you were created to experience the full measure of God's joy in you. But we live in a broken world. And if you're anything like me, your joy gets squelched too easily by too many things. What's squelching your joy today? What's depleting your heart? What's making you feel empty inside?

First of all, know that you're going to be okay. God lives inside you. (How amazing is that?) When you know Jesus, you have Him right there in your heart. Also, know that it's okay to be wondering why your joy disappears sometimes. There is value in evaluating what's stealing your joy. We have a real enemy on the prowl (1 Peter 5:8), and his focus is to steal our joy. He's sneaky and manipulative, and he's working around the clock to squelch our joy. But when we stand firm in the truth that we are daughters of Christ with Christ living in our hearts, and that we were made for joy, we can live above the taunts of the enemy.

Today, notice what little things are robbing you of the joy that is yours for the taking, and pray about them. Ask the Lord to renew your mind and thoughts. When He does, your joy will bubble up again. The joy is in there, but sometimes you have to pause and notice what things are squelching it.

Lord, in those moments when my joy is squelched, remind me to take
some time to bring any negative thoughts to You in prayer. Keep me alert to
the enemy's schemes to steal my joy, and help me to rejoice in You all day long.

The Lord wants you to have His full measure of joy.
Notice today what's squelching your joy, bring the concern to the Lord,
and watch for His love and joy to refill your heart.

A STRONG WOMAN OF GOD

I run in the path of Your commands, for You have set my heart free.
Psalm 119:32, NIV

The greatest calling on our lives is to know and love God. And out of that, vessels are raised up for His glory. He wants to use *you* as a vessel—a mighty one! You don't have to apologize for your gifts, desires, or dreams. The One Who made you is steering you, and He will steer those gifts, desires, and dreams. He will keep you on track with His beautiful plans for you.

The best guide to becoming a mighty woman for God is Scripture. God speaks through His Word, and when you open your Bible, He speaks to your heart. Those impressions you feel as you read a verse or that word that pops out at you when you read Scripture is a prompting from the One Who loves speaking truth into the depths of your soul. He has truth for every situation you face. All of God's Word is true, alive, and applicable to your life.

God is raising you up to be a mighty woman of God. With Scripture in your heart and as your guide, He leads you into the good works He created for you to do. Whether God uses you on a stage or behind the scenes, be excited about God's calling on your life to participate in His purposes. Our generation and the generations coming up behind us need women who love Jesus, who love His Word, and who stand firm in the callings He has set before them. He doesn't want you agonizing over how you look to the world or over what people will think. No, He's inviting you to dance free in the light of His presence, strong and mighty, with your feet firmly planted in Scripture.

Lord, sometimes I feel the opposite of a strong woman of God. I feel weak, insecure, and insignificant. It's hard to comprehend that You could use me to impact others for Christ. Today, I hold on to the truth that You do in fact use me in ways that I cannot see right now. Help me to keep looking to You day in and day out and trust that You are shining Your light through me in all kinds of ways.

God is using you to display His love and grace to the world around you—even when it doesn't feel like it, even as you read your Bible in your jammies and slippers, even when you have no makeup on, even when your mission for the day is to conquer the laundry and dirty dishes, and even when it feels like you're not making a difference.

A THANKFUL HEART

Give thanks to the LORD, for he is good; his love endures forever.
Psalm 118:1, NIV

Thanking God stirs up our affections for Him. As we look back over how God has been faithful to us, both in His gift of salvation and eternal life and also in our everyday relationship with Him, thankfulness rises up in our hearts and stirs up our love for Him. As we reflect on His love, His nature, His faithfulness, and His activity in our lives, we become even more aware of His presence. Find a quiet place, grab a hot tea or coffee (I'll have a vanilla latte), grab a notebook or piece of paper (or simply answer these questions in your heart), and let your heart grow thankful. I pray these questions will bless you today.

- How has God revealed Himself to you in a tangible way in the last year?
- What is a prayer request that God has answered in the last few months?
- How has God comforted you recently?
- How has God pulled you up out of discouragement lately?
- Name some blessings from God that simply bless your soul every day (they can be spiritual things or practical things, or even silly things).
- Who is a person that God has placed in your life who always makes you feel loved?
- In what ways has God surprised you in the last year?
- What doors has God opened for you this year that you are thankful for?
- What doors has God closed this year that you are thankful for?
- What are some tangible ways God has ministered to your soul in the last week?
- Which memories from the last year are your favorite?
- How have God and His Word ministered to your soul this year?

Lord, thank You for the many ways You have intersected my life
again and again. Grow in me a thankful heart so that I am more aware
of Your activity in my life. Your constant company is my joy and delight.

*May your heart grow in affection for God as you
see His handprints all over your precious life.*

WHEN GOD TUGS ON YOUR HEART

Let the beloved of the LORD rest secure in Him, for He shields him all day long, and the one the LORD loves rests between His shoulders.

Deuteronomy 33:12, NIV

Our hearts and souls seem to give us hints when we need God. The hints show up as fatigue, stress, or angst. These signs of spiritual dryness signal our hearts to return to God. Our hearts and souls were designed to need and crave God. Only He can fill us. God pursues our hearts completely. He keeps tugging on our hearts until we grab hold of the truth that our hearts are most at home with Him. He calls us ever deeper. He wants us to feel free, fully alive and present, and deeply connected to Him in ways that often our souls are crying out for, but that we don't quite recognize as God-thirst. Nothing is worth missing His presence. As we turn our hearts toward Him, He satisfies and settles our hearts into a deep contentment that stems from His presence and company.

Practically speaking, what noise can we turn down in our lives so that we can hear the Lord? What clutter in our minds and hearts need to go so that we can have space and room to feel His love? Our hearts function better when they have time and space to get quiet with God. A quiet heart is a content heart. A content heart is a joyful heart. God gladly teaches us these simple truths when we run to Him instead of other things. It is only when we run to Him that we find true peace and joy. He will gladly continue to guide us as we step into a new way of living, one that is in step with Him. The more space in our hearts we give over to God, the more He will show up in our everyday moments. Or perhaps, the more we will sense His presence, because He's always there.

**Thank You, God, for continuously tugging on my heart.
Thank You for not letting me miss You.**

*Lean into those moments when you
feel a tug on your heart toward God.*

RHYTHMS OF GRACE

Learn the unforced rhythms of grace.
Matthew 11:29, MSG

There are good things about being busy, but sometimes busyness can simply overwhelm our hearts. Sometimes the busyness causes a deeply rooted stress that slowly, if suppressed long enough, depletes our joy. We have a strong enemy who would love for us to feel defeated and who would prefer that we stay entangled in stress and weighed down by anxiety. Our human nature and our culture tempt our hearts to hustle and strive our way through life. But something divine resides inside us, a whisper that when we get really quiet, we hear. It is God's gentle, quiet, reassuring voice inviting us to *cease striving, be still, trust God, and pray.*

Hustle leads to stress, and stress leads to burnout. We long to find a new rhythm of grace. We long for grace over perfection. Abiding over striving. Leaning on God over hustling. Peace over stress. Prayer over worry. Rest over anxiety.

We were never meant to do life on our own. We were never meant to carry the burden of running our lives. We were never meant to try to do it all. Instead, we get to do life *with* God. Today, remember that prayer diffuses stress and breaks the tension of anxiety. Prayer sorts out your heart and draws you closer to your Father. When your heart is pulled in close to God, busyness and stress lose their hold on you. That sense of feeling overwhelmed is shattered when you invite God into your day to help you handle your load.

Lord, thank You that I don't have to do my day in my own power.
Show me what it looks like to step into Your rhythms of grace.
Show me how to lean on You throughout my day.

*Invite God into your day. He will empower you
with His peace and presence as you lean on Him.*

BRIGHT EYES

Consider me and answer, LORD my God.
Restore brightness to my eyes.

Psalm 13:3, CSB

In today's verse, David was literally running for his life. He was asking the Lord to help him escape from real, live enemies that were after his life. He was in serious trouble and needed serious help from God. While you may not be hiding in a cave today and running for your life, God wants to be your Deliverer each day.

What's your current cave? What things are you running from? In what ways is the enemy coming after your heart? What things are dimming the light in your soul and in your eyes? So many things can dim the light in us: to-do lists, busy schedules, distractions like social media, TV, and the news, comparison, stress, striving to live up to the expectations we put on ourselves, physical exhaustion, insecurity, circumstances that feel impossible. Think through what is dimming your light, because, sweet one, you were meant to glow. And I don't just mean on the outside, but from within.

When these obstacles take over and overwhelm our souls, we feel it. We feel the tension. We feel the weight. But we always have hope. We can always, every day and in any situation, call on the Lord like David did. We can bring Him everything that concerns us and overwhelms our hearts. We can bring God every impossible circumstance and turn it over to Him completely. We can tell God exactly what is causing us to feel stuck. We can tell Him exactly what is depleting our joy. And when we do, He begins to return our joy, comfort our hearts, build our faith, and restore the brightness back to our souls and our eyes. God brightens our hearts and faithfully delivers us out of any darkness we find ourselves in. He wants us shining from the inside out. So, like David, ask Him for light. Ask Him to restore the brightness to your eyes today.

Lord, restore brightness to my soul and eyes today. Thank You that I can lay all of my cares and concerns before You. You are my hope and light.

When you bring your whole heart to God,
He will gladly stir up light in you.

BECOME MORE
FULLY YOU

For You created my inmost being.
Psalm 139:13, NIV

One thing I love about being married to the man I began dating as a high school junior is that I don't have to try to be a better version of myself for him. In fact, he sees me at my absolute worst. He hears me say things that are just plain wonky. He gives me grace when I plummet into a bad mood over silly things, and he loves me when I'm sporting my favorite big, blue sweatshirt, hair in a bun on top of my head, and makeup washed off at the end of a full day. He loves me being me. And I'm most at home being myself with him.

Today, I want to encourage you that there is One that loves you being you. There is One Who delights in you being you. There is One Who doesn't need you to perform, to better yourself, or to strive harder. He wants you to rest in the simplicity, joy, and freedom of just being yourself. We become most fully ourselves when we live for an audience of our One and only God. When we live for Him, for His eyes, for His glory, and for His name, we get to lean back into the freedom of being ourselves. It's actually quite exhausting to try to mimic others or to better ourselves in our own power. But when our aim is to mimic Christ, our hearts wind up full, overflowing, and rich in simple joys. When He is our aim and our focus, we don't have to analyze how we are measuring up or living our unique dance through life. We just dance it.

You being you blesses God's heart. You can be comfortable in your own skin when in the depths of your heart you truly believe that God meticulously formed that very beautiful skin of yours. You can live from a place of rest because your heart is growing more in love with Jesus, and He's showing you that He's got all aspects of your life under control. You can live in the Spirit, with eyes and heart centered on God. This is how you can be the best version of yourself.

**Lord, thank You that I get to be me. Help me to embrace
who You made me to be—quirks and imperfections and all.**

*God loves you just the way you already are.
He showers you with His perfect grace every moment.*

THE BEAUTIFUL GRASS RIGHT UNDER YOUR TOES

Trust in the LORD and do good;
dwell in the land and enjoy safe pasture.
Psalm 37:3, NIV

Life is a mix of seasons, transitions, fresh starts, and changes. Just like the seasons of the weather change, so do our lives. Sometimes the unknown steps ahead make us feel antsy and restless. Sometimes we get stuck in a cycle of wishing for the next thing or that thing over there instead of enjoying the beautiful grass right under our toes. Today, know that the beautiful grass right under your toes is precisely where God has positioned you for your good and His glory. Cultivating gratitude for that beautiful grass right under your toes releases your heart from discontentment.

- Your life is intricately shaped by the Creator, and to appreciate your life and everything about it is to worship God with your life.
- When you enjoy where God has you—what you get to do each day, where you are, the pleasure of God's company—that joy trickles into the lives of your loved ones and the people around you.
- Enjoying where God has you is actually a step of faith and obedience that says, *God, I trust You with the lot You've given me, the position You have me in, and the special assignments You have placed before me.*
- When you soak in where God has you, no assignment is too big or too small.

Wherever you are today, I want to encourage you that when you take the step of faith to appreciate where God has you right now, you will find a sweet freedom and joy that perhaps your soul has been aching for. And you will find a new level of intimacy with the Lord as you begin to love the beautiful grass He has put right under your toes. Don't believe that the grass is greener somewhere else or that you will finally be happy when your circumstances change. Instead, believe that you are right where God wants you to be.

Lord, thank You for the beautiful grass right under my toes. Guide me today in appreciating, loving, and enjoying where You have me. Pull out the weeds of discontentment that I have allowed to grow, and bring me into the freedom of loving where You have me. Thank You for Your grace.

Where you are this very moment
is right where God wants you to be.

TAKE A STEP TOWARD HIM

The Lord is near to all who call on Him,
to all who call on Him in truth.

Psalm 145:18

If you're not sure what step to take next, just take a step toward God. Pursue Him. Because when we pursue Him, He shines a tiny bit more light onto our path. The goal isn't to know all the details of God's plans for our lives; the goal is to know Him more. When knowing God is our goal, our number one, our highest priority, then we will find purpose, meaning, and joy in the everyday. When you feel a little lost on your journey and you're needing some direction from God:

- Pray. Pull your heart up close to God and tell Him what's on your heart. He will listen, and He will relieve that pressure you feel to figure it all out.
- Start a list of all the blessings in your present season. Sometimes we get so excited about and anxious for the future or for the next season that we actually miss the beauty of what's right under our feet. Dig your heels into the grass under your toes and praise God for all His sweet gifts.
- Do the things that are right in front of you. What do you know God is calling you to do today? Love your husband? Love your kids? Take care of your home? Study? Teach? Lead? Do what is right before you.
- Trust that God will get your attention if you are taking a step outside His plans for you. Trust that He will keep your heart on course with Him as you seek Him.
- Celebrate that you long to know God's plans for you. That's a beautiful thing! It delights Him that you desire His plans for your life.
- Embrace the mystery of God and the mystery of His calling for your life. He's not trying to hide anything from you; He's simply longing for you to be dependent on Him for every step.
- Keep your blinders on. Don't look right or left, too far forward, or backward at the path you've already traveled. Be right where you are with God. Love the dance He has given you.

Lord, thank You for being my constant guide and companion through life.
When I'm not sure what step to take next, help me to focus on taking steps
toward You. Help me to make my relationship with You my highest goal.

A step toward God is a deep dive into His peace.

GOD IS GUIDING YOUR SOUL

*For you were straying like sheep, but have now
returned to the Shepherd and Overseer of your souls.*

1 Peter 2:25

Do you ever wish God would send you an email with an outlined agenda for your day, your week, your month, your year, or your whole life? It's tricky to navigate life without a detailed plan. It's hard to decipher what steps God wants you to take next when He doesn't speak with an audible voice. Maybe you are feeling a bit discouraged today as you try to figure out what steps God is asking you to take or you wish He would speak a little louder to your heart so that you could know—really, really know—what He is asking you to do. I know. Hold on to this today:

God is the Shepherd and Overseer of your soul. He's guiding your soul, intricately shaping your life, and leading each and every one of your steps.

Maybe instead of focusing so much on what He is trying to tell us or how He is leading in a particular situation, we can focus on pulling our hearts up close to His. As we draw near to Him, He draws near to us (James 4:8). As we focus on nearness to Him and intimacy with Him, His plans for us (all the good stuff we would like an email about) will unfold day by day. The gift is that we don't have to manufacture, analyze, or stress over our lives—we can simply focus on drawing close to the Lord and spending time with Him in His Word and in honest conversation with Him.

I know that doesn't solve the dilemma of wanting an exact outline from God. But I hope it puts your heart at rest a bit today to know that He's got you, He's got your life, and He's got every step that you take. When you find yourself feeling uneasy about it all, let that be a signal to your heart to draw close to Him. When you draw close to God, He will do what only He can do—He will bring your heart peace about future steps, next steps, and all the steps in between. He will gently remind you that He's got it all.

**Lord, thank You for guiding my life and for being the Shepherd and
Overseer of my soul. Help me to trust You with my life—to trust You to
lead my steps and guide my soul. When I am tempted to take control,
remind me that I don't have to manufacture Your plans for me.**

*Surrender control to God. Follow Him like a sheep
follows its shepherd, and you will experience
greater peace than you ever had before.*

HEART MAKEOVER

I will give you a new heart and put a new spirit in you; I will remove from
you your heart of stone and give you a heart of flesh. And I will put My Spirit
in you and move you to follow My decrees and be careful to keep My laws.

Ezekiel 36:26-27, NIV

Maybe today your heart feels a bit hardened toward God, toward a person, or simply from the wear and tear of living in a broken world. Maybe your heart feels tender from disappointment, weary from struggles, or simply a bit overwhelmed.

God sees your heart. He knows it. He knows every crevice, every corner, every nook that feels unseen. He knows the patterns and thoughts that sit inside you, and He wants you to know that He wants to be the One to handle your heart. He longs to lead you, to comfort you, and to restore your weary heart. He has the power to give you a heart makeover. The makeover begins with allowing His love for you to be the focus of your life. God wants to tenderly bless your heart. He wants to free you from every entanglement and set you free to enjoy His presence in your life. Bring God your whole heart today. He will gladly refresh your spirit.

Jesus, here's my heart.
Here's everything that has it entangled.
Remove any hardness in it, and give me a
new heart that is full of Your beautiful Spirit.

We were not made to handle our hearts on our own. Between the pull of
the world, the enemy at work, and our own human nature, our hearts
are in trouble apart from God. He is the one who created your heart.
Let Him free you from the burden of managing your heart.

HAVE FAITH TODAY

The fundamental fact of existence is that this trust in God,
this faith, is the firm foundation under everything that
makes life worth living. It's our handle on what we can't see.

Hebrews 11:1, MSG

Faith is trusting God when you would rather take the situation into your own hands. Faith is giving God as much time as He needs to work in a particular circumstance instead of jumping ahead and taking care of things by yourself. Faith is bringing your heart to God in prayer instead of running down the trail of worry and fretting. Faith is an opportunity to watch God work. Faith is trusting that God really, truly is at work behind the scenes of your life.

Whatever it is in your life and on your heart that has made your heart feel wobbly and unsteady, bring that to the One Who loves to steady your heart. Bring it to the One Who works tirelessly on your behalf. He is for you.

Faith is trusting God and believing in Him. Walking with a God you can't see, touch, or feel is challenging to say the least. Believing in a God you can't audibly hear or meet face-to-face requires faith. The fact that you are choosing to have faith in God is cause for celebration today. You are doing the hard thing. You are choosing faith over fear. Faith over worry. Faith over control. Faith over doing life on your own. You are choosing God's way. When you feel a bit unsteady in your faith, remind yourself that it's okay. Having faith is hard sometimes. God knows this. But as you choose faith, He will make Himself more and more real to you every day.

Lord, oftentimes it's hard for me to have faith when I can't see You.
Help me to trust You more and more every day. Even though I can't see You
face-to-face today, help me to trust that You are with me every second of the day.

Have faith that God is constantly at work on your behalf.
Have faith that God is present in everything you are doing today.
Have faith for this life and the eternal one to come.

GOD ALWAYS SHOWS UP

In the morning, LORD, You hear my voice;
in the morning I lay my requests before You and wait expectantly.

Psalm 5:3, NIV

What is twisting your heart around in knots and causing anxiety deep in your soul? I want to hold out a bit of encouragement to you about that from Psalm 5.

I know what it is like to feel like you cannot shake something that's nipping away at your peace. It's like a little bee flying around your head that you keep swatting at, but it always seems to find its way back to you. It won't go away, and the more you swat at it, the more it seems to buzz around you. Remember that we can bring *everything*—whether it is big, small, or somewhere in-between—to the Lord in prayer.

Our God is so personal. Sometimes I get all wonky inside because I feel like the cares that I bring to the Lord are pretty silly and petty in comparison to the big things going on around me in the world. But Psalm 5 tells us that God doesn't care how big or small our petitions and cares are, He simply cares that we bring them to Him. Sometimes after we bring Him our cares, we still feel the inner angst in our hearts. The very last bit of Psalm 5:3 says, "and wait expectantly." My heart seems to forget that waiting part. We must wait in expectation for God to move in our situation.

Wait for the Lord. He's working. Relief is coming. Peace is on its way. That thing will get worked out. You don't have to figure it out. God's handling it. Keep praying. Keep bringing it to Him. Keep trusting Him. Keep rehearsing truth. And then expect Him to show up. God loves to work in and through the situations that weigh on our hearts. So keep bringing it all to Him and asking for His help. And then wait in sweet expectation.

Lord, help me to remember that You always show up in my life.
Help me to wait in expectation and hope, not worry and angst.

Bring every care to God, then wait in hope for Him to
work things out. He cares about what you concerns you.
Nothing is too insignificant for Him.

YOUR DIRECT LINE TO GOD

*Tremendous power is released through the passionate,
heartfelt prayer of a godly believer!*
James 5:16, TPT

Sometimes we can get stuck in the mindset that our prayer time has to be this *one* time of day where we pray about everything all at once. We think our prayer life needs to look a certain way. But God invites us to pray all throughout the day—any time and any place—and to let our prayer life be a constant conversation with Him. He doesn't require that we have a formal prayer time. There is no certain number of minutes we are required to pray in order to get a check by our name. There's no right or wrong way to pray—we can pray in all kinds of ways. The important thing is to find ways to make prayer a priority.

Remember today that you have a constant, direct line to the God of the universe. You will never be put on hold. The line is always open, and prayer is what keeps us closely connected to our heavenly Father. There will be days when your day is so busy that quick arrow prayers to God on the go is your prayer plan for the day. That's beautiful. There will be days when you have more margin to sit on your back porch—sun shining, birds singing, coffee steaming—and list out your prayers in a journal as you pray through each and every request. That's beautiful. There will be days when your circumstances have drained every ounce of your faith and you're desperate for God to intervene so you drop to your knees in your closet and cry out to God, not sure how to word your requests. That's beautiful. The way you pray is precious and beautiful, powerful and effective. Your prayers move the heart of God, affecting generations to come.

**Lord, help me to pray throughout my day and to
remember that my prayers are powerful and effective.**

*You always have a direct line to God.
He delights in hearing from you.*

LET GOD SPEAK INTO YOUR LIFE

Our help is in the name of the LORD, Who made heaven and earth. Those who trust in the LORD are like Mount Zion, which cannot be moved, but abides forever.

Psalm 124:8–125:1

Sometimes I get so busy telling God all the things I need Him to do in my life, all the people I need Him to encourage, all the dreams I need Him to intervene in, and all the energy I need Him to infuse into me for my day that I forget to let Him speak into my life. I imagine Him grinning a bit as I type these words today: *Yeah, she talks a lot. But when she's ready to listen, I love speaking life into her.* He's patient and kind. And did I mention patient? He loves me and laughs with me, and I am pretty sure He goes with the flow of my very human nature. What grace. What love!

Maybe you feel like you have been doing a lot of praying lately, but in the very same breath, you feel thirsty to hear from God. Sweet one, I want you to know that God does hear you. And He provides His Word as an instrument to give His response. When you feel thirsty to hear God's voice, pour over His Word. When you long to get some direction from Him, let His Word pour into you. Saturate your heart and mind with His Word, because that is His instrument to speak to your heart, along with His Spirit.

Don't worry about following a program. Simply open up the Bible and start where you are. To hear God's voice every day, we must open His Word every day. When we tune our hearts to His Word, He tunes our hearts to Him. When we read Scripture, He infuses our hearts with truth, peace, and guidance. When we long to hear His voice, He will gladly and tenderly speak through the pages of Scripture. Dear friend, just open it up. As we get lost in the Word, God will speak truths to our hearts. Let your mind feed on His love letter to you.

Lord, remind me to listen for Your whispers.
Help me to look to Your Word when I need to hear from You.

May you sense God's gentle whispers over your life.
He is your Help. With Him and His Word, you cannot be shaken.

March

WHEN YOU NEED STRENGTH AND COURAGE

Have I not commanded you? Be strong and courageous.
Do not be frightened, and do not be dismayed,
for the LORD your God is with you wherever you go.

Joshua 1:9

Do you need strength and courage today? Are your circumstances overwhelming? Do you feel inadequate for the tasks before you? Are you wondering how you're going to tackle all that you face this week?

You're going to be okay. Wait, scratch that. If I could, I would look you straight in the eyes over coffee and say this: You're not just *going* to be okay. You *are* okay right now, in this moment, because God has you this very moment. He knows you're overwhelmed. He knows all that is on your plate. He knows where you feel dread and anxiety in your life. He knows the things that are causing stress in your heart. He makes you okay. But not just okay—He helps you thrive and live abundantly with joy and purpose.

God will give you the strength and courage that you need today. He does not want you to live in fear, discouragement, or a state of overwhelm. He invites you to be strong and courageous by leaning on Him. He makes you strong for the things He has called you to do. How can we gain His strength? By admitting that we are weak without Him. By admitting we can't do our day or our week in our own strength. By admitting, *Lord, I need Your help.*

Today, whatever is in front of you, surrender your heart to the Lord and let Him guide you and help you to be courageous. Keep your heart soft toward Him, always listening, always attentive. He will gladly lead you.

Lord, thank You that You are always with me. Thank You that
You provide me with the strength and courage for my day.
And thank You that You are always with me in everything.
Make me strong and courageous, and keep my heart attentive to You.
Show me how to lean on You instead of trying to do my life in my own strength.

You don't have to do your life in your own strength and
power. Bring your anxiety, dread, or sense of overwhelm
to the Lord. He will gladly take your burdens and
help you operate in a way that brings peace and joy.

WHEN YOU NEED
A LITTLE MORE FAITH

But the angel said to him, "Do not be afraid,
Zechariah, for your prayer has been heard."

Luke 1:13

Do you ever find yourself wanting a little more affirmation from God regarding His plans for you? After Zechariah receives this incredible audible message from an angel, his very first response is, "How shall I know this?" It almost makes me chuckle, because I want to hold Zechariah by the shoulders, look him in the eye, and say something like, "Zechariah! An angel literally delivered a message straight from God! Didn't you hear it?" Even with a meeting with an angel of God, Zechariah had doubts. He had questions.

I would have responded to the angel in a similar way. *Can I get a double confirmation that that was really God speaking to me? Can you just check on that real quick and get back to me and just make sure you're sure that's what God said?* It's like we want double confirmation of God's plans for us. We want a few more specifics. We think we sense God's promptings correctly, but then we question ourselves, wondering if we heard God correctly.

While I don't think God looks down on us for our lack of faith, I do believe He wants to stir up our faith. Zechariah's story shows us that it's better to exercise faith than to wallow in doubt. How do we stir up our faith and cancel out our doubts? The Word of God is our pathway to more certainty about who God is and what He is calling us to. Doubt will always be a temptation, so it will take faith to believe God, believe His Word, and believe the revelations that He speaks to our hearts.

May we choose to believe God and take Him at His Word. May we walk in faith instead of doubt. In those moments when you wish an angel of God would land in your living room and just spell out God's plans for you, may you choose faith in the One Who has a beautiful plan for your life by finding certainty in His Word.

Lord, help me to have faith in You today. When doubts creep
into my heart, may Your Word re-center my faith in You.

Choose faith over your doubts.
Faith in God will bring peace to your heart.

TEND YOUR SOUL AND FLOURISH

Only take care, and keep your soul diligently.
Deuteronomy 4:9

Our bodies and our souls signal to us when they need some care and pampering. Sometimes we don't realize all that we are doing and accomplishing in a day or a week or a month, or we don't realize all the emotion we have put into something. God designed our bodies and souls to signal us when we are depleted.

Our physical bodies as well as our souls need tending. In the physical realm, we may need rest, fuel, water, exercise, or sunshine. In a heart and soul sense, we may need time with Jesus—off the program, off the reading plan, just the two of you talking things out and finding comfort in His Word. Our bodies, souls, hearts, emotions, and minds are all connected. When one aspect of us is out of balance, we can feel completely depleted.

Where do you feel depleted today? Is your body trying to tell you something? How can you listen to your body so that you can flourish through your daily dance of life? I encourage you today to be gentle on yourself. Our God is so sweet to not demand a life of pushing ourselves to the point of exhaustion day in and day out. His way is easy. His burden is light (Matthew 11:28-30). He wants to partner with us through our days. He invites us to be gentle on ourselves, take care of ourselves, and rest. We cannot do the things He is calling us to do when we are depleted. We cannot dance when our bodies are fatigued. But when we tend to our souls and take care of ourselves, we flourish. Accept the invitation to be gentle on yourself today, to take care of yourself, and to tend to your soul so that you can flourish!

Lord, You know the state of my body and soul today. Thank You for designing our bodies in such a glorious way. Help me to listen to my body and soul and take care of myself so that I can be my best. Show me what I need today.

Be gentle to your body. Be kind to your soul. You're working so hard day in and day out. Don't forget to take care of yourself.

STEADY MY HEART

Truly He is my rock and my salvation; he is my fortress, I will never be shaken….
Yes, my soul, find rest in God; my hope comes from him.

Psalm 62:2, 5, NIV

So often we put our hope and our strength in everything but God. Or we put our hope and strength in God plus something else with Him. But Scripture implores us to put our hope in Him *alone*. When I think of a fortress, I think of a secure, sturdy, impenetrable blockade that nothing can get through. That's what God wants to be for us. But we tend to make other things be our fortress.

Instead of looking to earthly things for satisfaction, I long to take a holy pause and point my soul right to God's heart and say, *Hey, soul, wait in silence for God to fill you up. Because your hope is from Him.* Instead of looking to things to fill me up, I long to bring all my neediness to God so that He can satisfy my heart. Otherwise, I get tied up in all the wrong things instead of securing my footing in the strong fortress of God.

Today, grab hold of God as your strong fortress. He is like no other! He will keep you strong and on your feet. And when you find yourself in a heap, feeling like a mess—and that will happen sometimes—remember to reach up for Him. Remember to take a holy pause and let Him fill you like nothing else. Then stay strong, not in your own might, but in His. Let God steady your heart every day as you look to Him alone as your strong and mighty fortress.

Lord, may I look to You as my strong fortress. May my soul find its hope in You alone. Help me to lay aside the things I try to put my significance in, and instead find security in knowing that You are my fortress. Steady my heart. Steady my footing. Secure my hope.

Look to God alone to satisfy your heart's needs.

MADE BY GOD

In the same way, the Spirit helps us in our weakness.

Romans 8:26

It is so easy to think, *If I just had her body, her hair, her talent, her house, then I would be truly happy.* Insecurity and comparing ourselves to others accomplish nothing, they simply rob us of our joy. Sometimes we just need a little reminder to get our minds in line with God's perspective.

There is no one on earth like you! God made you, and you belong to Him. He cares so passionately about each one of us. He designed us perfectly. Every gal is like a unique, beautiful flower—each carrying beauty in our own way. In our world, it's way too easy to compare. One hop on social media, and suddenly we are not enough. One look around, and suddenly we crave more. One hop of comparison, and suddenly we feel lost. The more we look around and compare, the more we forget who we are as daughters of Christ. Where do you feel the pull of comparison in your life?

We have access to the Perfect Source for help. The Spirit helps us in our weakness. We have One Who will help us stay glued to the truth that God not only made us in a unique way, but that He want us to embrace the way He made us. He wants us to let go of comparing and be who He made us to be. Sometimes our hearts just need a little pep talk to get us back in line with the grace of embracing who we are. Embracing the grace to be ourselves releases us from the chains of comparison.

Today, remember that God made you and you belong to Him. Hold on to that simple truth and, with His help, step away from comparing thoughts when they try to sneak in. Trade them for the truth that God made you just the way He wanted. Embrace the beautiful woman God made you to be—inside and out.

Jesus, today please help me to let go of my insecurities and stop comparing myself to others. Help me to be thankful for the way You made me and the fact that I am Your daughter.

When you catch yourself comparing yourself to others, stop that thinking trap by reminding yourself that the God of the universe dreamed you up in His heart.

STEPS OF TRUST

*Whether you turn to the right or to the left, your ears will
hear a voice behind you, saying, "This is the way; walk in it."*
Isaiah 30:21, NIV

In this dance of life, God asks us to take steps of trust. Often those steps can feel like blind leaps of faith, and we would kind of rather not take them, you know? Life is this twisting, turning, constant motion of ups, downs, and all arounds, but thankfully we have a calm center inside of us—God Himself—who guides us through. We don't have to navigate. We don't have to steer the ship of our lives. What relief and grace and freedom there is in knowing that God navigates and steers us. We can let go of trying to control everything, and instead take grace steps of trust and of faith.

Dear one, when you let go of navigating and steering your life, something beautiful sweeps in to cover you, calm you, and center you. It's a grace, a power, and a presence—His Grace, His Power, and His Presence. The Lord takes over and just leads. And He loves to lead! What if you let go of leading and just took steps of trust today? What blessings and goodness and sweetness might God have for you on the other side of a step of faith? A step of trust is uncomfortable and feels foreign at first, but on the other side is His peace. He invites us to step toward Him, allowing Him to navigate and steer our lives, so that we can experience His leading presence. Steps of trust become steps of joy as we relearn how to trust God. He is guiding all of your steps. He has each one planned out. He guards them all.

Today, trust. Trust the Lord's lead of your life. Trust His care of your heart. Trust that He is right there with you. Trust that He cares about all the details of your life. Today, take one step of trust. His strength will meet you in your weakness with His beautiful grace.

**Lord, at times I forget to let You lead my life, and instead I power
through my day without checking in with You. Help me to look to You
for guidance. Help me to let You take the lead of my everyday steps.**

*That beautiful grace-filled sweet spot of abundant
life is found when we let God lead our steps.*

LIFE IS BEAUTIFUL

Then you will look and be radiant;
your heart will throb and swell with joy.

Isaiah 60:5, NIV

Life is beautiful. There is so much to love: the joy of new babies, the scent of flowers, the thrill of a new adventure, the love between a husband and wife, the precious things our kids say, the here and now, the hope of heaven, the security of salvation, the constant knowing of our Savior's presence. Life is filled with hard things too. You know it—you've walked through them. There will be hard things, dear one, but there is always light on the other side of it. And so we allow ourselves to feel the hard things. We let the tears fall, and we sit in God's lap. We trust when we can't understand, believe when we can't see, and hug a friend when we don't know what to say.

From brokenness and loss to wonder and happiness, our lives are a bundle of mountains and valleys, highs and lows. Here on earth in these temporary bodies and temporary homes is where we can find God and know Him intimately. We can experience His presence on the mountaintops of the beautiful moments of life, and we can experience His presence in the valleys of life. And one day we will step over into heaven and there will be no more sadness, no more darkness, and no more pain. Until then, we keep dancing in step with our Savior, holding His hand through the good and through the hard, and He remains faithful through it all.

Lord, thank You for reminding me that life is a mixture of mountains and valleys.
You know where I am today. Give me Your perspective for my life.
Help me to see that You are with me through all of life's joys and trials.
Thank You for filling my heart with joy as I look to You.

May you always keep looking up for God's
light in the hard moments, and may you keep
dancing with joy through the good moments.

BRING HIM YOUR MESS

The LORD builds up Jerusalem; he gathers the exiles of Israel.
He heals the brokenhearted and binds up their wounds.

Psalm 147:2-3, NIV

God's truth and grace are like a big, tall, drink of flowing water—a spring that always seems to find us. The Holy Spirit constantly draws us back in step with Him. Truth says, *You're enough, just as you are.* Grace says, *Your broken things—those frustrating struggles—are perfect opportunities to lean on Me.* So in all our feelings of not-enough-ness and frustration, we can cling to God's truth and grace. His truth and grace place us right back in step with Him.

I know that at times you're frustrated with things in your life that seem to always be a struggle or maybe even feel like a mess. Jesus says, in a sense, *bring Me your mess.* He invites us to bring Him our messy hearts. *Here's my same old stuff, Lord. Here's the same old mess. Here's the same old things I am stuck in again.* We bring Him our whole hearts again, but get this: His grace, truth, blessings, help, and love wash over us again and again. He sweeps us off our feet again. He dances with us, getting us right back into step with Him. He whispers something like, *Your mess is not too much for Me.* And His whispers make our heart dance.

God loves you in your mess. He loves you in your seemingly weak moments. Without those moments, dear one, perhaps you wouldn't feel like you need a Savior. What if just today, when faced with your weakness, you whispered back, *Thank You for my messy heart, Lord, because my messy heart gets to know the joy of being revived, renewed, and restored by You.* God builds us up continually. He gathers us again when we stray. He heals every broken heart. And He binds up every wound. He will never stop wooing us toward Himself, and the pathway to Him is often through our messes.

Lord, here's my messy heart again. Here's the same old thing.
Thank You—yes, thank You for my weak spots. For where I am weak,
You are strong in me. Meet me in my weak spots and bring me back in
step with You. Thank You for coming back for me day after day after day.

LOVELY THOUGHTS

Whatever is true, whatever is noble, whatever is right,
whatever is pure, whatever is lovely, whatever is admirable—if
anything is excellent or praiseworthy—think about such things.

Philippians 4:8, NIV

What we think about matters, and Scripture implores us to watch our thoughts. But it can feel so impossible to think about what we are thinking about, you know? How can we be intentional about our thoughts? How can we think lovely, sparkling, good, holy, precious thoughts when our human nature tends to lean toward negative thinking? We have a zillion little moments every day to dwell on negative thoughts, but we also have a Helper who loves us, and He will empower us to guard our minds if we let Him. You can think lovelier thoughts with the help of the Holy Spirit. And this change in your thoughts will impact your entire day.

When you find yourself stuck in a negative line of thinking today, or when you find yourself caught in a mood, pause a moment and ask the Lord to help you track down that pattern and bring your thoughts back in line with Christ. Replace the negative thoughts with truth. Remind yourself that God is good, that you are His daughter, and that He is at work in you. Instead of sweeping negative thoughts under the rug, bring them into Christ's light.

Jesus wants us to guard what we think about because what we think about affects how we feel and how we live. Today, may you look to the Lord to help you think lovely thoughts. He loves you dearly and wants His joy to flow through you.

Lord, help me to be aware of my thought life today. Help me to catch
the negative thoughts and bring them into Your light. Help me to replace any
negative thought patterns with Your truth. May my thoughts be lovely today.

Bring back lovely thoughts, bring back prayer,
bring back casting your cares on the Lord, and enjoy your day.

KEEP PRAYING BIG

Let us then approach God's throne of grace with confidence, so that
we may receive mercy and find grace to help us in our time of need.

Hebrews 4:16, NIV

Keep praying big! Sometimes I slip into kind of a small-faith mentality in my prayers. I hate to bother God with things that seem kind of surface, dreams that may not matter in the grand scheme of life, prayers that are just fun things that I am hoping for or would love to see come to fruition. But this perspective is not a correct view of God's heart. The truth is, God loves it when His daughters pray. He loves it when we talk to Him and ask Him for the things we feel Him nudging us to ask. He loves it when we pray because prayer is intimacy with Him. He does not roll His eyes at us when we ask for those things that are dear to us. You know, I think maybe He simply smiles and His heart swells up with joy because He knows that for us to ask these things in prayer means that we have faith in Him. We trust Him. We love Him. We know He will answer in the way that He sees fit, even if it's different than we desire. Thankfully God shapes and refines our desires as we look to Him. He knows that our desires can be deceiving and take us down the wrong paths.

So pray with confidence, pray with honesty, and trust the God of the universe to answer in the way He sees fit. Pray for those impossible things, pray for those silly things, pray casual prayers, pray funny prayers, and pray big prayers. What are you praying for today? Grab your coffee, find a porch, and pray on, sister in Christ!

Lord, thank You that I can bring anything that's on my heart
to You in prayer. Thank You for grace to pray! Help me to bring
You every concern on my heart, and may my prayer life be the
catalyst for deeper intimacy with You. I want to know You more.

Pray throughout your day. No prayer is too silly or small.
As you keep the line of prayer with your heavenly Father open,
you will feel His presence throughout your day.

WHEN YOU NEED TO KNOW
THERE IS ALWAYS HOPE

Hope deferred makes the heart sick,
but a longing fulfilled is a tree of life.
Proverbs 13:12, NIV

Give up or keep hoping? A sweet gal wrote me an email about similar questions going on in her heart: "I am afraid to hope, you know?" Yes. I know. Sometimes when our hopes don't turn out the way we want, well, it simply hurts. Hopes that don't pan out hurt. And so we stop hoping or dreaming because we don't want to feel that hurt. But keeping our hopes down also keeps our joy down. And keeping our hopes down robs us of peace, of energy, and of excitement.

Hope deferred (put off, delayed) makes the heart sick, but a longing fulfilled (keeping that hope in God up) is a tree of life (a thriving, well-established, growing, healthy soul).

I don't know what has got your hopes down today, but I want to encourage you to let your hope dance again. In that dream, in that relationship, for that prayer request, with your God, let your hope dance again. Believe that God has good things just for you today and every day. Watch for those little sparkles of hope. God is all around you, at work in your day, sprinkling your day with hope-filled moments. Watch for them, sweet one.

Lord, You know the hopes of my heart.
Keep me hoping in You every day.
Thank You that because of You,
there is always reason for hope.

Know today and every day that there is always hope
in everything and every situation because we have
the Wonderful Counselor, Mighty God, Holy One in our
midst all the time. He always wants us to keep our hopes up!

GOALS, ACCOMPLISHMENTS, REWARDS

Fill my heart with joy.
Psalm 4:7, NIV

I don't know what you are putting your hope in, but be encouraged, be reminded, be nudged to put your hope in God every day. Let go of the striving, the climbing, the outdoing, the quest for more, the chasing for more. We can rest deeply in the sweet relief of knowing that Jesus fulfills like nothing else. He keeps our hearts in line with His heart, which is the most fulfilling place for them to be.

Let go and lean back into His grace, love, peace, and presence. Those gifts are the greatest goal, the sweetest reward, and the best accomplishment. He is where our hearts find true rest from the chase of life and learn to dance through the journey and to truly enjoy it. The goals, the rewards, and the accomplishments, while they are exciting, fun, and rewarding are not the end goal. Our hearts won't find full, true, deep peace when we reach the things we are striving for. True joy lies in the journey of walking in step with our Savior.

Let go of finding fulfillment in the results. Let your true fulfillment be in the journey of partnering with God through the dance of life. Let His presence, company, help, love, and grace be your reward. Where have you been seeking fulfillment? Is it draining you? What might happen if you let go of that and sought fulfillment in Jesus alone?

**Lord, show me where I have been seeking fulfillment
outside of You. May I look to You instead.**

Your heart will find fulfillment when you look to Him alone.

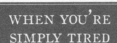

WHEN YOU'RE SIMPLY TIRED

Come to Me.
Matthew 11:28

Sometimes we are going, going, going, and we are suddenly hit with an overwhelming sense of fatigue. Physical fatigue is something we know what to do with. We know we need rest. We know we need to prop our feet up, go to bed earlier, and turn down the speed of our busy pace. But emotional and mental tiredness are a little bit harder to define and recognize. What things seem to deplete your time, your joy, and your energy? For me, it's the little things. Spending too much time scrolling through the newsfeed makes me tired. Keeping up with my to-do list makes me feel tired. Worrying about life makes me tired. Take note today of exactly what is making you tired. Is it physical? Is it emotional? Is it mental? I encourage you today to grab a pen and paper and write down what things are making you tired.

Seek rest in the One Who offers the truest kind of rest. There is a remedy to our emotional and physical fatigue—Jesus. Sometimes our fatigue actually leads us to surrender our try-hard life. Sometimes our fatigue is actually a good thing because it gives us an opportunity to acknowledge, *Lord, I can't do this on my own. I desperately need your help.* Fatigue reminds us that we need a Savior. And sometimes instead of fighting our fatigue, what we really need is to let God fully into our day. To pray, *Lord, I really need your help.*

God invites us to let go of the pressures, the stress, the burdens, and the busyness, and to let Him lead us. When He leads our day, our energy is restored, our joy is built up, and our hearts are revived. Let your fatigue be a signal that what your heart is really longing for is simply to rest in your Savior—to spend time with Him without any expectation of doing more or being better. Let it simply be a time to be refilled. He loves to refill you. A tired heart is sometimes a good thing because it leads to a surrendered heart. What does your tired heart need today, sweet one? Bring your heart to the Lord and allow His Spirit to pinpoint those little things in your heart that may be contributing to your fatigue. Then rest in Him. Let Him have your tired heart.

Lord, when my heart and soul feel tired, help me to turn to You for the restoration I need. Thank You that I don't have to do my day on my own.

Rest your weary heart today. Sip tea on your back porch.
Keep your Bible close. Take a nap. Surrender your day to the Lord.

WE NEED YOUR ART

I have filled him with the Spirit of God, with ability
and intelligence, with knowledge and all craftsmanship.

Exodus 31:3

In a world that's broken, hurting, scary, big, and chaotic, we need the joy of what you do. We need your beauty. We need that thing that God has put in you that makes you unique. We need you to do those things you do so well, but that maybe you feel don't matter much. Those things are your art—the beautiful ways God has gifted you. Whether your art is dancing on a stage, working behind the scenes, arranging flowers, taking photos, hosting a dinner gathering, or being a mom, we need your art because your art brightens our hearts. Your art lightens our load, takes our mind off the hard stuff, and breathes fresh light and hope into our world. Whether your art feels "spiritual" or not, know that it's all spiritual because God can use your art to bless other hearts in ways you may not see.

As you use your gifts, you grace the world around you. The way you use your gifts brings blessings to our hearts and allows us to take our minds off the world for a while. Sweet one, do the things you love and that God has wired you to do, because they bless our hurting world. Your gifts bring light into the world around you, and just a little bit of light can change a life. Keep doing what you're doing so God can use you to keep us inspired, to bring joy to our hearts, and to brighten our lives. Sometimes we all just need a little lift, and your gifts give us that boost. Keep shining brightly.

Lord, most days I don't feel like I contribute anything amazing to the world around me. But today You have reminded me that You have indeed gifted me in unique ways to bring light to a hurting world. Help me to tap into the things that I love to do and feel wired to do, and help me to trust that You are using me to bring light, even a little, to those around me.

The meal you make, the dance you dance, the art you create,
the words you write, the call you make, the love you offer, the house
you keep, the story you read, the note you send—it's all spiritual.

THE WORK OF GOD'S HANDS

*O LORD, You are our Father; we are the clay, and You
are our potter; we are all the work of Your hand.*

Isaiah 64:8

You are the work of God's hands. I know the dance of striving to make yourself something. Striving to become better, hustling and toiling to be better at "the Christian life." Oh, I know this dance, and I know how it makes a heart feel heavy. Today, may you remember that you are the work of God's hands. You don't have to strive to make yourself something. You don't have to strive to become better. You don't have to hustle and toil to try to be a better Christian.

Instead of trying hard, what if He's asking us to just be held? Instead of striving, what if He's asking us to be moldable? Instead of hustling and toiling, what if He's asking us to just be?

We are the work of His hands. Our job, our work, is to surrender to the Lord, allowing Him to mold us into who He created us to be.

Today, may you fully rest in the sweet knowledge that You are a royal, divine work of God. Let Him do the growing, the becoming, the bettering. Let Him do a mighty work of art with your life.

Lord, I find myself at times striving so hard to be a better version
of myself. Instead of striving, hustling, and toiling, help me to rest in
You and surrender to Your ways of growing me into the woman You had
in mind when You made me. Thank You that I can let go of striving.

*Instead of striving, hustling, and toiling,
be held by God today. Rest, dear daughter of Christ.
You don't have to force the growing and becoming.*

FINDING GOD IN
YOUR DAILYNESS

Behold, I am doing a new thing; now it springs forth, do you not perceive it?
I will make a way in the wilderness and rivers in the desert.

Isaiah 43:19

A text popped up on my phone from a friend I hadn't talked to in a long time. Her text asked me a simple question: "What's new?" I started to text her back with "nothing much," but then I got stumped. There's so much in "what's new?" I texted her a short version of the life moments that filled my days.

We are getting a puppy! My sister had her first baby. Navigating my dreams with God. We planted a garden in our backyard, and it makes my heart full! God keeps reminding me to pray about anything and that His peace comes when I pray something through. I fold laundry a lot. I wash dishes a lot, but I wouldn't change a thing! I sit on my back porch a lot. I walk the same route in our neighborhood most days, not really for exercise, more for soul-refueling. Music gives me a boost when I am cooking dinner. We read stories at night for bedtime, lift up friends, puppies, and math tests to God in prayer, and when the alarm goes off the next morning, we pop chocolate chip waffles in the toaster.

That's just the short of it. My "what's new" is full and good and overwhelming all at the same time. My "what's new" is full of imperfection, mistakes, and lots of grace, full of mess-ups, fresh starts, trials, busyness, and reminders to slow down. There's so much in a "what's new with you?" isn't there?

So, what's new with you, dear one? What's going on in your life? How is your heart, really? God sees you in all of it and is in every moment with you—celebrations, struggles, joys, issues, hang-ups, hurts, and habits. In your daily happenings, God is in your midst. When you see your daily life as walking with God, everything from folding the laundry and doing dishes to the celebrations and joyous moments link together to add up to a life of purpose. Abundant life and purpose aren't out there somewhere, they are happening right where you are. God keeps pursuing your heart in the everyday things.

Lord, remind me that You are in every moment.

As you go about the simplest things today,
remember that God is right there with you.

WHEN YOU NEED MIRACLES IN YOUR DAY

This, the first of His signs, Jesus did at Cana in Galilee,
and manifested His glory. And His disciples believed in Him.

John 2:11

The very first miracle that Jesus performed according to Scripture sits in John 2. Tucked away in a short chapter that takes place at a wedding, it happens so fast that it almost sounds nonchalant. It wasn't a miracle of life-saving proportions. The guests were out of wine. Jesus took this very practical, normal, and somewhat mundane need and turned it into a divine miracle. He took the most ordinary, common thing—water—infused it with the flow of His power, Spirit, and care, and did something that was supposed to be impossible. He transformed water into wine. He could have planned a more life-altering miracle to present Himself publicly for the first time, but He chose a practical one. He chose to point out that He wants to do everyday miracles in our own lives with our own very practical needs.

Jesus loves to take your ordinary, normal, and even mundane everyday needs and infuse them with the flow of His power, Spirit, and care so that you can experience His miracles in your life. No need or detail is too small. There will be days we experience "bigger" miracles, but He invites us to see the everyday ones too! Your everyday needs and cares are miracles in the making.

Will you talk to Him about your details? Will you invite Him to make miracles out of your heart needs? Will you step into the sweet dance of inviting the Wine Maker into your most common details, practical needs, and heart-felt questions? Be on the lookout for miracles in your life, sweet one, because if Jesus can turn water into wine, there's no telling what He can do in your life.

Lord, I give You all the details of my day. Thank You that You care about each one.
Lord, wake me up to the miracles You do each and every day in my life.
Thank You for loving me so intimately and for wanting to help me in so many
ordinary ways. You make ordinary things into miraculous moments. Thank You,
Jesus, for the ultimate miracle of salvation, but also for going beyond that.
You want to dance with me every day through the details and needs of my life.

Remember that Jesus wants to do miracles in the tiny
details of your day. Watch for His miracles today.

EVERY NEW DAY IS
A CHANCE TO DANCE

The steadfast love of the LORD is from everlasting
to everlasting on those who fear Him.

Psalm 103:17

Daughter of Christ, the Creator of the universe is creating beautiful things in and through your life. He knows the order of it. He knows the next step and the step after that. He knows how it's all supposed to fit together.

Every new day is a chance to invite God into our day and let Him lead us through it. Every new day we can start our day with Him. Every new day we can pray. Every new day we can invite the Holy Spirit into our day. Every new day we can follow God's perfect lead. Every new day we can trust that He knows the right thing for us to do because He created us, as well as each of our days.

This day is a precious day that was appointed by God for you personally. He is creative and orderly in and through your life. He is specific with you, planning everything with you in mind. He is detailed with you, not leaving anything to chance. God is creating the beautiful dance of your life one step at a time, and every new day is a chance to dance with your Savior.

Lord, thank You for Your steadfast love in my life.
May I see each day as a new day to walk hand and hand with You.
May I treasure every day and see each one as a gift.

God wants to dance with you through this day. He wants to lead you
step by step, moment by moment. Follow Him one step at a time.

A DANCE OF SURRENDER

In the world you will have trouble. But take heart!
I have overcome the world.

John 16:33, NIV

In this dance of life, we don't like to give up control of our plans, our schedule, our day, or our dreams. Giving up control feels scary—backwards, almost—and really, really hard. It's easier to trust God with the small stuff, the easy stuff. But when it comes to the big stuff, don't we all tend to want to take it in our own hands? We want to handle it. We want to hold on to it. We want to be in control.

But what if we took God's hand in this dance of surrender—whether it's of our dreams, our plans, or our agenda—and gave control to God? What beauty might He have for us on the other side of surrender?

Today, I don't know what area of your life is rubbing you the wrong way or maybe distracting you from having a peaceful heart. The thing is, we will always have things that try to steal our joy: worries, burdens, pressures, and decisions.

Jesus is clear: we will have trouble. But He invites us to *take heart* because He has overcome the world. "The world" covers all our days, all our troubles, all our stuff. He covers it all, dear one. Will you step toward Him, trust Him, take heart, and offer up your heart in surrender?

Lord, You know where my heart is today. You know the thing that I want to control and hold on to. But You offer beauty on the other side of surrender. Lord, I want to hand this thing over to You because You are showing me that I can trust You with all my worries, burdens, pressures—all my stuff. I choose to take Your hand in this dance of surrender.

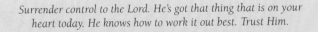

Surrender control to the Lord. He's got that thing that is on your heart today. He knows how to work it out best. Trust Him.

GRACE TO GO OFF
THE PROGRAM

Since we live by the Spirit, let us keep in step with the Spirit.
Galatians 5:25, NIV

There are days when our quiet time with Jesus feels like it needs a little refreshing. Sometimes in my quiet times with the Lord, I try really hard to stick to a reading plan so that I can get through the whole Bible in a certain amount of time. But often my heart longs to go off the program. My heart longs to feel close to God and hear His whispers. My heart longs to go deeper than checking my quiet time with God off my list for the day. Over the years I've learned to listen to that little heart nudge and lean into grace to go off the program.

Sometimes we need to mix things up a bit to keep our quiet time with Jesus fresh. He wants that time with Him to be exciting and new every day. He loves to refill us. He loves to show us new things. He loves to surprise us. He loves to speak to us. He loves to woo us. But sometimes we have to notice when our time with Him has grown mundane and dry—when it's become a program—and let Him swoop in with grace and get us off the program and closer to His heart.

How is your time with the Lord going? I want to encourage you today to mix it up a bit if it feels dry. Let Him lead your quiet time. He might lay a certain verse on your heart or a particular devotional to read. He may nudge you to just be still and listen, or He may nudge you to pray. He is not putting an "X" by your name if you don't stick to the reading plan or you don't read for a certain number of minutes. He is not tracking when and how long you are spending time with Him. No, Jesus just wants you to come to Him and experience the deeper waters of His grace. So don't be afraid to go off the program and follow the Spirit's leading. Your time with Jesus fills you up with Living Water. When you feel that ache, that void, that empty feeling you don't know what to do with, grab your Bible, grab a pen, grab a journal, find a porch, and just meet Him there. He will do the rest.

**Lord, refresh my perspective of my quiet time. Help me to follow
Your leading and remember that my time with You is building my
relationship with You and giving me everything I need for this day.**

*Be encouraged to go off the program today in order to
find a fresh perspective in your quiet time with the Lord.*

THE FIRST THING GOD WANTS YOU TO KNOW

*In the beginning God created the heavens and the earth. Now the earth
was formless and empty, darkness was over the surface of the deep,
and the Spirit of God was hovering over the waters. And God said,
"Let there be light," and there was light. God saw that the light was good.*

Genesis 1:1-4, NIV

In the very first paragraph of the Bible, God wants us to know something right off the bat. He wants us to know that He takes *formless and empty* and turns it into *light and goodness*. He took a dark, formless, empty, unformed world and brought it light, form, fullness, and life. Have you ever felt formless and empty? Maybe your version of formless and empty looks something like:

- uncertainty about who God made you to be
- feeling unclear about what you're supposed to do with your life
- feeling unfulfilled, unsatisfied, thirsty for something more
- being unsure if God will come through

Take this to heart, dear one. The very first thing God wants you to know about Him is that He takes the places you feel empty and turns them into goodness and light. You may feel like no forming or growing or shaping is taking place in your heart. You may feel like the garden of your life is just rocky and full of weeds—formless. You may not see the beauty yet. But hold on to this—God sees the beauty. He sees your formless places. He sees your empty places. And He is working hard behind the scenes on your behalf. He is fixed on fulfilling His purposes for you, set on guiding you on His beautiful path for you, and determined to bring the beauty out. He sees it, and as you let Him lead and guide you, He will bring forth goodness and light in your life.

**Lord, here are all my formless places. Here are all my empty spots.
Give me fresh hope, fresh perspective, and fresh faith that You see me, take me,
and remake me. May I step forward in faith, knowing that You see the big picture.**

*Be encouraged today, dear one, that God sees you
and is at work in you, around you, and for you.*

LET GO OF TRYING TO FIGURE IT ALL OUT

I will praise the Lord, Who counsels me; even at night my heart instructs me.
I will keep my eyes only on the Lord. With Him at my right hand,
I will not be shaken. Therefore my heart is glad and my tongue rejoices.

Psalm 16:7-9, NIV

God has you. I know you often wonder what God's plan for your life is. I know you often struggle to believe He is really in the details—guiding you, leading you, showing you His way. I know you often wonder if you're in the center of God's will or if you've strayed so far outside of it that you are way off God's course for you.

Today I want to encourage you that God wants you to know His will for your life even more than you want to know His will for your life! He is working tirelessly to guide you, direct your heart, shape your desires, and lead you into becoming all that He created you to be. You can relax. You can lean back. You don't have to manipulate your dreams or your desires into happening. No, you can trust Him to shape your dreams and desires. You don't have to analyze and strategize over the future. You don't have to try and figure out God's will for you and how He wants to use you.

You can let go of trying to figure it all out, and you can simply make your purpose, your goal, and your dream to know Him. Make knowing Him your highest purpose, your greatest pursuit, and your greatest goal.

Lord, You know my tendency to try to analyze and figure out my life.
Remind me today that You counsel me. You're always with me.
I can't be shaken because You are as close as my right hand.
Help me to let go of trying to figure out and analyze my life.

He's got you, He knows you, He pursues your heart,
and He loves you. You can let go of trying to figure out your life.

PRAY ABOUT YOUR FEARS

Perfect love drives out fear.
1 John 4:18, NIV

One evening our little family was eating ice cream with a football game on in the background. My youngest son, who was five years old at the time, announced, "Mommy! Last night I prayed to God before I went to sleep that I wouldn't have bad dreams." With the biggest smile ever across his face, he said, "and last night, I didn't have bad dreams!" And back to his chocolate ice cream he went.

In that moment, God reminded me that we can pray about *anything*, including our everyday fears. So, dear friend, what's the fear that's wearing you out? Is it a fear about parenting? Is it a fear over something you've heard on the news? Is it a fear of stepping outside your comfort zone to move toward a dream? Will you take a moment today to name that fear, bring it to the Lord, pray about it, and let Him do the mighty work of driving out that fear?

God's perfect love drives out fear. And dear one, you are perfectly loved. As you step toward God, bringing Him your fears, He will bring you the peace you need. You don't have to live in fear. Our Perfect Love is in your corner. You don't have to just try and suppress your fears. Instead, you can add them to your prayer list and start praying that God would drive them out.

Lord, thank You that I can bring my fears to You. Here is every one …

Release your fears to the One Who promises peace.

WHEN YOU NEED DIRECTION

The Lord makes firm the steps of the one who delights in Him.
Psalm 37:23, NIV

Sometimes I look through my stash of old journals as a way of remembering God's faithfulness. My heart always needs reminders that God is at work and that He has been nothing but faithful in the past. He's got me. Always, He's got me. And He's got you.

As I read my old journals, I notice a theme. So many times over the years I have asked God for direction—which way to go, which way to turn, whether to move forward in this opportunity or whether to let it go. It has always felt like a dance. And the more I dance with Him, the more I realize that things go so much smoother when I let Him lead.

God will get us where we need to go as we plant seeds of prayer and make knowing Him our top priority. As we spend time with Jesus, He guides us. He leads us. He shows us new things. He teaches us about His Word. He strengthens us. He directs us. We don't have to fret that we will make a wrong turn if we keep our hearts connected to Him. He will get us where we need to go.

We will always need direction in our lives. Who we choose to get our marching orders from will determine the course of our life. Who will you look to for direction? The world? Other people? Yourself? What if you let God lead your life completely? He will get you where you need to go. And that place, that journey, that path, is the best path for you because your Creator knows just what you need. He delights in giving you an abundant and full life, one that finds delight in letting Him lead.

Lord, remind me to seek You when I need direction for my life. You know what's best for me. May I always turn to You.

It is in seeking God's direction and company that we find abundant life.

TIME WITH GOD WILL CHANGE YOUR LIFE

Draw near to God, and He will draw near to you.

James 4:8

Time with God will change your life. It will feed your soul, brighten your outlook, and give you the strength you need for each day. Time with God clarifies your purpose, directs your path, and equips you for the callings He has for you. It satisfies your heart, calms your anxiety, and sets your heart, mind, and soul right. Time with God completes you. So if you're in a rut or haven't really figured out how to have a meaningful quiet time or how to get something out of your quiet time, I hope these little tidbits will inspire you.

- Mix it up. Sometimes I get in a rut in my quiet times because I am tired of doing the same thing—the same reading plan, the same Bible study, or the same devotional book. Take a break from the plan. Go off the program. Ask God what He wants you to read.
- Let the Spirit lead. Ask God to come into your time with Him. Ask Him to speak right straight to your heart, and He will.
- Find a favorite spot. Make your time with God special. Grab your favorite mug of tea or coffee and find a spot that feels a bit sanctuary-esque. For me, it's my back porch. For you, it could be a coffee shop or your favorite corner on the couch. Find a spot that's reserved for you and God.
- Get creative. Moms with little ones, I know how hard it is to find time/space/quiet for a quiet time. Your quiet time may not be so quiet! I have definitely had lots of "quiet times" during episodes of *Wild Kratts* and *Little Einsteins*. Do whatever works!
- Be flexible. Some days your quiet time will be in the morning. Some days it will be late at night. Some days you will get hours, some days you will get just a few minutes. Run in grace. Know that God sees you. Know that He's always pursuing you, and He's always available.
- Keep the conversation going. Talk to God in the car and talk to Him on a walk. Check in with Him whenever you can. Keep a Bible in your purse.

**Lord, thank You for the gift of a personal relationship with You.
May I never get over the wonder it.**

*May you be inspired today that time
with God will truly change your life.*

LISTENING FOR GOD'S VOICE

This is the way, walk in it.
Isaiah 30:21

On a typical morning, I put on my slippers and head straight to the kitchen while the house is still quiet. As my coffee is brewing, I grab my journal, pen, and Bible. Once the coffee making is complete, I head straight to my back porch. I curl up on my favorite chair, take a few minutes to quiet my heart, and then start praying about the things on my mind.

But sometimes I forget to *listen* to what God wants to say to my heart. I pray, read the Word, and then move into my day. It can feel unproductive to sit still and listen for God's voice. We wonder if we're really hearing Him, or we wonder if He's even there. I wish there were a simple formula to follow. I can't give you that, but I can offer you some tips that have helped me.

- Be in God's Word.
- Know that God can speak through His Word, through people, through your circumstances, and through gentle promptings in your heart.
- Give God time and space to speak.
- Have faith when you think He's speaking to you. Believe that it's Him.
- Always make sure that what you hear lines up with Scripture.
- Remember that God isn't trying to hide from you. He wants you to hear His voice.
- Know that God's voice will be kind, not condemning. Gentle, not harsh. Clear, not confusing.
- Ask God to help you hear His voice.

God is speaking to you in all kinds of ways today. Listen for His voice. Watch for the little ways He grabs your attention. Notice the little love notes He sends throughout the day—that butterfly that nearly lands on your nose, that answer to prayer that shows up in your day, that hug from your loved one at just the right time, that Bible verse that brings tears to your eyes, that nudge in your heart that you are loved unconditionally. It's a blessing to be able to pray about anything, but I want to never forget that it's a blessing to be able to hear from God too!

Lord, help me listen to You throughout my day. I long to hear Your voice.

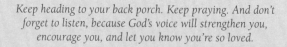

Keep heading to your back porch. Keep praying. And don't forget to listen, because God's voice will strengthen you, encourage you, and let you know you're so loved.

GOD IS ON THE MOVE FOR YOU

In the Lord I take refuge.

Psalm 11:1

Today, maybe your heart needs a reminder that God's plan for your life is good and best.

When the path ahead is unclear, when the trail you've been walking suddenly seems to take a U-turn, when the road ahead seems foggy, don't let discouragement have its way in your heart. What if we saw that U-turn, that fork in the road, that fogginess as a sign that God is on the move? What if we saw that sudden stop sign in our plans and our dreams as a yield sign? *Daughter, yield it all over to Me. Let go of your plans, let go of your dreams, and yield. Let Me pass in front of you, let Me get back in the driver's seat, let Me take over in your life.*

God wants to orchestrate. He wants to lead. He wants to work things out in His way, His timing, and on His terms because He cares for you. He doesn't want you to miss His beautiful plan for your life. So today, when your heart is tempted to doubt and to give in to discouragement, instead, rejoice that God is on the move for you. Take refuge in Him, entrusting your life to Him.

Lord, let my heart take refuge in You today. Remind me that Your plan is best. Remind me that You are and always will be at work in my life. Help me to yield my plans to You, and to trust that Your plan is far better.

A fork in the road, a roadblock, or a stop sign in your life may be just the things God is using to lead you to His best for you.

ROOM TO BREATHE

Do not fret.
Psalm 37:1, NIV

Pour out all your concerns to the Lord to make room for the peace He offers. Find a place to tell Him what's gnawing at you. Pour out your heart to Him so He can put your heart back together.

Find a spot, perhaps your back porch, and tell your concerns to the Lord so your heart has room to breathe and soak in His peace, His stillness, His rest, and His answers. We do not have to fret (although it's seems so much easier for some reason). Instead, we can be still, wait on God, and pour out every concern in prayer.

God wants us to live with a whole heart, not a fretful one. He makes wholeness possible as we pour out all our pieces to Him. He frees us to live right there in the moment with Him.

Lord, You know the things in my life that are causing me to fret.
Big things, small things, silly things, and stressful things—there are
so many details to handle, but You help me handle them all. Instead of
fretting over my concerns, help me to pour out each one to You in prayer.

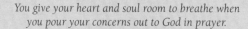
*You give your heart and soul room to breathe when
you pour your concerns out to God in prayer.*

WHEN YOU NEED TRUTH TO WASH OVER YOU

The law of the LORD is perfect, refreshing the soul.
Psalm 19:7, NIV

Some days we simply need to sit on the back porch and soak in the truth that we know but that maybe have forgotten. Let God's truth wash over you:

- **You are stunningly beautiful**. Yes YOU! "How beautiful you are, my darling! Oh, how beautiful." Song of Songs 4:1, NIV
- **You can be confident because God is in control of your life.** "For I know the plans I have for you," declares the LORD, "plans to prosper you and not to harm you, plans to give you hope and a future." Jeremiah 29:11, NIV
- **You can enjoy solitude, rest, and time to be renewed**, and you don't have to feel guilty about needing or wanting that time. "I will refresh the weary and satisfy the faint." Jeremiah 31:25, NIV
- **You are loved no matter what**. "I have loved you with an everlasting love; I have drawn you with unfailing kindness." Jeremiah 31:3, NIV
- **You are forgiven.** You don't have to keep confessing that same sin over and over again because it's paid for. Be free. "Blessed is he [or she] whose transgressions are forgiven, whose sins are covered." Psalm 32:1, NIV
- **You are good at what God has gifted you to do.** "For You created my inmost being; You knit me together in my mother's womb. I praise You because I am fearfully and wonderfully made ..." Psalm 139:13-14, NIV
- **You have a constant Helper, ready to listen and to guide you.** "Since we live by the Spirit, let us keep in step with the Spirit." Galatians 5:25, NIV
- **Those prayer requests on your heart have been heard, and an answer is on the way.** "Pray continually." 1 Thessalonians 5:17, NIV

**Lord, thank You for the truth of Your Word.
Let Your truth wash over my heart today and refresh my soul.**

*When the truth of God's Word washes over you,
your soul feels right again.*

WHEN YOUR HEART FEELS THIRST FOR THE "MORE" YOU CAN'T QUITE NAME

When I called, You answered me.

Psalm 138:3, NIV

Any heart thirst we feel—for whatever we think we are missing—can lead us back to deeper intimacy with the Lord. If you feel a thirst today—an angst, a stress, an unsettling feeling of not being able to quite name the ache in your heart—run to Jesus.

Grab your Bible, a pen, and a journal, break away from your schedule, and get alone with the One Who offers bread for your soul and living water for your heart. Take your soul right to Him and tell Him, as best you can, what you think is causing your angst. Let Him sort you out. He sorts out the emotions we feel, the stress we hold, and the deep angst we sometimes feel.

God is the one and only perfect fuel for your heart. He will satisfy you when your heart feels thirsty for the more you can't quite name, because as you draw near Him you will see that what your soul is actually craving—what you can't quite name—is *Him*. Our hearts crave more of Jesus. We want to know Him more and let Him know us more.

When I feel thirsty or anxious for that something "more"
that I can't quite pin-point, Lord, remind me to run
to You for the satisfaction that only You can give.

Let your thirst, angst, stress, or need be a signal to you
today that your heart is craving to sit with Jesus.
Sit with Him and let Him fill you back up.

A REMEDY FOR EVERY NEED

*And my God will meet all your needs according
to His glorious riches in Christ Jesus.*

Philippians 4:19, NIV

What does your heart need today? Is it a prayer request to be answered? Is it a solution to a problem going on in your life? Is it a need that you can't quite define? There is a remedy for our every need. The sweet remedy is prayer. But sometimes we skip over it because it's hard to take the time for it, we don't see quick results, or we take the human nature route: we worry through our problems.

Take it to prayer. Take a step of faith by believing that when you pray, God is there. When you pray, God hears every word. When you pray, you invite God into your situation. When you pray, He moves on your behalf. When you pray, your need will be met. But here is an important key: you have to *keep praying.*

Don't stop praying when the answer doesn't come. Don't stop praying when you are tired of praying. Prayer takes time. It takes persistence and waiting. Indeed, the waiting becomes praying. Some answers will come quickly. Some answers will seem like they take forever. But believe today that the answers will come.

Praying is nurturing your relationship with Jesus. It's hanging out with the One Who completes your soul, gives you life, and satisfies your every need.

**Lord, thank You for the gift of prayer. Remind me of its importance and its power.
Remind me that bringing each and every need of my heart to You is the
answer to all my worry. Thank You that You meet all my needs—every one.**

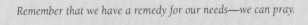

Remember that we have a remedy for our needs—we can pray.

April

EMBRACE YOUR CALLING

… the unfading beauty of a gentle and quiet spirit,
which is of great worth in God's sight.

1 Peter 3:4, NIV

I want to encourage you today that the things God has called you to in this life, whether they involve big stages with lights and an audience or the quietness of home where no one sees the details you take care of every day, they matter. Don't let anyone or anything make you feel like your calling is insignificant. Your calling may feel less than or small or not impactful, you may see others following callings that look much more glamorous than yours, but hold on to this, dear sister: the seemingly small stuff matters. A quiet life matters. A gentle and humble spirit matters. Your work—even though it may not look like "real" missionary work or important work—matters. Your work is spiritual work.

Where God has you right now is your mission field. You delight God by leaning into your calling. You make Him smile when you embrace it. Don't look around and compare what you are doing to anybody else; embrace your calling.

Lord, help me to make getting to know You my greatest purpose.
Thank You that the work and the callings You have given me are all spiritual work,
and they all matter. Thank You for gently reminding my heart that I am significant
to You, and that when I focus my life on You, I am free to be me—no one else.

Be you. Seek Him. Make getting to know Him your purpose,
and He will delight to remind you day in and day out
that what you do is absolutely significant. He wouldn't
want you doing anything else but being yourself.

WHEN YOUR HEART HAS QUESTIONS

He will cover you with His feathers, and under His wings you will find refuge; His faithfulness will be your shield and rampart.

Psalm 91:4, NIV

You can bring all the questions of your heart to your Maker. Your heart is aching for a divine touch. For divine direction. For divine love. Let the ache and uncertainty that you sometimes feel in your heart lead you to Jesus. He knows your heart because He made your heart, and He knows what you are designed to do and be. As You press into Him by daily asking for His guidance and bringing all your questions to Him, you will become the woman of God He created you to be. Little by little, step by step, as You lean into God, each moment brims over with purpose because You know it all matters.

You will find your purpose when you put your significance in Jesus and remember that you belong to Him. And when your heart feels down, confused, or unsure throughout the different seasons of your life, He will continue to pursue your heart. Choose to ask God your questions. Choose to ask Him for direction for your life. Choose to want His will above your best plans. The promise of His good plans will be the adventure your heart longs for, the perfect fit for you. In Jesus, you have a forever refuge—a constant shield from the hard moments of life.

Take a step toward Him today. What does taking that step look like? Grab a pen and a journal and scribble your thoughts down as a prayer to God. Open your Bible and search for verses that touch your soul. Take some time to sit down with God. Pray to Him in your heart. Read a verse or two, and let His Spirit speak to you. Start small, take baby steps toward Him, and watch Him come closer.

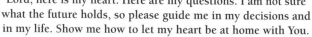

Lord, here is my heart. Here are my questions. I am not sure what the future holds, so please guide me in my decisions and in my life. Show me how to let my heart be at home with You.

Jesus cares about the questions of your heart. Bring every one to Him.

WHEN YOU FEEL SPIRITUALLY DRY

My soul thirsts for God, for the living God.
When can I go and meet with God?

Psalm 42:2, NIV

Maybe you don't feel God's presence in your life lately. You may wonder where God went or if He's still there. You may feel like your passion for Him dissolved, your fire went out, or your zest for the things of God has become weighed down with trials. There will be days when you feel far away from God, where you can't seem to find Him, hear Him, or feel Him. There will be days when your passion feels ho-hum, your excitement feels worn down, and your heart feels heavy. It's okay, dear one. Those feelings are absolutely normal.

If we were always on top of a spiritual mountaintop, we might never feel our need for a Savior. If we never experienced the valley, we would never ache for relief. Jesus doesn't just revive our hearts once. He does it over and over and over again. He keeps reviving your heart throughout your whole lifetime.

So in those moments when you feel burned out in your faith, hold on. Ask Him to revive your heart. Tell Him how you feel. Then wait, watch, wait again, and watch some more. He will renew you. He will restore you. He will make you dance with joy when He reveals new promises to your heart and new revelations from His Word to your soul. You can't ever wear out God. You can't ever learn everything you need to know about Him. He will always have fresh encouragement for your heart. But know that there will be days and moments—we all have them—when you feel spiritually dry. In those times, hold on, dear sister, because breakthrough will come. You can count on it.

Lord, when I can't feel You, when I feel far away
from You, remind my heart that again and again,
You will revive my heart. Thank You that breakthrough, relief,
and joy are always on the way. How gracious and good You are.

May you walk through this day with fresh faith that
God will refresh you where you feel spiritually dry.

THE PATH TO THE MOST FULFILLING PEACE

Cease striving and know that I am God.

Psalm 46:10, NASB

Our hearts are bombarded with the message from the world that the more we have, the better off we will be. This makes life more complicated than it needs to be, and our hearts get crowded with the angst of an unfulfilled heart.

God is always pursuing our hearts. He is inviting us to experience a peace so calm, so warm, so joyous, that we hesitate to take His hand because we wonder if that kind of deep peace is really possible. We twirl around life, fixing our hearts and eyes on other pursuits that we think will fulfill our hearts because that's our human nature. As humans, our hearts are prone to wander, as the old hymn goes, prone to look to anything but God to fulfill us.

The path to the most fulfilling peace is choosing to let God fill that part of your heart that longs to be filled. Run to Him instead of things that don't satisfy. The path to peace is putting God first in your life. It's making Him your go-to, your number one, and your all in all. If you want peace, let go of striving your way through your life and instead surrender to Him.

Lord, I have put my value into many things other than You,
but I have come to realize that those other things only leave me
feeling empty. Nothing satisfies like You do. Thank You for pursuing my
heart constantly. I want to know Your peace, Your joy, and Your ways.

*As you look to God for fulfillment,
your heart will find true peace.*

YOUR SUPPORT

When I said, "My foot is slipping," Your unfailing love,
Lord, supported me. When anxiety was great within me,
Your consolation brought me joy.
Psalm 94:18-19, NIV

God is our strong foundation. He supports us throughout our entire day. We can operate out of that love. But when we operate out of stress, trying to manage everything in our own strength, anxious from worrying, we miss out on the freedom to enjoy life and to know deep peace.

So how do we operate out of God's love rather than in anxiety and stress? We simply invite Him into the details of our day. We invite Him into our plans, our ideas, and our dreams. We ask for His help in the big stuff and the little stuff. Prayer doesn't have to be formal. We can talk to God anywhere and anytime. As we invite Him into our lives, we will feel His love supporting us throughout the day.

Jesus, thank You for Your love that supports me through each day.
May I let my life rest on the foundation of Your love instead of on my own
strength. Let me operate from Your love and Your peace. Here is every worry
on my heart and every concern on my mind. Come into the details of my day
so that I can live in freedom and confidence. Thank You for loving me so deeply.

When you feel your foot slipping, your heart sinking,
your mind despairing, or your thoughts going downhill,
remember that God is one simple prayer away.

WHEN YOUR DREAMS GRAB HOLD OF YOUR HEART

Delight yourself in the LORD, and He will
give you the desires of your heart.

Psalm 37:4

God is the Dream Planter. He loves to plant little seeds of dreams in our hearts that He will use to lead us through life, give us great joy, guide us into living out our gifts, and use to make an impact in the world. So bring those desires, dreams, and ideas to God. Write them down in a journal and talk to Him about them.

As You delight in the Lord, get to know Him, and walk through life with Him, He will convince you that His plan for your life is far better than anything you can think, dream, or imagine. God is the Pursuer of your heart. He is knocking on the door of your heart because He wants you to know that His plan for your life is the best plan you could possibly imagine. The way to live out that plan is to delight in Him and get to know Him. How can you delight in Him?

- **Spend time reading the Bible.** The Bible is His letter to you, and He wants to talk to you through His Word.
- **Talk to Him.** Pray on a walk, journal your prayers, talk to God in the car, or just sit quietly and talk to Him in your heart.
- **Worship Him.** Put on some praise music and sing to the Lord.
- **Honor Him.** Listen to those little ways that He is asking you to be obedient to Him.
- **Thank Him.** Thank Him for all the gifts He has brought you.
- **Choose Him.** Choose time with God over other things that seem urgent.
- **Trust Him.** Ask the Holy Spirit to help you choose to trust Him instead of worrying.
- **Enjoy Him:** Take delight in the fact that He's got you.

The path to following our dreams is taking delight in God. Then, whether that dream comes true or another one surfaces, you can have peace that the Dream Giver is in control.

Lord, thank You for planting desires in my heart.
May I bring each and every one of them to You. Shape and
mold my desires to be in line with Your best plan for my life.

As you delight in God,
He will shape your desires and dreams.

THE DANCE OF WAITING

"My thoughts are nothing like your thoughts," says the Lord,
"And My ways are far beyond anything you could imagine."

Isaiah 55:8, NLT

What are you waiting for? It may be a prayer request to be answered, it may be affirmation from God about some decision you have to make, or it may be word about something important to you. The waiting may feel like the elephant always in the room, dominating your day and distracting you from peace. We go through lots of seasons of waiting, and it isn't fun! For me, waiting feels like my mind can't fully rest. I know I need to remember that God does not want me to live in a state of emotional stress. He wants me to live free of angst and worry, as if learning to trust God with everything in my life is a kind of dance. Waiting is a reminder to trust in God's timing, His ways, and His plan. As we wait, we can soak our hearts into God's love by:

- Diving into His Word when our hearts are hungry for an answer.
- Talking to God in prayer (on a walk, in the car, through journaling, or simply sitting outside and letting our hearts settle into His faithfulness).

God's got you. God's got me. And He's got a plan for our lives. He knows what is best. His timing is best. He's at work behind the scenes of your circumstances. I like to think that He's most actively at work on our behalf on the days we feel like our prayer request may have gone unnoticed. His love for us is deep and personal. He is passionate about us, and He has surprises up His sleeve and just around the corner. The challenge is not to rush Him. The challenge is to trust that His timing is best and that it will be worth the wait. He will answer, and then our hearts will dance with joy as we look back and see how He worked it all out. But in the meantime, live like He's going to answer. He is the God of joy, and He wants us to live joyfully even in the waiting seasons of life.

Lord, You know what I am waiting for. Help me to live joyfully
in the wait. Help me to trust that You are working out the details
behind the scenes in ways that are far better than my plans.

*Your heart will feel God's peace as you remember
that His timing and ways are good.*

WEEDS OF MY HEART

Create in me a pure heart, O God,
and renew a steadfast spirit within me.

Psalm 51:10, NIV

Recently the weeds in my little garden were literally weighing down my flowers, crowding and choking the things I had planted. I had walked by the weeds bunches of times over the last couple of weeks, but the thought of clearing them out felt a little overwhelming. But one afternoon something came over me, and I just started pulling them out, one by one. The flowers underneath seemed to come up for air. Some looked pretty lifeless and fragile. All of them seemed relieved to be free from the weeds!

It occurred to me that there are weeds in my heart that keep me from growing, blossoming, and moving toward God's purposes for my life. Weeds can be lots of things. They can be negative thoughts, comparing thoughts, self-focused thoughts, anxious thoughts, stress, or overwhelm. When we are so full of those kinds of "weedy" thoughts, there is no room for good thoughts.

When we uproot the weeds of our hearts, we make room to focus on God and His love for us, and then the joy blossoms. What weeds in your heart need to go so that you can fully bloom today?

Lord, I want to let go of the weeds in my heart in order
to make room for You. Show me what needs to go.

Whatever weeds are crowding your heart—negative
thoughts, anxiety, a sense of overwhelm—hand
those burdens over to the Lord today.

DIVINE HELP

In repentance and rest is your salvation,
in quietness and trust is your strength.

Isaiah 30:15, NIV

Sometimes in this frantic world we feel too busy to stop and pray, as if when we stop, our world, our calendar, and our schedule will unravel. So we keep plowing away at our to-do list.

Meanwhile, the Savior of the world waits patiently, knocking on the door of our hearts, waiting to provide us with all of the love, grace, and peace we have been looking for. He saves us eternally. What grace, what love, what mercy—Jesus died so that we could live in heaven! He reminds us of that over and over in little grace moments on earth: sunsets, rainbows, mountains, the birth of a baby, the love between a husband and a wife, a prayer answered—grace moments that point us to the reality of heaven.

At the same time, He waits for us to ask for His help in the day-to-day stuff. He wants us to ask for His help in the littlest things: decisions, strength to overcome, problems, everyday things we encounter here and now on this earth. He wants to partner with us in this dance of life. He doesn't promise an easy life, but an abundant one, an adventure. Don't let your to-do list and busy calendar keep you from drawing close to God. Sit with Him. Rest in Him. Sit with Him awhile today and receive His peace, know He's there, and ponder the wonder of the truth that God is real, heaven is real, and God's presence here on earth is real.

Lord, I forget sometimes how real You are!
Help me to soak in the reality of Your presence.
Help me to catch Your little hints of heaven.
Help me to see You in this day.

Jesus wants a relationship with you—not just a transaction for
salvation. He wants to hang out with you. He wants to help
you through your day. He wants to be the One you turn to.

GRACE TO BE TIRED

Do not fret.
Psalm 37:8, NIV

Sometimes fatigue overtakes us. We can be going, going, going—absolutely gung-ho and resolved to exercise, eat right, get enough sleep, and do all the things that are supposed to make us feel good. We can be taking our vitamins, drinking plenty of water, even having our quiet time with God. We may be doing all the "right" things, but for whatever reason, some mornings we wake up, and we just feel—drumroll, please—tired!

I had one of those mornings recently. My to-do list was staring me down, trying to capture my attention. The more I ignored it, the longer it seemed to grow. Procrastination set it. Then guilt set in for procrastinating. Then pure frustration sets in because I was just plain mad at my fatigue. Inside I thought, *Hey, body! Let's go! What do you need? More coffee? A nap? A walk? What's going on with you today? I thought we had a good thing going—eating right, exercising—what's up?* I kept waiting for my energy to kick in, but my body was hinting at something that I needed but I didn't think I had time for: *rest.* That afternoon, laundry still piled up and the house a bit of a disaster, I gave my boys the okay to hold down the fort while I snuck off into my bedroom for a "quick power nap." That power nap became a two-and-a-half-hour nap of wonderfulness, and my kiddos got imaginary stars and brownie points for letting Mommy sleep.

Women get tired. But sometimes we are too busy to notice, and our bodies have to get our attention somehow, so a heavy fatigue sets in. We often feel guilty for taking time to take care of ourselves. Instead of fighting through the fatigue, we need to listen to the signals our bodies are giving us. So be gentle on yourself. Give yourself grace to be tired some days. On those days, curl up with a good book. Take it easy. You will be back to your productive self another day, but for now, your body is trying to tell you something.

**Dear Lord, on the days that I feel tired, help me to
embrace the grace to rest and be gentle on myself.**

*This week, give yourself grace to be tired. When fatigue sets in,
do something good for yourself: take a walk, make a cup of tea,
or take a nap on the back porch. The extra rest will do your soul
so much good. God will keep the world running; you rest, dear one.*

A SERVANT HEART

Honor one another above yourselves. Never be lacking in zeal,
but keep your spiritual fervor, serving the Lord.
Romans 12:10-11, NIV

Christ calls us to a completely different way of thinking and living. His way goes against our competitive, me-focused nature. It requires self-control, faith, love, and hope. It requires a servant heart even in an incredibly self-focused world. Christ had a servant heart, and He wants to cultivate a servant heart in you, too, so you can be a light to those He has put around you.

Does this mean you let people walk all over you or take advantage of you? No. Does this mean you never speak up or stand up for yourself? No. Does this mean you wallow in self-doubt or low self-esteem? Absolutely not! But it might mean a change of attitude in those moments when you feel heated, and it might mean being more aware of the needs of those around you.

A servant heart is an overflow from your relationship with Christ. You don't have to manufacture it in your own strength. His Spirit in you will help you, and as you draw closer and closer to Him, your heart will want to serve. When you see your day as an opportunity to serve Christ, which in turn will bless and serve others, your whole day will feel different. You will feel joy and a sense of purpose rising up in your heart as you bless others with a heart like Christ.

Dear Lord, show me how to have a servant heart like You.

Make your day one of worship and serving Christ. See how
that little change of perspective lights up your heart.

DANCE WITH THE FATHER

*The LORD is like a father to His children, tender
and compassionate to those who fear Him.*

Psalm 103:13, NLT

Your heavenly Father embraces you no matter what your past has been like. Your heavenly Father cares for you more deeply than you could possibly fathom. Your heavenly Father pursues your heart because He knows what you need. Your heavenly Father offers support, encouragement, and guidance in your life. Your heavenly Father wants to meet every single need of your heart. Your heavenly Father has compassion on you no matter what you have done or where you have been.

And because of His Son Jesus, we can know the Father. Jesus paves the way for us to know Him. Remember today that there is a Father in heaven who loves you deeply, who is passionate about you, and who has a plan for your life. He offers His hand to you and invites you to dance with Him through life. And He wants to take the lead. Will you let Him lead?

**Heavenly Father, thank You for Your love for me.
Help me to grasp how great Your love for me is, despite my past,
my sins, and my failures. I want to take Your hand and let You lead my life.**

*God really is here with you this very moment.
And He will never leave you. His love for you is constant.*

RENEWAL

Therefore, if anyone is in Christ, he is a new creation.
The old has passed away; behold, the new has come. All this is
from God, Who through Christ reconciled us to Himself and gave us
the ministry of reconciliation; that is, in Christ God was reconciling
the world to Himself, not counting their trespasses against them.

2 Corinthians 5:17-19

There is One Who knows exactly where you are. He notices you. There is One Who knows every detail of your day. He knows what you are going through. There is One Who knows what struggles you are facing and what obstacles are defeating you. There is One Who knows the doubts in your heart. There is One Who knows exactly where you have been and exactly what you have faced. There is One Who knows the nitty-gritty details of your story that make you feel insecure and alone. He also knows what you are facing today and tomorrow. There is One Who knows when you feel alone. He knows that you struggle to find purpose. He knows that sometimes you feel like giving up. There is One Who knows you feel like no one gets it. There is One Who knows the guilt you feel for wishing things were different. He knows you feel like your past is too messy. He knows you don't feel good enough to deserve His love. There is One Who knows you wonder where He is. There is One Who knows you wonder if there is a God at all.

Jesus is knocking on the door of your heart. He gets you because He made you, and He wants to give you a fresh start today. He is relentlessly pursuing your heart. Jesus wants to make you into a new creation today! He's your constant source for renewal.

Lord, here's my heart. Renew it today.

No matter where you've been or where you are,
Christ will gladly renew you.

WHEN YOU'RE WAITING FOR AN ANSWER

Consider how the wild flowers grow. They do not labor or spin.
Yet I tell you, not even Solomon in all in his splendor was dressed
like one of these. If that is how God clothes the grass of the field,
which is here today, and tomorrow is thrown into the fire,
how much more will He clothe you—you of little faith!

Luke 12:27-28, NIV

When you are waiting on an answer to prayer, don't give up hope. There are moments when we wonder if God hears our prayer. Have you been there? Sometimes it can feel like He doesn't hear us, or we're afraid He thinks our prayers are silly. Sometimes it is hard to believe that our prayers are effective. When you feel stuck in your prayers, what do you do?

Keep praying. Don't give up. Keep taking your prayer requests to the Lord. As you continue to pray, even when it feels like the answer is far off, you wind up drawing closer to God. Remember that He is always listening, and He hears you. The answer is on the way. It may look different from the answer you are hoping for, or it may be exactly what you are hoping for. It may come when you least expect it or after many years of praying. The answer to your prayer is riding the waves of God's perfect timing. He is never early. He is never late.

In the meantime, keep bringing your prayers to Him. And just like the wildflowers, which seem to bloom at just the right time with effortless grace, resting in the sweet timing of their Maker, God will send His answer to you at just the right time. Keep praying, my friend.

Dear Lord, I am honestly anxious for an answer. It's hard to wait.
It's hard to be patient. Give me peace in the wait. Build my faith. It's tempting
to give up praying about the cares of my heart. It's tempting to think the answers
will never come. Help me to hold on to You, trust in Your timing, and not lose
heart. Help me to keep praying when the answer seems far off. Thank You for
Your very perfect timing. Help me to trust You, and help me to keep on praying.

God knows you're anxious for His answers. Trust that His timing
is for your good. Trust that He has an answer on the way.

GOD IS AT WORK
IN YOUR LIFE

*Jesus said to them, "My Father is always at
work to this very day, and I too am working."*

John 5:17, NIV

As you go about your day today, remember that God is at work in your life. Watch for His activity. Invite Him into the details of your day. It is easy for us to just ask for God's help in the "big" stuff, but He wants us to invite Him into the seemingly "little" stuff. When we leave Him out of the details, the stress of carrying it all on our own two shoulders becomes heavy, and the pressure squelches the joy out of our day. But when we let Him in, He carries our burdens on His shoulders, and we are free to live in His grace.

Know today that God is always at work in your life, even when you can't feel it. And many times, just when you think God is far off and not doing anything about your prayers, He will surprise you, just to let you know that He's there. What details of your day do you need to give over to Jesus today?

**Dear Lord, sometimes I feel bad asking for Your help in the little
things because it feels like I should be strong enough to handle that
kind of stuff on my own. But Lord, I am tired of carrying everything
on my own shoulders. I want to feel joy as I go about my day, and I need
You to show me how to let You in. So Lord, please come into the details
of my life, and let me know today that You truly are at work in my life.**

*Whatever that thing is today that you're carrying—that thing that is
sapping your joy, causing you stress, or depleting your energy—know
that God has it covered. He's at work this very moment on your behalf.*

WHO IS YOUR GOD?

I am the way, and the truth, and the life.
No one comes to the Father except through Me.

John 14:6

Many religions have their own higher power, but there is only one true, saving God. There is only One Who is chasing after your heart. There is only One Who is powerful enough to make a way for you to know for sure that when you pass from this life, you will not die, but live forever in heaven with Him. His name is Jesus. God, out of love, sent His only Son to earth to live and then die on a cross for you and for me so that not only could we have eternal life with Him, but we could also enjoy a personal relationship with Him. It is too wonderful for words. This is the greatest love.

Maybe you have been searching for something that is real. Maybe you have been questioning if there even is a God. Or maybe you have not felt convinced that there is only one way to heaven. Maybe you have thought that if you are just good enough and kind enough, maybe God will somehow show a little love and let you into heaven. Maybe at times you doubt that God even exists. No matter what your life has looked like up until now, no matter what you have done, no matter where you are, God has provided a way for you to know Him. He wants you to have a personal, close relationship with Him and to know with absolute certainty that you will spend eternity with Him in heaven.

Just as there is this beautiful everlasting place called heaven where God will restore our earth and bring a new heaven and a new earth, there is this horrible, everlasting place called hell. God sent His son, Jesus, to rescue you from that.

You may be wondering, *How can I know Him? How can I know for sure that I will go to heaven?* You simply ask Him into your heart. You simply tell Him that you believe that what He did for you was true. And when you invite Him in, His Holy Spirit will take up residence in your heart. His Holy Spirit is your comforter, your guide, and your counselor.

Lord, thank You for reminding me of the
wonder and glory of salvation in You.

YOUR WHOLE DAY
IS SPIRITUAL

Because You are my help, I sing in the shadow of Your wings.
Psalm 63:7, NIV

The Lord has a beautiful day laid out for you today. He will walk you through the day, carry you through any obstacles that come up, and stay with you through each and every moment. Remember today that God is in *all* the moments of your day. He isn't just in the "spiritual" parts of your day, when you're reading your Bible or enjoying your quiet time, when you're at a church or Bible study. No, he's in *all* the moments. He's in the seemingly unspiritual things—the tasks of the day, the meals you make, the people you come across, the beauty outside, the mundane, everyday things. He's there when you're brushing your teeth and making breakfast. He's there when you're driving your kids to school or when you're driving yourself to a doctor's appointment. He's there when you're watching the news and when you're loading the dishwasher. He's there on the back porch just as much as He is there at the kitchen sink.

No matter the busyness or stress pulling at your heart today, you can return again and again to Christ. He will re-center your heart throughout the day as you turn to Him in your everyday moments. Jesus is where you will find the nourishment, encouragement, joy, and fulfillment you need for your day. When you feel depleted, return to Him, and He will set your heart, thoughts, and emotions right again, and you will leave that time refreshed, ready, and rejuvenated. So in all your moments today, know that Jesus is with you the entire day. Your whole day is spiritual, sweet sister.

**Thank You that You are my help, and that I can come to You for
soul-strengthening. May my soul cling to You and enjoy the quiet,
deep soul rest that comes from centering my life on You.
Help me to remember that You are in all of my moments.**

*Christ energizes, strengthens, and centers
you for a day that's full of His presence.*

PRAY

Very early in the morning, while it was still dark, Jesus got up,
left the house and went off to a solitary place, where He prayed.

Mark 1:35, NIV

Sometimes it can feel counterproductive to pray when we have so much that needs to get done. Or we can grow desensitized to how amazing it is that we can pray to the God of the universe about absolutely anything.

Jesus snuck off to be alone with His Father many times during His life on earth. He prayed. He talked to God about the cries of His heart. I imagine He asked God for direction, for guidance, for wisdom, for clarity, and for strength. There were times when He cried out in anguish, and there were times when He thanked God for being in control. I would love to have been a fly on the wall in those moments of intimacy with His Father. Jesus walked away from those times of prayer refreshed, renewed, recharged, and rejuvenated. And God can do that for you, too. And the Scriptures give us a taste of that sweetness by encouraging us to go to God in prayer about anything and everything.

God invites us to make prayer a part of our day. We can take the pressure off of ourselves to sit down and pray for a certain amount of minutes because He invites us to a relationship with Him, not a set of rules. Think of prayer as just talking to God. He wants us to talk to Him throughout the day. We can pray while we are folding laundry, driving, exercising, or doing the dishes. Our entire day can be an endless conversation with the Lord. Some days we will feel the need to sit down with the Lord for a longer period of time out on our back porch or to take a long walk with Him. There is no right or wrong way to pray. Pray for whatever is concerning you in order to build your relationship with God, and then watch God do miracles in your life! Prayer will refresh, renew, recharge, and rejuvenate your heart, mind, soul, and life. Think of prayer as just talking to God. Reaching out to Him in prayer will begin a journey of intimacy with Christ—the One Who made you, loves you, and wants to help you in everything.

Thank You that You are the answer to every cry of my heart, every dilemma,
every issue, and every need. Help me to make prayer a priority in my
everyday life and to remember that praying to You is spending time with You.

Talk to the Lord as you go about your day.
Your prayers delight His heart.

PEACE FOR MY SOUL

The LORD is my shepherd; I shall not want.
He makes me lie down in green pastures.
He leads me beside still waters. He restores my soul.
Psalm 23:1-3

Sometimes it can feel like darkness is winning. The weight of the stress of life can deplete our souls and worry our minds. Anxiety can grip us. Fear can deeply affect us. Whatever that thing is today that's causing you to feel even the slightest bit of despair, that weight that is causing the slightest bit of stress or worry, that anxiety that has gripped you, or that fear that is deeply affecting you—there is peace awaiting you today. Even when the darkness of our world feels like it's winning, we can still have peace in our souls.

You can have hope even in chaos. You can have peace even in pain. You can have joy even in struggle. The Lord is watching over you, even in this thing that you are going through. Look up. He's waiting for you. He wants to help you and lead you—you just have to look up.

Jesus offers you peace like a river—a quiet, constant, flowing, and melodic trickling of rest for your soul. He quiets your heart. His love is constantly flowing toward you, and His joy will flow into your heart when you let Him lead your life. He will help you when it feels like darkness, stress, anxiety, and fear are winning.

So wherever you are, whatever you have been through, look up. The Lord wants to lead you. And you will find out that His lead is best—good, comforting, freeing, and peaceful.

Lord, thank You for being the Shepherd of my life.
Thank You for being my calm in chaos, my light in darkness,
and my constant hope. You know where I am. You know what
I am dealing with. Help me to look up. Help me to take Your
hand and let You lead me beside still waters and restore my soul.

With Jesus, darkness never wins.

WHERE DOES GOD HAVE YOU RIGHT NOW?

You make known to me the path of life; You will fill me with joy in Your presence, with eternal pleasures at Your right hand.

Psalm 16:11, NIV

Do you ever find yourself living for tomorrow? Do you ever catch yourself coasting through today because you are anticipating tomorrow? Remember that *today—this* moment—is where God wants you to live. He knows your past and your future. He sees the big picture. But in order to get you from your past to your future, He needs you to take His hand in the *now*. He waits for you in *this* moment. He is always beside you, ready to lead you. Our world moves at a fast pace, and we are distracted by so many things that feel urgent. But as we slow our pace and plant our feet in the present moment, we are able to connect with God more deeply.

So, where does God have you *right now*? It's so tempting to wish for tomorrow, to constantly try and figure out the future, and to miss the very precious day right under our toes. But living in the moment with God will fill you with joy and with the assurance that God has you in the palm of His hand.

Ask the Lord to help you live in the moment. Press into where God has you *right now*. Don't wish you were anywhere else. His path brings life and His presence will bring you joy.

Lord, thank You for where You have me in this season
of life. Show me what is distracting me from living in the
present moment. Help me to live in the present with You.
Help me to see Your blessings in my current season.

Don't miss the beauty of this day.

DRAW NEAR

Draw near to God, and He will draw near to you.

James 4:8

How is your soul today? On busy days when I feel productive and set into my routine, I don't think too much about how my soul is doing. The flow of daily life keeps me at a pace that never stops, and so I ride those waves of productivity, and I think *all is well*. I love those days!

But what about the days where we feel alone in our struggles, emotions, or circumstances? Although it feels as if you are all alone in whatever you are currently going through, there is One Who gets it—who gets *you*. There is One Who is always with you. Christ invites you when you feel alone to crawl into His lap of grace, love, and comfort.

Sometimes we do everything but go to God in our struggles, or we busy ourselves so we do not have to think about how we are really feeling.

God invites us to draw close to Him in those moments. When we draw near to Him, He will draw near to us. So when you feel alone, consider grabbing a journal, a pen, and your Bible. Find a cozy spot and tell God exactly how you feel. Tell Him what is going on with your soul. And ask Him for His comfort. Write down anything He impresses on your heart and any Scripture that applies to your situation. When you come to Him, expect comfort. Expect peace. Expect to not feel alone.

Walking with God does not guarantee a problem-free life. We need Him every day. We need to draw close to His heart so that He can comfort ours.

Dear Lord, You know how I am feeling today. I bring my soul's struggles to You. When I feel this way, help me to run to You, not other stuff. Help me to make time with You my go-to Source for comfort when I feel alone.

You are never alone in your trials and circumstances. Take a step toward God today. He will deliver comfort, peace, and His presence to your heart.

BEAUTIFULLY AWARE

*Forget the former things; do not dwell on the past. See, I am
doing a new thing! Now it springs up; do you not perceive it?
I am making a way in the wilderness and streams in the wasteland.*

Isaiah 43:18-19, NIV

When I was dancing as a ballerina, I learned a vital lesson that not only took my dancing to a new level, but also affected the way I want to live my life outside of pointe shoes and tutus. We were working on a ballet called *Giselle* at the time. My director approached me after the dress rehearsal to tell me that I did a good job with the steps, but I was missing the emotion behind it all. Ugh, not good feedback. He told me to go talk to one of the older, more experienced dancers and find out how she got to that place of character and emotion that I was missing. So, embarrassed, I asked an older dancer what she was thinking when she danced this role alongside me. Expecting a short answer, she took me by complete surprise when she described in full detail all she was thinking and imagining when she was dancing. She described shadows, darkness, willowy trees, fog, mystery—a haunting, eerie sadness that lurked through these dark woods that we, the willies, were dancing through. She lived it on stage. She was not herself on stage; she was the role she was dancing.

I realized I had to think like my character would think, and I had to feel and be and see all that my character would feel and be and see. I realized that I had to fully step into that role and be present in the moment. That was the only way my character would be believable to the audience. It changed the way I danced, and it makes me think differently about the way I live.

I want to step fully into the roles God designed for me, to be fully present and aware of His beautiful gifts—not just coast. God is doing a new thing in your life; will you step fully into His loving care? It will spring up if you fully lean on Him. Coasting through life is our natural inclination. But He calls us to wake up, come alive, and live abundantly with great joy. He wouldn't call us to it if it weren't possible. Indeed, He makes it possible. He will help you.

**Lord, wake me up to the amazing gift of knowing You. Help me to be fully
present in each moment, beautifully aware of Your constant presence.**

*Today, may you be aware of God's presence in
you and around you. Be fully in each moment.*

PEP TALK

To You they cried and were rescued;
in You they trusted and were not put to shame.

Psalm 22:5

Do you feel spiritually dry? Do you feel tired? Do you just feel a sadness in your heart? Do you feel restless? Do you feel alone? Do you feel yourself questioning? Do you wonder if God is there at all? Tell Jesus. Find a quiet place, sit down with Him, and talk to Him.

When you sit down with Jesus, you can talk to Him like He is your closest friend in the world. You can talk to Him just as you would talk to your closest friend at a coffee shop. You can be honest with Him about how you are feeling. When you cry out to Him with honesty, He will answer you with His peace. Your trials may not be resolved in that moment of prayer, your obstacles may still be a roadblock in your life, but as you turn your thoughts over to the Lord, trusting Him with what's concerning your heart, dear one, you will not be disappointed with the outcome.

So I encourage you today to enjoy a pep talk with Jesus—a one-on-one conversation with the One Who loves you so dearly and personally. You do not have to be eloquent; you do not have to say the right words; you do not have to pray for a certain number of minutes. Just talk to Him. Then watch for Him to work. He delights in cheering you up and taking care of your burdens. Watch for Him to surprise you throughout your day with little bursts of His peace washing over your heart. Notice anxiety losing its hold on you and joy swelling up in your soul. Look for His encouragement throughout your day. Watch for God to be at work in your life because He cares so much about you that He wants to answer your every concern.

Lord, thank You that I can bring You everything that weighs on
my heart today. Sometimes it feels easier to hold it all inside,
but quiet my heart today so that I can honestly bring You my heart.
Help me to trust You with all that concerns me today, Lord.

Honest prayer leads to peace.

MADE BY GOD

Then God said, "Let us make man in Our image, in Our likeness."
Genesis 1:26

What if you remembered today that you were thought up, imagined, created, and formed by the God of the universe? How would it affect your day if you held on to the beautiful truth that God designed you, wired your personality, and shaped your heart? He knew the world would need you, so He gifted you with your talents, skills, and character to touch the people in your sphere of influence. He made you out of the deep well of His love.

Oh, how we forget! We get caught up in how we need to improve ourselves or how we need to be a *better* version of ourselves. You know the deep angst in your heart about what you wish you could change about yourself. Sometimes I think we get so used to this thought pattern of wishing we were more this or more that, that it just becomes our natural inclination of thinking. We grow desensitized to how damaging these thought patterns are to our souls.

In Genesis 1:26, we are given a glimpse of the divine conversation of the Trinity—Father, Son, and Holy Spirit. God said, in effect, *Let's make a living, breathing, being, and let's make him/her similar to us.* This is mind-boggling—God envisioned you as being *similar to* Him! Like a daughter reflects her daddy. Like a son reflects his mom. Similar mannerisms. Similar character. Similar demeanor. Think of the glory of what God is hinting at—you are made In God's image.

You reflect God, sweet sister. You are similar to Him. Your laugh reveals a glimpse of our Creator God. Your eyes show His heart. Your smile oozes with heavenly sparkles. You reflect your Creator. Today, remember that not only are you made by God, but you were created to reflect Him—like Daddy, like daughter.

Lord, thank You that You made each of us to reflect You. Help me to let go of the thought patterns that drag me down into thinking I'm not good enough, smart enough, or beautiful enough, and imprint Your truth on my heart. Help me to walk through this day with joy as I linger on the thought that I am Your daughter.

*Let the truth that you are a beautiful
reflection of God sink in today.*

FILL UP AND JUMP FOR JOY

You will go out in joy and be led forth in peace.
Isaiah 55:12, NIV

In your walk with the Lord, Jesus wants you to come to Him daily to be filled up with Him. Your time with the Lord on Monday, while it is better than no time with Him at all, will not last the whole week. Without the bread of His Word each day, you will start to feel empty and depleted. God has something special for you in His Word every single day. You can pray, *Lord, give me just what I need to read from Your Word today.* And He will give you just what you need. You can trust Him to do it.

And when you spend that time with Him, enjoying His company, *you will go out in joy and be led forth in peace.* Sign me up! I want that! Every. Single. Day. What a privilege it is to be able to go about our day in joy and be led forth in peace by the God of the universe.

In the busyness of this season, take the time to be with Jesus first. Take the time to fill up so that you can live with joy every single day, no matter what the day holds.

Dear Lord, give me just what I need from Your Word for today.
Help me to make time with You my first priority, because I know
that Your Word is where I gain wisdom and strength for every day.

Time with God daily will fill your heart to fullness.

MY CONSTANT GUIDE

*Trust in the LORD with all your heart, and do not lean on
your own understanding. In all your ways acknowledge Him,
and He will make your paths straight.*

Proverbs 3:5-6

I do well with driving if I can avoid major highways, but put me on several highways with lane changes, crossing over and under other highways, and it puts a little tension in my bones. One night I was following my dad home from an event on the outskirts of Dallas in an area I was unfamiliar with. As we headed out, I felt a sense of calm, knowing that I was following my dad in his big red truck. All of a sudden, though, he exited the highway, and I could not get over fast enough to exit with him. So I just kept driving, having no idea where this highway was leading me.

Had it just been residential streets, I probably wouldn't have panicked, but we were on a highway surrounded by what seemed like lots of other highways, and I couldn't just pick up my phone and look up directions while driving. Deep breath. My phone rang. It was my Daddy. In the most calming, reassuring voice, he told me not to worry and to stay on the phone and let him guide me where to go. He guided me back on course, back on track, and back on the correct route. Even better, within ten minutes of my little detour, He was pulling up in his big red truck right behind me. He had come to find me, make sure I knew where I was, and guide me the rest of the way home. It hit me that I just needed to follow—not worry, not try to figure it out, just follow.

That's just like my heavenly Father's love: big, strong, protective, and surrounding me at all times. He is with me every moment, and He is my compass and constant guide. He leads me to where I need to be. He gets me off the wrong path and points me back in the right direction. My job is to follow and to trust that He knows what He is doing and where He is leading. Your heavenly Daddy is your constant guide. When you get a little lost, He will come find you and get you back on track. Take a breath. Just follow Him.

❧

**Thank You, Father, that You are my guiding light. Thank You that
You lead me every step of every day. Thank You that I can trust
Your leading. Help me to trust You, knowing that You know best.**

*When your circumstances feel shaky, keep your eyes
on the One Who constantly leads you. Trust His lead.*

THE FATHER'S LOVE

The Lord your God is in your midst, a mighty One Who will save;
He will rejoice over you with gladness; He will quiet
you by His love, He will exult over you with loud singing.
Zephaniah 3:17,

As women, we love to celebrate the people we love. We celebrate birthdays, anniversaries, graduations, new babies, and weddings. We cook, plan, and decorate in order to make the person we are celebrating feel special and loved.

The God who knows you intimately—all the good and all the parts of yourself that feel messy—loves you completely no matter what. He hoots and hollers over you in every little step that you take as you are learning to lean on Him.

God is cheering you on, step by step. You delight Him and make Him smile. You give Him such joy. He is watching you every moment, and He is throwing a party and celebrating every time you choose Him. In the moments when you feel like a mess, run to Him and just say, *Okay, God, I cannot do this on my own. Please help me. I need You.* That makes His heart glad, because that's what it is all about—recognizing that you cannot do it on your own. So in your day today, remember that God sees your choices, your decisions, your prayers, your kindness. And He is celebrating each and every step you take in His grace.

Thank You, Jesus, for showing me that I delight You.
Thank You for showing me that I make You smile,
celebrate, and laugh with joy! Don't let me forget it.

May you know today that God is celebrating you!
He is cheering you on. You absolutely delight His heart.

RELY ON HIM

By this we know that we abide in Him and He in us, because He has given us of His Spirit.
And we have seen and testify that the Father has sent His Son to be the Savior
of the world. Whoever confesses that Jesus is the Son of God, God abides in him,
and he in God. So we have come to know and to believe the love that God has for us.
God is love, and whoever abides in love abides in God, and God abides in him.

1 John 4:13-16

Rest and freedom are two words that our souls ache for, wouldn't you agree? Our human bent is to orchestrate our lives apart from God, analyze our future forgetting that God is in control, and attempt to figure out ourselves and our lives by sheer determination. But in all of that orchestrating and analyzing, we forget the most important thing—we don't have to do all that! We can rely on God and let Him work out the details, let Him handle all the pieces of the puzzle, let him manage our lives. Therein lies the way to freedom and rest.

What are you trying to figure out today? What problem or issue are you wanting to take into your own hands, in your own time frame? What are you trying to do or handle in your own strength? What if you took that to God today and let yourself rest in His agenda, His time frame, His way, and His will? Will you allow Him to work it out?

God invites you to rely on Him in everything. What a gift! He wants you to have the freedom and the rest and the peace that only He can give. He wants peace to wash over you as you let Him into your daily agenda. And not only will you feel His peace, but you will feel His love.

Here's my agenda today, Lord. Everything in my nature wants to handle it all, analyze it all, and do it all on my own. Everything in me wants to figure it all out. But I want freedom and rest and YOU more than I want my own way. Help me to rest in YOUR agenda. Help me to let go and let YOU in. Help me to rely on YOU.

Before you set out for your day,
take a moment to turn everything over to the Lord.

HE'S REALLY THERE

God is within her, she will not fall;
God will help her at break of day.

Psalm 46:5, NIV

As you go about your day today, remember that the God of the universe—the Creator of this huge, big world—is pursuing your heart. He is always with you, and He will not let you fall.

I love how today's verse says, *God will help her at break of day*. As soon as your day starts, He is actively helping you. So whether your day starts at five in the morning feeding a newborn baby, or at a later hour like seven or eight, He's right there waiting for you.

Invite God into your day. Start the day with prayer—even a short prayer. Keep the conversation going throughout the day. Ask Him questions like, *Lord, how should I handle this? Lord, what should I do here?* This ebb and flow of conversation with the Father is like a dance. He leads, we follow, and there is a beautiful synchronization of living in step with Him.

You may be thinking, *Sometimes I don't feel close to God…. I can't feel His presence.* James 4:8 says, "Draw near to God, and he will draw near to you." Move toward God. Just take one step toward Him. Maybe for you that means praying throughout your day, maybe it means memorizing a verse, maybe it means just sitting in a comfy chair and thinking about Him. I recently read that the most important thing our children need from us is not training and correcting, but our company. I can't help but relate that to our relationship with Christ. Yes, we need training in godliness and correcting in our behavior so that ultimately we can glorify Him with our lives, but more importantly we need His company. He wants to capture your heart with His love and grace so that you can live a life of faith, joy, and peace.

Lord, thank You for loving me. Show me one thing I can do today to step toward You. Thank You for Your company. Thank You that I am never alone.

You are loved by God, and He will never let you stray too far away
from Him. Step toward Him. Trust that He'll show up in your day today.

SOMETIMES I FORGET

Then they said, "Ask God whether or not our journey will be successful."
"Go in peace," the priest replied, "For. the Lord is watching over your journey."

Judges 18:5-6, NLT

Sometimes I need a gentle reminder—no, sometimes I need a loud reminder—that God is in the details and that He is on this journey through life with me. I need to know that He is working behind the scenes. And sometimes I forget, and I get caught up in worry, fear, doubt, and uncertainty. Those emotions drain my faith.

Remember today that God is watching over your journey.

God sees your whole journey, and He is working tirelessly on your behalf. He is orchestrating, intervening, and working in all of the details of your life. He is busy, even when you feel like nothing is happening.

So don't lose heart, dear friend, when you feel like you are waiting for an answer to prayer, or waiting for God's direction in your life, or just waiting for His peace to pour over you. Talk to Him about what is on your heart and know that He is at work on your behalf.

Dear Lord, You know how easily I forget that You are at work in the details of my life. Help me to remember that You are always watching over my journey. Thank You for Your constant work in my life, and when I lose sight of You, draw me back to You.

God is working even when you can't feel it or see it.
Have faith that He is guiding your journey day by day,
and that He will never leave you.

May

ENOUGH

Lord, You alone are my portion and my cup;
You make my lot secure.

Psalm 16:5, NIV

I just want to encourage you today that God is enough. I know you feel scattered sometimes; I know you feel spread thin because of your commitments, the things on your to-do list, and your responsibilities. I know sometimes you feel like you do not have time to think, dream, or pray, and I know sometimes it feels nice to just do nothing, but it is hard to give yourself the grace to do that. I pray that today, in those moments when you think, *Okay, what do I need to do next?* that you will take a moment to seek the Lord. Rest in the fact that some days are going to be super productive days, some days are going to be days to rest, and some days are going to be a mixture of the two. Some days you feel super joyful, happy, and content, and other days you feel tired, defeated, or discouraged. Some days are full of appointments and activities, jam-packed with places to go and people to see. Other days are quieter, with no schedule and nowhere to be. There is one common denominator in each day.

Jesus is enough.

So whatever you need, whatever you are doing today—He is enough, and He will meet your need.

He's got you today. Go in His peace.

Be in my day, Lord. Remind me that You are enough
for any need, any struggle, any schedule, or any issue.

The Lord will provide everything you need for this day.

CHRISTMAS IN MAY

But the fruit of the Spirit is love, joy, peace …
Galatians 5:22

I know it's May, but today, let's talk about Christmas morning! Christmas morning feels like a little slice of heaven on earth, doesn't it? Growing up, Mom and Dad made Christmas morning so special for us. As my siblings and I sat at the top of our staircase, anxiously anticipating our descent down the stairs and around the corner to see what Santa had brought, Mom and Dad joyfully bustled around downstairs—Mom whipping up cinnamon rolls or eggs and Dad taking care of last-minute Christmas details. I bet you carry special Christmas morning traditions in your heart too.

Christmas is a mixture of joyful anticipation, a little magic in the air, and a bit of heaven crossing paths with our everyday life. This past Christmas, a thought crossed my mind as I drank my coffee in front of the glowing lights of the Christmas tree: *I want to live every day like it's Christmas morning.*

I want to live with as much joy and holy anticipation today as I do on the morning that holds wrapping paper and twinkling lights. I want to anticipate God's sweet gifts and surprises as much every other day of the year as I anticipate them on Christmas morning. I want to ponder God and how He sent His Son to cross paths with our everyday life as much in May as I ponder it during the Christmas season. I want to live with Christmas joy every day of the year. Maybe you're thinking, *Is it possible to live with such joy and expectation?* I believe it's possible to keep our joy and zeal for God and this life He's given us, and to live with a holy anticipation of God intervening in our lives. I believe it's possible to be full of Christmas—full of Christ—every day of the year.

Maybe all it takes is a quiet moment each day to acknowledge that every day is a gift to unwrap, to marvel over, and to thank God for. Every day is a gift because God resides in us, and by His Spirit, He produces joy in us. What if you lived every day like it's Christmas morning?

God, thank You for the gift of Your Son.
Keep the joy of celebrating Him in my heart all year long.

Keep Christmas in your heart all year long.

COME REST

Come with Me by yourselves to a quiet place and get some rest.
Mark 6:31, NIV

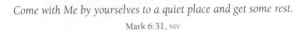

Come to Jesus when you feel restless, when you're too busy, or when your thoughts are stirring up your anxiety.

Sometimes I wind up trying to do this Christian life in my own strength. I try to do the right things, say the right things, be the right person, not do the wrong things, check off all my to-dos. Then, add in eating right, exercising, and encouraging my children, plus my car needs gasoline, and, oh yeah, I need to go put the clothes in the dryer, and where's my son's other shoe? Then add in thoughts of, *I feel tired, but I'll just fight through it. I have a dream to do this, but I'll never have time to do that. Oh, homework, we need to make sure homework is done, and oh, the laundry!* It all can lead to feelings restlessness and angst. I often shove those feelings down because, well, I don't have time to stop!

Does this pattern sound familiar? And do you know this restlessness? This uneasiness of the mind or the heart? What do you run to? Jesus invites us, *Come with Me by yourselves to a quiet place and get some rest.* Maybe that involves going on a walk and just pouring out your heart to Him. Maybe it means reading His Word on your back porch with your coffee in the morning. Maybe it means praying to Him when you're going to sleep. It may look different every day. But the point is, Jesus is the answer to your restlessness. He solves it, soothes it, and melts it away. He brings rest when you come to Him.

Jesus, help me come to You daily, because You set
my heart at rest. Thank You so much for loving me
and for caring so deeply for me that You give me hope.

*When God is your daily fuel, when you make that time with Him
each day vital, your heart can be at peace and you can enjoy life.*

O MY SOUL

*Praise the LORD, my soul, and forget not all His benefits—Who forgives
all your sins and heals all your diseases, Who redeems your life from
the pit and crowns you with love and compassion, Who satisfies your
desires with good things so that your youth is renewed like the eagle's.*

Psalm 103:2-5, NIV

As you go about your day today, remind yourself to stop every once in a while and remember all the beautiful benefits of knowing the One Who saved you by His grace. Nurture your soul by remembering:

- Any sin you have ever committed—past, present, and future—is completely forgiven because of Jesus.
- He is your healer.
- He has saved you from eternal separation from Him and crowns you with His love and compassion so that You can one day spend an eternity with Him and so that You can live an abundant life while on earth.
- He satisfies your desires with good things that make you feel young! I love that!

What an awesome God we serve. How amazing it is that we do not have to earn our salvation. How amazing that our God wants us to have fun and enjoy life. How amazing that we can talk to the God of the universe at any time. How amazing that He will help us with big issues and little issues. How amazing!

**Jesus, words cannot fully express my thanks to You.
Help me to better understand Your beautiful benefits. Help me
to think on these truths that I am forgiven, You are my healer,
You crown me with love and compassion, and You satisfy my desires.**

*Praise Him as you remember His benefits,
and be prepared for your soul to be filled!*

UNDESERVING

*He does not treat us as our sins deserve or repay us according
to our iniquities. For as high as the heavens are above the earth,
so great is His love for those who fear Him; as far as the east is
from the west, so far has He removed our transgressions from us.*

Psalm 103:10-12, NIV

We are truly set free from our sins. The beautiful work that the Holy Spirit does in us through helping us recognize our sins is a process that we will go through again and again on this side of heaven. There is always going to be a sin in our lives— it's part of being human. And acknowledging and repenting of it is part of growing spiritually, part of leaning on Jesus. But in our growth process, may we remember that there is grace. May we remember that when God looks at us, because of Jesus, He does not see our sin and imperfections, He sees a clean slate. He sees purity. He sees us as forgiven. We are set free from sin, and He loves us more than words can possibly describe.

So when you're reminded of the sin that is hanging over your head, the one you feel guilty about or you cannot seem to conquer, ask the Lord for forgiveness, trust that You are forgiven, and keep growing in Jesus. He is bigger than your sin, and He can help you overcome it. He will keep showing you things that need pruning or shaping or changing, and then He will empower you to repent and move forward. We will never be perfect this side of heaven, but we can keep being attentive to His voice, allowing Him access to our hearts so that He can shape us into who He created us to be.

God does not treat us as our sins deserve. Let that sink in. He has removed our sins as far as the east is from the west—can you sense His grace?

Thank You, Lord, for Your beautiful grace.

*In Jesus, you are free from sin. Bring Him your struggles,
rest in His forgiveness and grace, and lean on Him for daily grace.*

GIFTED BY GOD

As each has received a gift, use it to serve one another,
as good stewards of God's varied grace.

1 Peter 4:10

Did you know that God has gifted you in a specific, unique way—different from anybody else in this world? He has gifted you, wired you, and designed you to be good at certain things. And He has given you specific works that only you can do. Do you know what your unique gifts are? Sometimes finding those gifts can seem like a big task. Sometimes we think that we are not good at anything. But if you look closely at the desires of your heart, your passion and desires for certain things usually point you to the gifts God has given you. Often it is more than one thing—a combination of several gifts that God has blessed you with. What is the purpose of these gifts? In today's verse, we are encouraged to use our gifts to serve others, faithfully administering God's grace in its various forms. I think there is a mystery here. Somehow, in a way only God can truly know, when His precious children embrace and use the gifts He has given them for His glory, others see the grace of God. They get a taste of Him. Your gifts point others to Christ.

What stirs your heart? What are you good at? What do you love doing? When do you feel God's pleasure? For me, I feel God's pleasure being a wife. I feel God's pleasure when I take care of my children and my home. I feel God's pleasure when I dance. And I feel God's pleasure when I write. I cannot explain it fully in words, but doing those things feels right.

God uses our gifts to help us experience more of Him and to help others get a taste of Him. So go forward with what moves you. Talk to God about the desires of your heart. If you are not sure what your gifts are or what you are good at, ask to Him about it.

Lord, thank You for the gifts You give us, the skills, the way You wire us to be good at certain things or to have certain character qualities. Thank You that we are all wired in such unique ways. Help me to look to You to discover my gifts and my calling and the unique ways in which You have wired me.

You are gifted by God for specific purposes.

LAUGH, SING, DANCE

*"Martha, Martha," the Lord answered, "you are worried and upset
about many things, but few things are needed—or indeed only one.
Mary has chosen what is better, and it will not be taken away from her."*

Luke 10:41-42, NIV

Life gets busy, and sometimes we forget to enjoy it. Sometimes we get so caught up in "getting things done" mode that we forget to watch the sunset and be reminded of how big our God is, or to throw the Frisbee with the kiddos instead of always doing the dishes, or to just be still while our coffee is brewing and thank God for a new day instead of checking our email. We can easily forget to notice the beautiful details of our day because we are moving too fast, plowing through all that needs to get done. Below the surface of busyness and activity, I think we long to get caught up in Jesus and be more aware of His precious gifts instead of getting caught up in distractions and to-do lists.

Mary sat at Jesus' feet. She stopped, paused, slowed down, and just listened to Him. I am sure she got up at some point to do what she needed to do, but she sat at His feet first. Work is good—thank God for work, and for giving us things to do, people to impact, and families to be a part of. But Jesus urges us to come to Him first. To put Him first. Then He will provide the strength and energy we need for the rest of the day.

We put so much pressure on ourselves to do, do, do like Martha. Jesus is calling us to enjoy being in His presence and to enjoy the precious gifts He has given us. Today, remember to enjoy His gifts and have fun! And as the sun comes up and rolls out another day, remember to laugh, to sing, to dance through your day with joy because the Maker of heaven and earth is with you every second.

Dear Lord, thank You for Your countless gifts, and forgive me
for letting myself get caught up in the lists of things to do.
Thank You for rescuing me from my tendency to plow through life.
Thank You for loving me enough to remind me to slow down.

*Enjoy the little things today. Watch for God's presence
throughout the day. Let God minister to you all day long.*

LIFT ME UP

I waited patiently for the LORD; He turned to me and heard my cry.
He lifted me out of the slimy pit, out of the mud and mire;
He set my feet on a rock and gave me a firm place to stand.
He put a new song in my mouth, a hymn of praise to our God.

Psalm 40:1-3, NIV

Burnout. It is not fun, but it happens to everyone. We can be going strong, feeling passionate and inspired, running on adrenaline, excited for what is going on in our life—and then somewhere, somehow, a little slice of discouragement creeps in.

Have you been there? During those times, it is easy to want to give up, to quit. What do you do when you feel that sense of burnout? Today's verse says we can look to the Lord, and He hears our cry. Tell Him how you are feeling. He will lift you out of that pit—that place of feeling burned out. He will give you a firm place to stand, and He will put a new song in your mouth or a new hop in your step. But notice the first part of the verse: *I waited patiently for the Lord.* Give Him time to work. Be careful about making a rash decision to quit something in a heated moment of frustration, or after a hard day, or when you are tired.

I want to encourage you to step away for some perspective. It is okay to take a break. Find a way to recharge, refuel, and rest. Take a break with the Lord. Go to His Word to let Him recharge you. Let Him help you through these waves of burnout. Let Him help you put things into perspective. Let Him give you the rest you need. You are working so hard, so many hours of the day, and there are going to be times when you are tired. Being tired affects your emotions and your motivation. So when you start getting that sense of burnout, run to Him. And then wait. He will refuel you and help you recapture the motivation to keep going. He will lift you up.

Jesus, I am feeling that sense of burnout. Please carry me through these emotions. Help me to step away for Your perspective and hold on to the promise that You will lift me out of this place.

The Lord lifts you up when you run to Him.

HIS DAILY INVITATION

Why, my soul, are you downcast? Why so disturbed within me?
Put your hope in God, for I will yet praise Him, my Savior and my God.
My soul is downcast within me; therefore I will remember You.

Psalm 42:5-6, NIV

When you are feeling down, how do you usually handle it? Who do you confide in? How do you get past it? How long do you stay in a slump? What do you run to? What makes you feel better?

We run to many things to fill that gnawing feeling inside us. I know I can easily run to something to distract me, like my phone or the television. Jesus invites us to run to Him each time we feel discouraged or down. What if we looked upwards at Him, talked to Him, and went to Him to let Him fill our need? What if we chose to put our hope in Christ? I think sometimes it seems easier to try anything else to satisfy us. But it is never enough, is it?

Let God surprise You today with a pure joy that only He can give. Give Him your troubled heart and see how He will fix it. Let Him sort it out. Anytime you feel down about something, try giving it to Jesus. He wants to carry each and every burden. Let Him carry your load.

Jesus, I bring whatever is bothering me today to You. Help me to
run to You, and nothing else, whenever I feel the slightest bit down.
I praise You, my Savior and my God! Thank You for loving me so much.

God is inviting you to bring Him every burden, concern,
and worry. He wants you to come to Him when your
heart aches. Run to the One Who can help you.

SURRENDER

Therefore I tell you, do not worry about your life.
Luke 12:22, NIV

What are you worried about today? What are you trying to control today? What do you hope will happen today? Take a breath. Jesus invites you into His amazing, indescribable peace, a peace you can have every moment of every day. Soak in the truth that you are His daughter, He loves you so much, and He wants to be in control of your life so that you do not have to be!

We can list a million things to fret about in our daily routine. Think about what kind of state your heart and mind get into when you are worrying. Jesus wants us to learn from the birds of the air and the flowers of the field. They are not hustling about, frantic to find food, or in a hurry to grow. They are in a state of surrender to their Maker because He can take better care of them than they can. After all, He made them, and He knows how they are designed to function. He made you, too. He knows how you are designed to function. He does not want you to live your life in a state of worry. All He wants is for you to release your grip, to surrender it to Him.

I hope you dance through your day with peace, resting in Christ's care and letting Him carry your worries.

Jesus, thank You that just like You take care of Your creation,
the birds and the flowers, You take perfect care of me. Help me to
daily surrender every burden, every worry, and every stress to You.
Thank You that the Holy Spirit helps me to surrender. Help me to
remember daily to surrender, because so often I forget, and sometimes it
feels easier to worry and try to control every situation. You are so good.

*Worry loses its hold on you when you
remember that God is truly in control.*

TUNING OUT
THE NEWSFEED

The LORD is my shepherd, I lack nothing.

Psalm 23:1, NIV

Comparison and not-enough-ness are struggles whether or not we are looking through a screen, but social media deeply magnifies the issue. The more we scroll, the more we must battle the beast of comparison. We set ourselves up for envy when we continue to look through the screens. And what is most problematic is that as we look through filters and images of other people's lives, we begin to lose the awe, wonder, and gratitude of what's right in front of us: our own lives. Your sweet heart is too precious for all that gunk. Your life is too beautiful. Your relationship with Jesus is too much of a treasure to be missed out on in favor of scrolling.

Today's verse says that the Lord is our shepherd. A shepherd carefully tends his flock. He provides for each individual sheep's needs. He knows their every move. He cares for every aspect of their lives. He runs after the one who veers off, and He carries the lambs in His arms.

Daughter of Jesus, He is your shepherd. He carefully tends your life. He provides for every one of your needs. He knows your every move, and he cares for every aspect of your life. He's running after you, sweet one, so that He can carry you in His arms. Sweet ones, you were not meant to live in the icky feelings of comparison, envy, not-enough-ness, despair, or depression. Don't let the newsfeed steal your joy. Do what you need to do to log off, sign off, deactivate, and unfollow.

Jesus, help me to tune out the noise of the internet so I can fully tune into You. Give me the strength to protect my heart from the onslaught of comparison and feelings of not-enough-ness. Help me to spend my time wisely. Help me to choose what's better—time with You. Help me to have a new appreciation for the life and sweet gifts that are right in front of me.

God wants to give you His joy. Tune out
the other voices so you can receive it.

RUNNING TO GOD
FOR SATISFACTION

He makes me lie down in green pastures,
He leads me beside quiet waters.

Psalm 23:2, NIV

Recently I was feeling the weight of distractions pulling at my heart quite deeply. I turned my phone off and threw it in my purse. I needed some peace and quiet and alone time with God. I needed brain space to think, ponder, and hear God. I put my golden retriever puppy on his leash, and we set out for a long, quiet walk. I looked at my pup, Shaka, and longed to feel as free and happy and undistracted as he is. I longed to soak in the beauty of my walk and to just be. On that walk, I told God I was tired of feeling the urgent pull of my phone and email inbox. I told Him that it felt like a hopeless endeavor to be fully free. And in the quiet of my heart, I sensed God's whisper.

Sweet Daughter, I am bigger than the internet and social media and your phone. I am more powerful than all that stuff. I needed to hear that. I needed to know that my God is bigger and stronger than the pull of all the fancy tools. As I processed this, I started to wonder, *But, God, how do I battle this struggle on my own? All the phone boundaries and unplugging apps and technology limits don't solve the problem.*

And here's what God started to impress on my heart: *Love Someone more.* Okay, I knew I needed to love Jesus more than all the fancy tools. But how? *Choose Me instead.*

I started thinking about how in those moments when I would typically run to my phone or check my email, perhaps I could find ways to choose God instead. I started thinking about ways that I feel most connected to God. I feel most connected with God when I journal to Him and write down meaningful Bible verses. Also, grabbing an old journal off my bookshelf and diving into old journal entries and Scriptures God showed me years ago helps me feel God's sweet presence.

So with God's help, I began choosing Him instead. In everyday moments, when that itch to run to the phone or computer came up, I grabbed a journal. And I dove in. When I chose God instead, peace came like a river. Joy rose up in my heart. Anxiety lessened and wholeness swelled. We have a tendency to run to things that do not satisfy, but when we run to God instead, we will find green pastures and quiet waters and a closer walk with Jesus.

Jesus, You are the secret to joy, to abundant life, and to overflowing peace.
In those moments when I typically run to the internet or my
phone to satisfy a deep longing, help me to choose You instead.

Choosing God leads to peace and satisfaction.

CHOOSING GOD
OVER DISTRACTIONS

Surely Your goodness and love will follow me all the days of my life,
and I will dwell in the house of the LORD forever.

Psalm 23:6, NIV

God's goodness and love will follow us all the days of our lives. He's never going to stop pursuing us. He will dwell with us forever—here on earth and eternally if we believe in Him. He has never left us or stopped pursuing us. But distractions can make us feel like He has left us. The busier and more crowded our hearts get with information, images, the next good read, urgent emails, dings and pings, scrolling, checking, clicking, liking, and swiping, the harder it is to feel God's nearness. He never left us, but the fancy tools make it feel harder to hear Him and sense His presence.

When we begin to turn down the noise, we begin to hear His whispers and feel His presence. I want you to know today that God has never left you. No matter how far away you have felt from God due to screens, distractions, or busyness, He hasn't pulled away from you. In fact, I believe He's pursuing you even harder because He wants you that much.

Scripture echoes, "Return to me … and I will return to you" (Zechariah 1:3).

It appears that God wants us to make the first move, to take the first step toward Him. And when we do, He returns to us. He hasn't left you, sweet one, but He's calling you closer.

I want more of You, God. Help me to choose You first, before the lure
of the world. Change me on this journey to crave You and to seek You.

No matter how far away you may feel from God,
He is always drawing you back to Himself.

THE BEAUTY OF
A QUIET LIFE

In quietness and trust is your strength.

Isaiah 30:15, NIV

Jesus modeled for us how to live in a way that helps us function best. Throughout Scripture, we learn that Jesus often withdrew to be alone with the Father. His pattern was to minister to people and then go to a quiet place and pray. Back and forth He went, from His busy life to solitude. After His quiet moments with God, Jesus returned filled up, refreshed, equipped, and strengthened. He wants the very same thing for you and me. In the quiet moments with God, we, too, can find soul-nourishment, satisfaction, and supernatural power.

It's in the quiet that we find His strength for the day.
We learn to trust Him with our lives.
We find release from stress, anxiety, and tension.
He grows us in our spiritual gifts so we can be women God uses.
We discover who God made us to be.
We get to pour out our hearts to God and turn over our worries.
We discover God's divine direction for our lives.
We hear God speak to us.
It's in the quiet that we find all we've ever needed.

When you feel that longing in your heart for something more, or you feel anxiety or stress taking over your heart, head to the quiet again and again, if necessary. Head to that quiet spot in your home where your soul finds rest and strength from the Lord. When we have a quiet place that we return to again and again, our tension begins to release as we sit down physically, but also sit down inside. As we sit before the Lord, our hearts calm down, our emotions grow still, and our minds lose their frantic pace. It's in the quiet that we find all that we need in Christ alone.

God, bring me back to the quietness of an unplugged life.
Increase my desire to protect my quiet moments with You.
Draw me closer, Lord.

He's drawing you back to quiet waters.

KEEP YOUR HEART ON HIM

Make it your ambition to lead a quiet life.
1 Thessalonians 4:11, NIV

Our culture shouts a message that we need to do more, be more, do better, be bigger, accomplish more, do something different, do the next thing, be more beautiful, be more fit, be more (you fill in the blank).

When I scroll through the feed or get lost in information overload, something creeps in my heart that makes me feel like I need to change. Sometimes change is good. But when culture is the one luring us in, we must be careful to guard our hearts. I don't think God intends for us to live in a constant state of needing more or being more or constantly looking to the next thing to fulfill us. I don't think He intends for us to live in a frenzied state of information crowding our hearts and notifications interrupting our days.

Culture shouts, *more, bigger, better.*

Scripture echoes, *lead a quiet life, be still, trust, rest.*

In today's verse, we are encouraged to make it our ambition, our quest, our goal, our desire to lead a quiet life. The verse continues with, "You should mind your own business and work with your hands."

God knows how to help us function best physically, emotionally, and mentally. He knows that when we lead a quieter life, we are relieved of unnecessary stress, tension, and anxiety. When we keep our eyes on Him and the good path He has for us, there's a sweet freedom and joy. There's relief from the pressure to do more and be more. When we put on blinders to the world and run the race God has for us, we live with focus, purpose, and joy. But when we are constantly looking around, we never quite find contentment, and a lack of contentment is stressful and leaves us feeling empty.

Today, keep your heart on God and your eyes on your own path. Your path, your life, and your heart are so beautiful. The quiet life you are leading—whatever that looks like—is gorgeous.

God, help me to make it my ambition to lead a quiet life. Help me to love
the path You have me on. Grow in me a heart of contentment and peace.
Help me keep my heart on You and my eyes on my own beautiful path.

God needs you to keep your heart on Him and your eyes
on your path. You will find the freedom of a quiet life,
and it will be sweeter than you could ever imagine.

THE BEHIND-THE-SCENES MOMENTS

I have learned the secret of being content in any and every situation.
Philippians 4:12, NIV

The behind-the-scenes moments of your life, the unseen ones where no picture is taken, no filters are used, no announcement is made—those are the sweet stuff of life. God sees all your behind-the-scenes moments. He's the only One Who sees it all.

Daughter, I see you.
I see you loving your kiddos.
I see you praying for your kiddos.
I know how many dishes you've washed and how many loads of laundry you've folded.
I see you working hard to make sure your family eats well.
I see you encouraging your husband.
I see all you do in a day.
I hear your prayers and I know your thoughts.
I see you.
Even when the rest of the world doesn't, I see you.

God sees your whole life. He sees behind the filters and screens to the good stuff. You are not less than. You are not unseen. The God of the universe sees it all.

So in those moments when the world is oohing and aahing over the facades on screens, ponder the wonder of being seen by the God who made you. Ponder the wonder of the secret, quiet moments between you and your God and your people.

God, I thank You that You see me completely. You see my every moment.
Help me to ponder the gift of being completely seen, known, and loved
by You. Guard my heart from the lies that say I need to be more,
do more, and be seen. I am seen by You—let that be enough.

You are seen. You are celebrated. Life through
filters and screens is not real life—the life
you're living is where the sweet stuff is.

FREEDOM FROM THE PHONE

I will walk about in freedom, for I have sought out Your precepts.
Psalm 119:45, NIV

The more time we spend on our apps, phones, and social media, the more depression, overwhelm, and stress take over our lives. I remember reading an article about how Steve Jobs, the creator of the iPhone, never intended for us to use our phones the way we do. He couldn't imagine how we use them now. He literally created iPhones so that we could make calls, text, and listen to music. That's it. I would so love it if that's all my phone did. Actually, I would still want to have google maps on my phone because I love not getting lost on the road!

I love a lot of things about my phone. My favorite thing is that my husband and I can stay in touch throughout the day while he's at work. I love knowing my teenager can get ahold of me if he needs me to pick him up. It is possible to live in the freedom of using our phones with wisdom and joy. It is possible to be in control of our phone use instead of our phones being in control of us.

Remember to keep God in the center of your quest for freedom. He's your Helper, Counselor, Guide, and Friend. He wants to free you from the chains of distraction. The secret is to replace your habits of distraction with something better and more life-giving. Simplify your phone down to only the apps that you truly need each day or go back to a more simple phone if needed. See your phone as a tool, not an escape. When you find yourself too invested in your phone, it's time to put it away. Turn it off for a few hours if you can. Put it in a drawer and walk away from it for a while. Put a screen saver on your phone of a Bible verse that reminds you to live free from the pull of the phone. Do whatever you need to do to keep your phone from running your day. Ask the Lord to help you put your phone in its place.

Thank You for giving me hope, freedom, and strength.
Free me from the entanglements of distraction, increase my joy
as I turn to You, and help me to continue to seek after You every day.

Release the distractions with His help.

TIME ALONE WITH GOD

Your word is a lamp to my feet and a light on my path.
Psalm 119:105

God designed us to need solitude. Whether we are extroverts, introverts, or some-where in-between, we all need moments of complete solitude, especially so we can connect with our Maker. I discovered the beauty of solitude and complete alone-ness with God when I was an 18-year-old living in Austin, TX. My career as a ballerina was just starting. I had moved away from home for the first time, and I felt alone in my quest to dance because all my friends had gone off to college.

I was living in a quaint little dorm room by myself. Outside my dorm room was a quiet, ivy-covered patio adorned with round iron tables and chairs. No one was ever out there, so I claimed it as my spot to connect with God. I stepped into the courtyard daily. Out there I felt so seen by God. It was just me, God, my Bible, a journal, and a good devotional book. It wasn't about having a quiet time, it was about seeking Him. It wasn't about checking my Bible reading off my to-do list, it was about being known by God. Over twenty years later, I sometimes miss that quiet, ivy-covered patio where it was just me and God.

These days, it's a little trickier to get completely alone with God—no distractions. You have to fight for solitude and quietness with God. I hope you're inspired to find the joy of hours alone with God. That time with God allows Him to be a lamp for your feet and a light for your path, as it says in Psalm 119. God wants to guide and lead your life. He has precious plans for you, but He needs you to spend time with Him so He can reveal them to you. He wants you to know Him. He wants you to find the satisfaction of a deep relationship with Him. And that takes time and space. Following Jesus' model of withdrawing to be alone with God is important. It may take some creativity, it may take some thought and intention, but it's possible and it's worth it.

Jesus, help me to guard my alone time with You. Meet me in the quiet of Your company, and give me a craving for more and more alone time with You.

Pull away from the world, step out onto your back porch, and get alone with God—just you and Him. He delights in your company.

HOT TEA FOR THE SOUL

The unfolding of Your words gives light.
Psalm 119:130

I remember one season in my life in particular when I discovered the joy of God's Word. One night a week, I drove through the hilly roads of Austin to a sweet mom's house in the hill country. She hosted a small group of gals from church at her cozy home. She always had fresh-out-of-the-oven brownies for us and chamomile tea by the cupful. We doused our tea in sugar and sipped on it throughout our time together. Just as the hot tea soothed my stress and made me feel so at home, so the time in God's Word together soothed my soul.

My Bible study leader guided us through God's Word week by week. It was nothing fancy, just a small group of gals diving into the Word. But that time together in God's Word got me excited about knowing the Word better. It helped me feel less alone to be able to talk about God and His Word. There was something so refreshing, good, sweet, and pure about those weekly nights studying the Word with other gals.

We need all the light we can get these days. We live in a beautiful yet very broken world. One look at the news and our hearts can sink into despair. We need the light of God's Word to be front and center in our lives. Remember today that the unfolding of God's Word gives light.

Lord, remind me daily that the unfolding of Your Word gives me true light.
Be the light of my life. Be front and center in my priorities. Make Your
Word come alive to me as I read, ponder, and think on Your promises.
Help me to set aside time each day to let Your Word seep into my heart.

As women of our generation,
we need the light of God's Word more than ever.

LOOK HOW FAR YOU'VE COME

The Lord will keep you from all harm—He will watch over your life;
the LORD will watch over your coming and going both now and forevermore.

Psalm 121:7-8, NIV

When I was a little girl, I loved snow skiing with my Dad. I remember how huge his skis looked next to mine as we swung our legs back and forth on the chair lift. I would follow him down the mountain, and every once in a while he would stop and wait for me to catch up. Then he would say with enthusiasm, "Sarah, look back at that mountain you just went down. Look how far you went!" Squinting from the glare of the sun, I would turn around and look at the mountain we had just conquered. From this view, it looked so steep and gigantic. But when I was skiing it with my Dad leading the way, it didn't feel quite so daunting. As long as I kept my eyes on him and followed his path, we made it safely down.

If I could look you in the eyes today, I would say, *Look how far you've come. You are journeying day by day with God. You're growing, changing, and transforming as you walk each day with your heavenly Daddy. As you follow His lead, He is guiding you through rough terrain, mountain climbs, and deep waters. Keep going. Keep following your Father's lead. Stay on this path with Him and let Him guide you day by day.*

Every once in a while it's good to look at how far you've come. Peer back a bit, read through an old prayer journal, flip through a photo album, or review Bible verses you have highlighted. Look how far the Lord has brought you, and allow His faithfulness to be your fuel for the journey ahead. As you look back at your spiritual journey, may you be reminded that God has never left you. May you discover with fresh faith that the Lord is constantly watching over your life.

Lord, thank You for being my heavenly Daddy. Help me to keep my eyes on You day by day. When I get anxious about the future or my present circumstances, remind me of Your faithful love and presence over the course of my life.

The Lord watches over you every second of your day.

GOD IS MINDFUL OF YOU

What is man that You are mindful of him,
and the son of man that You care for him?

Psalm 8:4

The God of the universe is mindful of you. He is paying attention to you, He's watching over you, and He cares about what you care about. He's tending your life. He cares deeply about you and your circumstances. And He will never leave you.

On one of our family walks recently, our little crew came across a butterfly that was on the ground with one wing up and one wing kind of crooked and layered with dust as it leaned into the dirt. One of my boys tenderly looked at it, wondering if it was dead or alive. He carefully nudged it with a stick to see if it would come back to life. Was she still flourishing, or was she kind of done? We all peered over her, willing her to come back to life.

I think we all have times in our lives when we feel like that butterfly—half alive in the dust. We desire to flourish and bloom and do all that God has called us to be, but we're weighed down by anxiety, busyness, or weariness. Just like the broken butterfly, perhaps we feel a bit broken inside. Hear me today: you're still flourishing as you seek God in your day-to-day life. God is at work in you. Right when you feel out of energy or motivation for what's before you, right when you feel defeated and stuck in the dust, God can pick you up and set you free to fly again.

So hang on, dear sister. You will come back to full life again. God will pick you up and restore your heart as you look to Him. He is in the business of restoration. You will bloom again, but what you may not see is that you're blooming now. God is peering over you, and He sees your whole beautiful life in the grand scheme of eternity. He sees you, and He's faithful to carry you through every difficult season.

Lord, in those moments when I feel broken,
weary, or just bogged down with life,
remind me that You are always mindful of me,
and You are always at work to restore my heart.

There is still flourishing and blooming happening
in your current season. Seeds are being planted and
roots are growing deeper. There will be blooming soon!

PULL OVER
FOR A REPRIEVE

You keep him in perfect peace whose mind is stayed on You,
because he trusts in You. Trust in the Lord forever,
for the Lord God is an everlasting rock.

Isaiah 26:3-4

Our golden retriever puppy often curls up in a cozy corner of our home, and as he plops down on the floor, he lets out a big puppy sigh that makes his lips kind of flutter—sort of like a horse. It's his way of communicating that he needs a break, a time-out, a reprieve from his daily walk, puppy playtime, and chasing squirrels.

We all need that kind of reprieve on certain days. The world and news around us feels heavy, and we're not sure what to do. Sometimes a big sigh, a big letting go of control, a big sitting down and letting God be God is just what we need. We can rest while God takes care of our burdens. We can take a break from the spinning news cycles and trust that He is working. We can take some time to be quiet in our hearts with God, trusting Him day by day and hour by hour to heal, comfort, and renew our hearts. When we let go of our anxious thoughts and cast them into God's care, we find the reprieve we're aching for. But we also want to help, to do something. When the news feels heavy and the problems feel unsolvable, we are not powerless. We can play a massive role in history and healing because we have a secret power as God's children: prayer.

We can pray.

We can find quiet spaces in our day to whisper healing prayers for whatever is on our hearts—prayers for our nation, prayers for our world. Prayers for our own hearts, families, children, friends. Prayers about anything and everything releases the power of God into our world and into our own lives. Prayer allows us to encounter God every single day.

Today, may you take some time out in a way that's good for your soul. May you pull away from the world and the news and linger in the presence of your God and Savior. May you pull over for a reprieve. May you feel God's nearness in a fresh way. May you feel hope and joy rising up in your heart as you remember that God has never once left you. May you steady your gaze on Jesus, and in return feel His peace wash over you. May you trust the One Who made the world and who will one day restore the world.

Lord, I'm pulling over today for a reprieve. Remind me that You are in control. Thank You that I can pray about anything. Here's everything on my heart …

Pull over for a reprieve and find
the rest that only God can provide.

YOUR RIGHT PATH

Show me the right path, O Lord; point out the road for me to follow. Lead me by Your truth
and teach me, for You are the God who saves me. All day long I put my hope in You.

Psalm 25:4-5, NLT

God has a specific and special path just for you. But if you're like me, you've probably heard that before. And maybe, just maybe, you've sort of stopped believing it. Or you feel like your path isn't as special as someone else's.

Let today be a fresh start for your heart in believing that God has a specific, good path handmade in heaven just for one specific gal's heart—*yours*. He wants you to find your footing on this specific path. And He wants you to stop looking to the right, to the left, far behind you, or way ahead of you. He wants you to look down at those two beautiful feet of yours and embrace the beautiful path right under your beautiful toes. Because it's *your* path. And when you begin to really embrace your path, you will begin to truly flourish.

This is a fork-in-the-road moment for you and for me. Imagine we're standing in a beautiful, wooded oasis, with a canopy of golden foliage from towering trees surrounding us on every side. We look down, and there are two paths. One looks like the road most people would take. It looks more well-worn, maybe a little easier, and maybe even a little safer. We turn to our left, and there is another path. It's not as fancy. It looks a little less traveled, a little less beautiful, and a little less inviting. But we know deep in our hearts that God is steering us toward that path. Will we choose the more common path, the one it seems everyone else is on? Or will we take a step of faith and set our feet on uncommon ground, into unknown territory, trusting that God will always be guiding us? Will we choose to keep going with the flow of the path the world tells us we should be on, or will we step foot into an adventure of faith with the One Who wove together a handmade path for our handmade hearts?

I know that deep down, you want God's best path for you. You want the right path. And today I want you to know that it really exists, and it's a very special path. It's your path. And it's time to set foot on it, trusting your Guide for the curves, turns, and hidden jewels along the way.

God, I am ready to step sure-footed onto the beautiful path You have laid out for me.
I want to desire the path that You have for me. Reveal Your specific, beautiful,
and good path for my life and help me to follow You one step at a time.

Take God's hand and trust Him to lead the way.
Your path is where God reveals His purposes and
plans for your life. Just take it one step at a time.

YOUR PRAYERS MOVE HEAVEN AND EARTH

Look to the LORD and His strength; seek His face always.
1 Chronicles 16:11, NIV

I woke up one morning with a sense of angst. The news of the day was the same—turbulent times, politics brewing, worries growing. I headed straight to the coffee maker. Lord, calm my anxious heart. It's so tempting to take in all the news of the day instead of tuning my heart to God. My phone waits there on the counter for me, ready to announce my to-do list and the news of the day. A lot of days I reach for it in an effort to stay aware of what's going on in the world and to make sure I haven't missed anything important. But I try, most days, to set the phone aside and tune my heart to God's company before the voices of the world start clamoring for my attention.

When worry over our world and the news gnaws at our hearts, the temptation is to want to fix it all. So we try. We analyze the latest news reports. We google all our questions. We pace and worry and fret. And where are we left? Anxious and weighed down by worry. Jesus provides a different way. A radical way. A quiet way. It's an unpopular route. A narrow road. He invites us to pray about everything, not just because prayer lifts our spirits and calms our anxious hearts, but because God moves through our prayers.

Our prayers move God.

Prayer is powerful and effective.

Yes, prayer lifts our spirits, calms our anxious hearts, eases our stress, and untangles our worries (amen for that!). But prayer also works. Your prayers move heaven and earth. Let's be a generation of praying women.

Today, when you feel the phone or the news sucking you in and vying for your attention, take a moment with your sweet God who cares so much for you and everything that concerns you. Lay down your cares and burdens before Him. Tell Him everything that's tangling you up inside. Believe that He hears you. Then watch Him move in your life.

Lord, remind me to pray instead of worry. When the news of the day causes anxiety in my heart, may I turn to You and trust that You are in control.

Your prayers move the heart of God.

TRUSTING INSTEAD
OF FRETTING

When I am afraid, I put my trust in You.

Psalm 56:3

I was having one of those frazzled kinds of days where I was fretting about the future. I was waiting on the Lord to answer my prayers, but I couldn't seem to find peace in the waiting. I opened my email inbox that day and found a note from a friend. She invited me to a grace-paced kind of waiting on the Lord. She wrote, "Choose gratitude. Stay present. Pray for God's peace." She reminded me to intentionally look for all the ways God had been working. She reminded me to stay in the present moment instead of mentally writing the story of how I thought my circumstances would turn out. She invited me to pray for God's peace for my heart as I waited on Him to answer my prayers.

I realized I had been so focused on the future that I had forgotten to thank God for the ways He had been faithful in my life. I had been so busy worrying that I was living outside the present moment. I had prayed hard for my circumstances to change, but I hadn't thought to ask God for His supernatural peace in the waiting. My friend's simple encouragement was just what I needed and gave me a newfound hope and peace to move forward with courage.

Maybe you're caught up in worry and anxiety today. Maybe you're writing the story of your circumstances before you really know how God will work them out. Maybe you're so stressed about future circumstances that you're missing your right-now life. Maybe your heart is full of angst and stress. Today, may I pass on my friend's words of encouragement as you wait on the Lord?

Choose gratitude. Thank Him for what He *has* done. Notice the ways He has come through. Let your heart think on the good things He has done in your life.

Stay present. Breathe. Be all here in this moment. Resist the temptation to think about tomorrow, to worry over your circumstances, or to look back and wish something were different. The present is where God is.

And *pray* for God's supernatural peace to wash over you. Yes, keep praying for your circumstances and the situations where you need God's guidance and direction. Something happens when we ask for God's peace in the waiting—He showers us with His peace in an unexplainable way.

Lord, instead of worrying in the waiting, help me to
choose gratitude and to stay present with You. Give me
supernatural peace as I trust You with my circumstances.

*When we stick in this right-now moment with God, allowing gratitude to
build our faith and His peace to steady our hearts, we find new strength
and courage because we're trusting Him again instead of fretting.*

QUIET-TIME GRACE

*The LORD your God is in your midst, a mighty One Who
will save; He will rejoice over you with gladness; He will quiet
you by His love; He will exult over you with loud singing.*

Zephaniah 3:17

We all know we should read our Bible and have our quiet time with God. But oftentimes the "should" outweighs our "want-to." The obligation steals the joy out of it. We set out with good intentions to have a meaningful quiet time. We strive to power through our reading plan, or we check our quiet time off our list for the day. We move on, but maybe we go through our day with this feeling that we don't feel any closer to God after that well-intentioned time with Him. We wonder what we're doing wrong. We wonder what it would feel like to have a perfect quiet time with God that would leave us feeling fueled up for the day.

What if instead we think of it this way: Your quiet time with God doesn't have to be perfect, just make it personal.

I've realized that oftentimes I'm striving to have my quiet time with God the right way. I think I need to stick to a strict Bible-reading plan or do an in-depth Bible study or pray a certain way, when really, deep down, the little girl in me simply wants to take her big coffee mug out to the porch, hair in a messy bun and still in her jammies, sit herself down on the porch swing next to a pot of flowers, and do quiet time the way that connects her most deeply to God. For her, that's journaling, pretty resources to help her study God's Word, sometimes a stack of devotional books to pinpoint a particular topic, a prayer journal, and her big fluffy golden retriever at her feet. This is breathing in God for her.

When you make your time with God personal, the pressure of perfect loses its grip. When you keep it personal, your desire and delight in spending time with God outweigh the obligation to spend time with God. Make it personal or pretty or cozy. Make that time with God something you look forward to in a way that's unique to you, and that's the place where you'll feel most deeply connected to God.

Lord, thank You that I get to spend time meeting with You,
knowing You, and sitting in Your presence. Help me to look
forward to spending time with You every single day, and help me
to let go of the pressure I put on myself to have a perfect quiet time.

*God simply wants your heart. He wants to shower you
with His love every day. Come to Him just as you are.*

SPACE FROM THE WORLD

Give ear and come to Me; listen, that you may live.

Isaiah 55:3, NIV

Sometimes we need a little space from the world to figure out what God is saying to us or how He's encouraging us. There's often a longing in our soul to hear from Him, but that longing gets drowned out by busyness and noise. Have you been there? Have you felt that deep ache in your soul to hear from God, to know His direction for your life, and to simply feel His presence? While I don't have all the answers, know that I feel it too. The ache to hear from God is uncomfortable, but it's the ache that leads us to Him. So today, when you feel that deep-down ache for more of God, press into it instead of burying it. Take a step of faith by turning down the noise in your life in some small way. Step aside from the busyness, and simply look to the One Who wants to be your peace, your strong center, and your delight. He will gladly meet you in the quiet moments of your day as you look for Him. He wants to be found by you. He wants to speak into your life and into your ache. He'll use the ache of your heart to draw you close to His heart.

So often we ignore our longings to hear from God because hearing from Him can feel impossible at times. It's easier, in a way, to go fill up with the next good read, the latest news report, or our social media feeds. It's easier to turn on the TV than to listen for God's still, small voice. It's easier to busy ourselves than it is to listen for the voice of our Maker. But what if we believed He is speaking to our hearts? What if we truly listened for His voice? What if we did the hard thing of giving ourselves space from the world, the news, the online world, our email inbox, the phone, and the TV and gave God space to speak? What might He say? What might He show us? How might He shower us with His love? I know sometimes it's hard to decipher our own thoughts. We wonder, *Is that just me thinking this, or is God speaking to me?* I have a feeling God knows we struggle to discern His voice. He knows it's a bit of a mystery. But He's not trying to make it tricky. He's not hiding from us. In fact, He never leaves us. I think He longs to speak to us as much as we long to hear from Him, and He simply needs us to make some space to hear from Him. Don't doubt yourself when you feel like God is speaking to you through His Word, through creation, through your circumstances, or through a friend. God speaks in a variety of ways to your heart every single day. Open your heart up to Him today. Make some space to listen. He will not let you down.

Lord, I long to know You are speaking to me today. I long to feel the assurance of Your sweet presence. Give me the power to push aside the distractions of the day and to listen for Your still, small voice. I'm ready to hear from You.

When we listen to God, we become fully alive.

YOUR SWEET SOUL

Only take care, and keep your soul diligently.
Deuteronomy 4:9

As women, we can be really hard on ourselves sometimes. We work hard to do and be all that we want to do and be. We strive to look better, feel better, and be better. We go, go, go, but how are our souls? How are you being kind to your own soul? What does your soul need this week?

Because we are as different from each other as one wildflower is from another, each of us needs different things to nourish our souls. When we take care of our souls, we flourish. When we take care of our souls, we slow down. When we take care of our souls, we feel God's grace. When we take care of our souls, we are energized. So what does your sweet soul need today?

Does it need:
To unplug from all the voices?
To go on a long walk?
To soak in a bubble bath?
To take your kiddo to the park and just play?
To snuggle up with a good book?
To grab coffee with a friend?
To take a nap?
To spend time with God with no agenda?
To create something?
To have a good laugh?
To declutter your home?
To drive through Starbucks, grab a vanilla latte, and go roam the bookstore?
Be kind to your soul. And as you do, you'll flourish, sweet one.

Lord, You know the state of my soul this morning. Sometimes I am going, going, going through my week, and I forget to slow down and give my soul some space to breathe. Show me just what I need today to care for my soul so that I can flourish as Your daughter.

Slow down today. Be kind to yourself. Slow your pace. Just breathe.

IDENTITY AND VALUE

Put on the new self, created after the likeness
of God in true righteousness and holiness.

Ephesians 4:24

It's tempting to place our identity and value in what we do as opposed to Whom we belong to. Daughter of Christ, what you do in life—your roles, your job, your accomplishments—are beautiful. But you don't have to depend on those things for identity and value. You are already valuable to God. You are identified with Christ. You belong to Him. He paid a price to make you all His. So enjoy what you do, but don't derive your value from those things. Place your identity fully in Christ.

God gives us special assignments and roles in life. He wants us to enjoy our assignments and roles and to feel like we have a purpose. But at the same time, He wants our number one purpose to be knowing Him. He wants our relationship with Him to be our sure foundation for everything else that we do in life. And as we make Him first, our identity and value are placed in the steadiness of Christ rather than our shifting roles in life.

That transaction of identity was made the moment we accepted Christ as our Savior; we are His no matter where we are currently placing our identity. As we grow in our faith, He begins to supernaturally shift our identity. It's not something we have to conjure up on our own—He does the work of helping us live as His daughters.

We were created with a desire to have an identity, to feel significant, and to feel valued. We want to know that we matter. We want to know who we are. And we will only discover who we truly are in Christ. How are you fleshing out finding your identity in Christ alone? What does that mean to you?

I am Yours, God. I belong to You. Thank You for what I get to
do and the things that give me purpose, but help me to place
my need for identity, significance, and value in You alone.

Today may you place your identity and value in Christ
alone. Know that you are significant to the God of the
universe. Your roles, jobs, and accomplishments are what
you do, not who you are. You are a daughter of Christ.

WHEN YOU'RE UNSURE HOW TO STUDY YOUR BIBLE & PRAY

*The friendship of the L*ORD* is for those who fear Him.*
Psalm 25:14

Spending time alone with the Lord is vital to cultivating a close relationship with Him. But being consistent isn't always easy. We can go through seasons where our quiet time feels fresh, exciting, and even exhilarating. The Bible feels alive and every page grabs our heart and refreshes us anew. Other times, we can't seem to get ourselves to sit down and spend time with the Lord. Our phone keeps us occupied, the laundry room is calling our name, or it feels easier to flip on the news and catch up with the world. Many times, when we sit down to study our Bible and pray, we feel stuck. We're not sure where to begin.

Today, let's take the pressure off ourselves to do "quiet time" a certain way or the right way. Let's take the pressure off ourselves to study our Bible in a formulaic way. Let's take the pressure off ourselves to pray perfectly. Let's move away from quiet time formulas and toward fearing God and enjoying His friendship. Friendship with God isn't formulaic. Just as we wouldn't sit down with a friend and follow a list of rules to get to know them, we shouldn't feel like we must follow a set of rules to get to know God. Just as we would spend time getting to know a friend, enjoying fun activities with them, and enjoying their company, we can do the very same thing with God.

Focusing on the gift of our friendship and relationship with God takes the pressure off how we spend our time with Him. Our time with God can look different from day to day or be more consistent, depending on our personalities and the ways we connect with God best.

Lord, You know that some days I feel stuck in how to study my Bible
or pray—so stuck that sometimes I skip my time with You altogether.
Would You help me to focus on the gift of my friendship and
relationship with You instead of rules and formulas for my quiet time?
Keep me amazed at the wonder of getting to be known and loved by You.

Today, may you break free from quiet time rules and formulas
and discover the sweet companionship of your friendship with Jesus.
May you read your Bible and pray with new delight as you
let go of pressure and formulas and embrace His grace and love.

WHEN YOU NEED TO TURN DOWN ALL THE NOISE

*Quiet your heart in His presence and pray; keep hope
alive as you long for God to come through for you.*

Psalm 37:7, TPT

Do you ever have days where you just need to turn down all the noise, clamor, and clatter? The pings and dings coming from your phone? The barrage of emails grabbing your attention and focus? The sense of overwhelm coming from your overloaded calendar? The endless stream of information coming from the internet and the news?

Your desire to turn down all the noise is a beautiful, good desire. The enemy would love for us to keep riding that treadmill of noise and keep living in a state of information overload. That way, we wouldn't spend time nurturing our relationship with God. If the enemy can get us to stay distracted by all the seemingly urgent pings, dings, emails, dates, and information, he can keep us from experiencing the goodness of the Lord's company and the blessing of a quiet heart.

Maybe today your heart and your soul are trying to tell you that they are on overload. And perhaps the Holy Spirit is nudging your heart toward Him. When you feel that soul-deep need for quietness, stillness, and time alone with the Lord, don't just ignore that desire. Listen. And move toward the Lord. Take one step of faith. Quiet your heart in His sweet presence.

I know that sometimes we aren't sure what to do when we do meet with God. Maybe we feel like we can never stick to our Bible reading plan. Or maybe we feel like a Bible study dropout because we can never follow a Bible study through to completion. Perhaps we feel a sense of overwhelm when we open our Bibles or sit down to pray to the Lord. Maybe it can even feel like we are spending our time with the Lord all wrong.

Dear friend, there is no wrong way to spend time with the Lord. Keep His Word in front of you, take some deep breaths on your back porch to quiet your heart, and let Him lead your time with Him.

**Lord, You know my heart today. I need a break from all the noise,
overload, and clutter. Give me strength to set all the noise aside and pull in
close to You. Help me to give myself grace as I spend time with You—grace
to just be with You and enjoy Your company. Quiet my heart, Lord.**

*Today, may you have the strength to set aside the surface
things that are robbing you of closeness to the Lord. May
you intentionally put it all away and trust God to fill the
empty places in your heart with His joy and satisfaction.*

June

WHEN YOU JUST FEEL OFF

When the cares of my heart are many, Your consolations cheer my soul.
Psalm 94:19

Do you ever have those days when you just feel "off"? Maybe your heart feels restless and anxious and you're not sure why. Maybe you feel unmotivated, weary, bored, or too busy. Maybe you're having trouble focusing or you get to the end of your day and feel like you got nothing done. Or maybe you're having one of those days when your thoughts are running a million miles per hour, jumping from one thing to the next.

It can be frustrating. You may even be hard on yourself, thinking thoughts like,
Why can't I stay focused on one thing at a time?
Why am I always overanalyzing everything?
Why can't I stay motivated?
Why do I feel so tired?

We can be so hard on ourselves for having days when we feel off. Today, remember that it's okay to have off days. It's okay to have hard days. In fact, we all have hard days, and without them, we certainly wouldn't need the Lord. We can give ourselves grace to have an off day. Keep in mind that a variety of things can contribute to our hearts feeling off. We could be in a particularly stressful season. We could be not getting enough rest and sleep. We could be anxious on the inside and carrying our burdens like a heavy backpack. We could be worried about a situation or a person. We could simply need some self-care—good food, good sleep, good downtime, and good company. Or we could simply need more of God.

When you have those days when you feel a bit off, take a few moments to turn to the Lord with the anxiety you are feeling. Even if you're not sure what is causing you to feel off, come to the Lord and let Him sort out your feelings. He made us to need Him, and He uses the off days to draw us closer to Him. He wants to be the One Who helps you through those harder days. He wants to brighten your path and refuel your heart.

Lord, thank You for reminding me that You are the One Who
walks me through the harder days. Thank You for the gift of being
in a relationship with You. Thank You that there is no off day that
You can't brighten. Help me to remember to run to You when I feel off.

Run to the One Who satisfies, strengthens, and refuels you.
Remember that it's okay to have a hard day.
We all have hard days. You are never alone in a hard day.

SUMMER SPACE FOR GOD

I will refresh the weary and satisfy the faint.
Jeremiah 31:25, NIV

Summer is a time to slow our pace, enjoy God's creation, and to hopefully give our hearts a bit more space to rest, dream, imagine, and play. For some of us, summer stays busy, but just knowing that it's summer seems to help us slow our pace a bit. Popsicles, swimming, summer sunsets, crickets singing at dusk, fireflies, bare feet, shorts and ponytails, longer days, grilling yummy food, no school! Summer is one of my favorite seasons, and it is a great time to slow down and check in with our hearts. How is your heart, really? How's your pace of life? How's the deep-down part of your soul, sweet one?

Summer is for building memories, playing, dreaming—and summer can also be a really sweet time to tuck our hearts in close to God and allow Him room and space to do a replenishing work in us. It's a time to set aside some things and to center our focus on the One Who guides our hearts. It's a time to know His grace in a deeper way as we trust Him for the spiritual growth and stronger faith we long for. So today, I simply want to encourage you to soak in the slower pace and make some room to let God into that summer space. Dream a little about your summer with me:

- What do you need from God this summer?
- What dreams and prayer requests are you trusting Him with this summer?
- In what ways do you want to grow spiritually?
- How do you want to spend your time?
- What do you need physically, spiritually, and emotionally this summer?
- What will you be glad you did or didn't do this summer?
- How can you make more room for God?

I'm learning that reflection with God leads to replenishment. As we bring our hearts and souls to God and give Him our cares and needs, He gently guides us with His Word and His Spirit, refreshing us in ways that we didn't even know we needed.

Lord, thank You for the slower days of summer. As I reflect over my life, show me ways I can grow spiritually and tune in to You more deeply.

Make space in your summer days to slow down and tune into God. He loves to replenish, refresh, and restore you.

A SIMPLE WAY TO FLOURISH

May the LORD cause you to flourish.
Psalm 115:14, NIV

I have two turquoise pots on my back porch. Both are currently filled with long stems of Angelonia—deep purple stalks of flowers. One pot had been sitting out in the sun for months, growing happily and flourishing in all its purple beauty. The other pot was nestled under the shade of the patio, and I finally realized it just wasn't flourishing. Instead of purple flowers, it only grew tall green stems. Puzzled, I continued to water it day by day to make sure it was getting enough hydration in the Texas heat. For the whole summer, I just kind of passed it by after I watered it, wondering why it was struggling to bloom.

It finally occurred to me one day that it wasn't getting enough sun. So I lifted the pot up out of its shady spot and transferred it to a sunnier spot on the back porch. I continued to water it throughout the end of the summer into the early days of fall. Meanwhile, the other pot of Angelonia continued to bloom and flourish in its sunny spot just like it always had. I didn't see any signs of flourishing for the newly placed pot of flowers for weeks. I started to think that maybe it just wasn't meant to flourish and bloom. Then one day when I stepped outside to do my normal watering routine, and hiding in the tall stalks of green I could see some purple flowers beginning to bud. Every day I could see more and more purple. The pot of Angelonia that had been stunted in its growth in the shade of the patio was finally blooming in all its purple glory. It just needed a little more sun. It wasn't quite getting all the nutrients it needed to flourish.

Don't forget about the healing, restorative, calming, and nourishing gift of God's creation—the sun, fresh air, butterflies, birds, sky, and gentle breeze. In our technology-infused modern times, it's easy to stay inside. It's easy to look for entertainment on TV instead of stepping outside. It's easy to search the internet instead of exploring God's creation. How easily we forget that God made the outdoors for us to enjoy. The sun literally infuses us with the vitamin D that we need in order to fight off disease and depression and to reduce stress. Just like that pot of flowers needed more sun in order to flourish, we need more sun and fresh air in order to flourish. God made the outdoors for you, and He wants to refresh your spirit with the beauty of His creation. Look around you today as you take a step outside, and let God speak to your heart as you linger in His beautiful creation.

Lord, thank You for Your beautiful creation. Help me to remember that stepping outside every day is healing and restorative. Help me to see Your beauty outside.

You were made to flourish and bloom. Allow God's creation to center your soul, refresh your heart, and rejuvenate your spirit.

LED BY THE SPIRIT

The Spirit said to Philip, "Go over and join this chariot."
Acts 8:29

Recently I sat down at my computer for a video conference call with one of my son's teachers. I nestled into my chair, coffee cup in hand, ready to take notes. Fully expecting the conference to focus on my son's academics and grades, I was pleasantly and sweetly surprised when the teacher noted, "I really try to listen to the Holy Spirit's promptings when I teach my students because He knows what they need best." Suddenly, academics and grades felt incredibly minute in light of this sweet reminder in front of me to listen to the Spirit's promptings. This grandmotherly teacher—wise, gentle in spirit, and tender with compassion—radiated a faith in the Lord that I needed to see that day. She reminded me that the Lord is in our midst. She reminded me that this is the day the Lord has made. And she reminded me that His Spirit helps, leads, and guides us every day because He knows how to make life work best. He knows what we need in each and every situation.

I easily forget how close the Lord really is. I easily forget that He's constantly prompting me through the Holy Spirit. I easily forget that if I will tune into His promptings, I will function better and be more helpful to those around me.

Dear friend, the Holy Spirit is available to you every moment, to help you live an abundant day with His help. In Acts 8, Philip tunes into the Spirit's promptings and winds up sharing the gospel with a eunuch and then continuing on to spread the gospel. The Spirit's promptings to Philip were so specific: *Go over and join this chariot.* One step at a time, the Spirit led Philip, intentionally and purposefully. The Spirit didn't give Philip the whole plan, only one step at a time. And Philip listened and obeyed, enabling him to experience the fruit of the Holy Spirit's guidance.

The Spirit wants to lead you today. That can feel like a big, mysterious, elusive concept. That's okay! We all struggle to know if we're listening correctly. We all struggle to remember that we have the Holy Spirit in us, happy to help and lead us through our day. But today, simply remember that the Spirit wants to lead you, and that His leadership is so, so good because He knows how to best help you handle any situation you face. Tune into His promptings and watch where He leads you and how He helps you. I think you will be pleasantly and sweetly surprised.

Spirit, lead me today and keep me aware of Your constant presence in my day. Help me to turn to You for wisdom and direction all day long.

Trust that the Holy Spirit wants to lead you today.
Ask Him for help to discern His promptings.

LIKE A TREE

*He is like a tree planted by steams of water that yields
its fruit in its season, and its leaf does not wither.*

Psalm 1:3

As you sit on your back porch today, take a moment to soak in the gift of your Bible. Delight in the truth of the Scriptures that you hold in your lap. Remember that the Bible you hold is your source for all hope and peace and joy and true life. Its pages are laced with grace and love and truth. Psalm 1 reminds us that the gal who delights in God's Word is *happy* or *blessed*. Someone who is happy and blessed is full of hope—hope that drips off the pages of Scripture inspired directly from the pen and heart of God. When we delight in God's Word, our hopes are lifted, our perspective is shifted, and our hearts become grounded in God's truth. When we delight in God's Word and think on it, linger over it, and meditate on it we become, as the Psalmist pens, *like a tree planted by streams of water that yields its fruit in its season, and its leaf does not wither.* Hope begins when we delight in God's Word.

Thank You, Lord, for my Bible and for the incredible gift of Your Word. Thank You that we get to hold the word of life in our hands! Lord, remind me of its power, promises, and truth for my life. Today, help me to delight in Your holy pages of Scripture so that my heart is like a tree planted by streams of water.

*As you allow Your heart to soak in Scripture day after day,
little by little, your heart will become rooted in Christ,
strengthened by truth, and flourishing in hope.*

HE KNOWS YOUR WAY

The LORD knows the way of the righteous.
Psalm 1:6

Much of our anxiety and stress comes from the unknown future ahead. We wonder what the future will hold. We fear what may come. We stress about future things and eventually drain our energy for the present moment.

What if we believed today, deep in our hearts, that the Lord truly knows our way? Daughter of Christ, you are His, and because of Him you are called *righteous*. Scripture tells us that *the Lord knows the way of the righteous*. He knows *your* way. He knows what lies ahead for you. He's constantly pursuing your heart, directing your footsteps, and watching over you as you walk through life with Him. There is no need to fear what's ahead. Will there be trials, struggles, and valleys? You bet. Will there be joys, triumphs, and mountains? Absolutely. And one thing is for sure—He will be with you in all of it. The Lord knows your way. He can see it because He dreamed it for you.

So today, begin a trust walk with Him and let Him lead you day by day. I know it's scary at times to walk into the unknowns. But God is with you and for you and beside you and in you. He's got you.

Lord, thank You for reminding me that I am Your daughter,
that I am righteous in Your eyes, and that You know my way. Lord,
help me to trust You today with fresh faith as I walk with You. Help me to
leave the future unknowns to You and enjoy the pleasure of Your company today.

*When thoughts of the future threaten to stir up your
anxiety today, take a breath and remember that God knows
your way. He has your future. You can rest. He's got it all.*

LIFTER OF MY HEAD

But You, O Lord, are a shield about me,
my glory, and the lifter of my head.

Psalm 3:3

I know that some days hope feels really hard. In fact, hope may feel impossible. The forecast may seem bleak. The world may feel dark. The answers you long for may seem very far off. This is a recipe for unsteady emotions.

Today, remember that God is a shield around you. He is surrounding you with His love. He is in front of you, behind you, beside you, in you, and over you. Just as a superhero's shield protects his body from the darts of the enemy, so God protects your heart from the darts of the enemy. All day, He is shielding you, sweet one. I know that the loss of hope is causing your chin to fall downwards. Perhaps you wonder where your joy went, and you are focused on your impossible circumstances. Take this in, dear sister: God is the lifter of your head. He gets on your level, reaches out to you through His Word and presence, and gently helps you look up.

So look up, dear sister. God is still God. He is still in control. He is in your midst. God knows everything that concerns you and is working while you're waiting. God is leveling your valleys, smoothing out your path, and managing all your cares and burdens.

God, keep me hopeful even when things around me seem bleak.
Remind me today that You are my shield, my glory, and the lifter
of my head. Keep me from despairing, and instead, help me to
stay hopeful that You will come through, just as You always do.

Let God be in control today while you rest your weary
heart. Let Him lift your chin. Look up, dear sister.
Hope is still alive because of Him.

THE LORD HEARS ME

The LORD hears when I call to Him.

Psalm 4:3

The God of the universe longs to spend time with you. He's not looking for you to check off your quiet time and scoot on about your day. He's not looking for you to read a certain number of Bible verses per day. He's not looking for you to complete a certain number of Bible studies per year. He's simply looking to meet with you and love you in the quiet place of His presence.

In the secret place of just the two of you, God longs to bring you the comfort, peace, and joy you're looking for. He's longing to satisfy your soul, quench your thirst for relationship, and fulfill your longing for purpose. In Him, you will find the fullness your heart is aching for. And in that place of intimacy with the Lord, He hears your every cry, your every prayer, and your every request. He hears you. Let that truth sink in.

The God who spread the stars in the sky and named them one by one hears you. The God who dreamt up oceans and placed their borders hears you. The God who breathed life into the first human hears you. And as you bring your heart to Him each day, you will hear Him. Throughout your day the Lord of the heavens wants to speak into and over your life.

Today, lift your voice to God and make space to hear from Him. Meet Him in a quiet place. Carve out time in your day to tune into Him and encounter the living God. Simply come, and He will do the rest. He hears you, daughter of Christ, because you are His.

Lord, thank You that You hear me. You know every inclination of my heart and mind and soul. You know every word of prayer that I pray before a word is on my lips. Thank You for hearing me. Build hope into my heart as I bring every distress to You. And give me grace to make space to hear You and to deepen my relationship with You by giving You more time and space in my life.

God is as real as the back porch you are sitting on, the coffee you are drinking, and the breeze you feel on your skin. He's right there with you. Believe He's with you today.

HE KNOWS MY WAY

Lead me, O LORD ... make Your way straight before me.

Psalm 5:8

Today, you can have hope that Jesus cares for you and is tending to every single detail of your life, down to the steps you take each day. He knows where He's leading you, and He's tenderly guiding your heart day by day. He made you and wired you in certain ways so that He can use your life for kingdom purposes. His plans and ways for you are far beyond anything you can dream up, and He wants to lead you there.

As you surrender to Jesus, you will experience the utter joy, good plans, and full abundant life the heavenly Father has for you. In surrender, there is true life. In surrender, there is full joy. In surrender, there is a path of abundant life. As you surrender, the Lord leads your steps and makes your way straight.

You can trust the Lord with your life. You don't have to make things happen. Instead, you can entrust your life to the One Who has a plan for your life that is more beautiful than you can fathom. An easy life? No. But a good, beautiful, full life? Yes. More full of God and full of joy than you can imagine.

Jesus, thank You that You know my way and my path. You know the steps of my life because You created me and You have an abundant life planned for me. I want that path. I want Your path for my life, not my plans. Guide my steps today and every day, and bloom hope in my heart as I trust You day by day.

Trust God with your path. Trust Him to lead you. Trust that He truly knows your way. Let the truth that God knows your way fill your heart with hope today.

HE KNOWS YOUR TEARS

The LORD has heard the sound of my weeping.

Psalm 6:8

What are the things that bring tears to your eyes in the season you are in? What things catch your breath and form a lump in your throat? What things turn the switch of your tears on? What things prick your heart?

Dear sister, the Lord hears your weeping. He knows what brings your tears. He knows when your eyes are springing with tears of joy, and He knows when your eyes are tearing up with sorrow. He knows just what is troubling your heart today and every day. You are His daughter, and He wants to bring comfort to the places in your heart that are hurting. He wants to catch every tear, bind every wound, and restore every ache of your heart.

Oftentimes, our tears bring us closer to the Lord as we let Him more fully into our hearts. When we are honest with Him about the things that hurt, we realize that He is the cure. When we let Him into our hearts completely and allow Him to touch the part of us that births tears, His healing waters wash over us.

Sometimes the act of simply telling the Lord the cause of our tears brings renewal. Other times we don't know what's behind our tears. But He knows. The Lord understands our tears and our hearts more than we understand ourselves. As we bring our tears to Him, whether they are tears of joy or tears of pain, He is the One Who brings comfort and restores hope.

Lord, thank You for the cleansing gift of tears and how they point me to what's really going on in my heart. Thank You that You see my tears. Thank You that I can bring every one to You.

May you sense today that the Lord knows your tears,
and He's always there to love you through them.

HE IS YOUR SHIELD

My shield is with God.
Psalm 7:10

When my sons were young, they often had a handmade sword in one hand and a toy shield in the other. They ran through the house with their superhero capes flowing behind them, and off they went to conquer the world and defeat their enemies.

As women in this world, we are in a real battle—a spiritual battle. Our enemy is always at work against us, constantly condemning us, defeating us, and misleading us. Sometimes we forget our enemy's influence until we run right smack into one of His lies. But we have a shield. And not just any shield; this shield is supernatural, powerful, almighty, a strong fortress, a mighty force. God is your shield around you—in front of you, behind you, beside you, and with you. He blocks the enemy's taunts, protects you from evil, and surrounds you with His love.

From the moment you wake up to the moment your head hits the pillow and every moment in between, the God of the universe is your shield. Every day we live in a real battle, but every day we have a real shield and protector.

**Thank You, Lord, that You are my shield every day and every moment.
Remind me today that You constantly surround me with Your
love and power. Shield me today from the enemy's taunts and lies,
and make Your presence real to me as I remember Your constant presence.**

*May you walk into your day knowing
that the Lord your God is your shield.*

HE IS MINDFUL OF YOU

What is man that You are mindful of him,
and the son of man that You care for him?

Psalm 8:4

Today, dear sister, may you deeply know and believe that God is mindful of you. God is *aware, watchful, alert,* and *wide awake* to you, your life, your heart, and your circumstances. You are not just a number on His list of creations. You are not a blob of matter to Him. You are His daughter, and He is your Daddy.

He cares so deeply for you—down to the steps you take, the cares of your heart, and the requests of your prayers. He watches over you with utter delight as you walk with Him day by day. He intentionally blesses you, encourages you, and pursues you. He cares for you, and He cares for what you care about. He is personal, and He wants a personal relationship with You. He wants to walk with you and talk with you. He wants to listen to you and speak to you. He wants to hold your hand through life and guide every one of your steps. He wants to be the One you lean on, the One you look to, the One you run to. As you go about your day today, remember that God is mindful of you, dear sister.

Lord, thank You that you are mindful of me. You see me and know
me and care for me. Thank You that You know me personally and
pursue me intimately even though You have the whole world to
maintain. Thank You that You see me. You see my steps. You see
my heart. Thank You for Your watchfulness and care over my life.

There is never a moment when God is not mindful of you.

HE IS YOUR STRONGHOLD

The LORD is a stronghold for the oppressed,
a stronghold in times of trouble.

Psalm 9:9

You may be in a time of trouble today. Your burdens may be heavy, and the load you carry emotionally and mentally may feel like too much. You may wonder when relief is coming. Today, know that God is your stronghold. Other Bible translations use words like *safe place, high tower, refuge, safe house,* and *shelter.*

Where is the place in your life where you feel most secure? The place where you can fully rest? The place where your soul finds shelter and peace? Maybe it's your back porch, a favorite cozy chair in your living room or dorm room, or a place outside where you see the sunset and feel God's presence.

Spiritually speaking, God wants to be your stronghold and safe place. He wants to make you feel safe, loved, known, and seen. He wants to be the place where you find the deepest rest. He wants to be the One you run to where you can let your guard down and fully be yourself. And when times of trouble come, as they do, He wants to be your shelter in the storm so that He can carry you through it. Today, may you experience the deep peace of God as your stronghold through troubled times.

Lord, thank You that You are my stronghold. Thank You that
You care for me so personally. Thank You that You carry me
through each of life's storms. Today, remind me to run to You.

In God's presence, you are safe, loved, and seen.
You can let down your guard. You can be yourself.
God knows everything about you and loves you completely.

WHEN YOU CRAVE REST

But Martha was distracted by all the preparations that had to be made....
"Martha, Martha," the Lord answered, "you are worried and upset
about many things, but few things are needed—or indeed only one."

Luke 10:40-42, NIV

Put your name in today's verses. For example, "Sarah, Sarah, you are worried and upset about many things, but few things are needed—or indeed only one." What's the *one* thing that is needed? Time with Jesus. He promises rest for our souls when we bring Him our burdens and spend time with Him.

Burdens can be big and heavy. But burdens can be a bunch of small things, too. The problem is that when we carry all of our burdens—big and small—it becomes too heavy. Christ wants to carry our burdens on His shoulders so that we do not have to carry them. He wants us to know the incredible peace and rest we can have in Him.

So how do we give Him our burdens, worries, and stress? First, I think we step away a little bit. Take a break from whatever it is that is causing you stress right now. Ask the Spirit to show you what that is. Then, we do some porch sitting or rocking-chair sitting (or whatever it is for you), and we just talk to Jesus. Tell Him everything on your heart. Pour it out to Him so that He can fill your heart up again. Because we all get dry, empty, and plain tired. Instead of plowing through all the things we need to do, what if we became more productive, effective, and peaceful by stepping away from the busyness in order to make space to spend time with Jesus?

Lord, I've been busy like Martha at times. Remind me to bring my burdens to You and to enjoy your company like Mary did. Thank You for the grace to slow down and to cultivate my relationship with You.

When you crave rest, remember that you will
find the greatest rest in Jesus' company.

LIFE UNCLUTTERED

If you seek Him, He will be found by you.
1 Chronicles 28:9, NIV

Sometimes what feels like physical fatigue is actually soul fatigue. What makes your soul tired? Is it busyness? Distractions? Information overload? To-do lists? Emails? Negative thoughts? Irrational fears? Insecurity?

Today, let soul fatigue direct you to the only One Who can refill and declutter your soul. Let it be the signal that points you to Jesus. Let it direct your heart to the One Who created your heart. Soul fatigue is a sign that our souls are too cluttered. But when we pull up close to the Lord, bringing Him all our cares and allowing His presence to still our hearts, we experience a deep decluttering of the soul.

Unload your cares onto the Lord's shoulders today. He is waiting to hear from you. He knows your thoughts and worries, but He needs you to bring them to Him so He can give you peace. Sometimes we hold on to the details of life until our souls feel like they are going to burst with a sense of overwhelm. We run through our day with hypothetical sticky notes attached to our hearts of all the things we need to get done, all the negative thoughts that need to be addressed, all the little things we need to remember for the week, plus all the cares and burdens we feel in our hearts. We carry around a load too heavy to bear. We run our race with a heart weighed down with worry. And we wonder why we're so very tired.

Today, take all those "sticky notes" on your heart to Jesus. Right there on your back porch, hand over the details of life and the daily stresses that are causing wear and tear on your soul. Ask Him to take on your burdens. Give your sticky notes of worry, stress, overwhelm, and negative thoughts to the Lord today. You will feel so much better. The sun will seem brighter, the flowers will seem more beautiful, and the sky will seem bluer. Best of all, your load will feel lighter and your heart will feel brighter.

Lord, I can hardly comprehend that You care for me so personally.
Thank You that You want me to bring every burden and care to You.
Oh, how often I forget and instead try and carry my load by myself.
What grace that You want to declutter my soul so I can walk in Your peace and joy.

There is joy and peace on the other side of prayer and surrender.

CLINGING TO GOD

My soul clings to You; Your right hand upholds me.
Psalm 63:8

When we pull our souls in close to God, He refreshes, restores, and rejuvenates our hearts. It may take some time for our souls to feel refreshed, but the second we pull in close to Him is the very second He begins His restoring work. So, daughter of Christ, when your soul feels thirsty, turn to God. Remind yourself that your soul's restoration is in Him alone.

Sometimes it takes us a while to recognize that our souls are indeed thirsty for God. Often we run to anything other than God to quench our soul thirst. But as we learn to recognize that thirst, it becomes a holy signal to cling to God.

Oftentimes we think that something new will satisfy our thirsty souls. We think we need a change of scenery, a new job, a new house, a new daily planner, a new outfit—anything to give us that renewed feeling. We think a new exercise program, a new Bible study, a new church, a new friend, or a new puppy will calm that sense of hunger and thirst in our souls. But of course the newness eventually wears off.

What if I told you that everything you need is already right in front of you? The lie of culture is that you need something more, better, or new. But the truth found in Scripture is that God is all you need.

That itch for something more—that longing that you can't quite put your finger on, that ache to be known are divine—signals that your soul needs a refill of God's presence, love, and care. Bring that longing to the Lord, and simply tell Him that your heart feels thirsty and you're not sure how to solve the angst in your heart. Then trust Him to fill you up throughout your day.

Lord, help me to run to You today when my soul feels thirsty. Oh, it's so hard sometimes in the moment to remember to run to You! Thank You that You never stop pursuing my heart. I want to run to You and cling to You instead of running to the world for satisfaction. Help me to remember to run to You.

Our souls were designed for God.
Clinging to God satisfies our deep soul thirst.

TRANSFER YOUR BURDENS

I will give you rest.
Matthew 11:28

What if you fully trusted God with your circumstances today? What if you truly believed that He is at work in your life? He is moving in your heart, and He holds your life in perfect working order. He's got you. What things are you holding on to today and trying to control? What things are you striving to make work in your life? What things are you trying to manage on your own?

One Sunday afternoon, I scanned my calendar for the week ahead. I had written in tiny handwriting so I could fit all the appointments, reminders, and meetings into the week. One look at my calendar, and I felt my blood pressure rising. A sense of overwhelm began to creep into my heart. The littlest details of the week—things that shouldn't overwhelm a gal—completely overwhelmed me. Somehow our week was crammed with doctor's appointments, teacher conferences, and other small things. Each little thing added up to a too-full calendar, and the stress of facing it felt like more than I could bear. Later in the evening, my husband picked up on my stress. He lovingly offered to take on some of the burden. He agreed to do a dentist appointment for one kiddo, a doctor's appointment for another, and two mornings of carpool. Transferring some of my load to his shoulders took the weight of overwhelm off my heart. My heart felt lighter, my stress began to dissipate, and joy began to rise up in my heart again.

In the same way, Christ wants to take on your burdens and overload. He wants to carry the things that feel too heavy for you today. He wants you to know that you don't have to carry all that's before you. Instead, you can transfer your load to His strong shoulders. So today, when you look at your schedule for the week, the month, or even just the day, take some quiet moments, right here on your back porch, and transfer the things that are feeling overwhelming and causing stress right into the Lord's lap. Hand those burdens over to Him in prayer. He will gladly lighten your load.

Lord, I cannot do it all and do it all well. Thank You that You don't call me to carry more than I can handle. Thank You that You offer to carry my burdens. Lord, I transfer every burden over to You today.

Transfer your burdens to the Lord. Your heart will feel lighter, your stress will dissipate, and your joy will rise up.

TAKE REFUGE IN THE LORD

He will cover you with His feathers, and under His wings you
will find refuge; His faithfulness will be your shield and rampart.

Psalm 91:4, NIV

Anytime tension rises,
    Anytime stress rises,
Anytime your heart feels depleted,
Anytime your heart feels overwhelmed,
Anytime you need refueling,
Anytime you need refreshment,
Anytime you need to settle some angst,
Anytime you need to sort out some thoughts,
Anytime.
Take refuge in the Lord. Seek Him. Sit down with Him. Tell Him what's going on in your heart and mind and soul. He loves to comfort, guide, tend, shape, help, and guard your heart. Remember today to take refuge in the One Who knows all your needs and who is able to tend to every single one.

Lord, I take refuge in You today. Thank You that You are
my safe haven and my refuge in every storm. When my
heart feels unsettled today, remind me to turn to You.

God wants to be your safe haven, your refuge, and your shelter.

KEEP THAT LITTLE-GIRL HEART

She laughs at the time to come.

Proverbs 31:25

With three growing boys, summer groove in the Marr household looks like Legos, Power Rangers, Hot Wheels, catching lizards, staying cool in the pool, walks, bike rides, staying up later than usual, baseball games, and eating ice cream. This is the good stuff of summer. Summer is about playtime. And for me, summer is also a time for our family to be together, to dream, and to reflect.

Today I'm reminded that even as a grown-up gal, it is good to play. Maybe it doesn't look like My Little Ponies or playing school, like it did when I was a little girl, but I still need to play. These boys remind me every day that playing is part of us, and it refreshes us. What does it look like to keep that sense of play as a grown-up gal, and why is it important?

Playing is getting lost in the things that make our hearts giddy. It's making time to do the things that fill us up. What are those things for you? The things you enjoy doing—those God-given likes, desires, and hobbies—can keep you young at heart.

So this summer, be sure to take some moments to be with the ones you love and the ones who love you back, to dream and imagine, to reflect on all of the good gifts and blessings God has brought into your life this year, and to just play. Play in ways that refresh you and uplift you. Although we are grown-up gals, we will always be God's little girls. He will always be our Daddy. Make some time to laugh, be silly, enjoy life, and play today. Your heavenly Daddy has your future, your assignments, your needs, and all that concerns you. He's got it all in His hands, so you can go play. Dance. Dream. Reflect. Enjoy. In all your growing up, keep that little-girl heart.

❧

Lord, thank You for the reminder to play and to tap into the things that delight my soul. Help me to make sure I am engaging in those things that I enjoy, because they uplift my heart and remind me that I am always Your little girl.

*The things you love to do are the ways
God designed you to feel His pleasure.*

LIKE A DANCE

Those who know Your name put their trust in You,
for You, O LORD, have not forsaken those who seek You.
Psalm 9:10

When a ballerina is learning a new piece of choreography, the choreographer typically teaches it to her one step at a time. When I was dancing, I would easily get overwhelmed if the choreographer threw too many steps at me all at once. I needed to learn the dance slowly, methodically, and step-by-step.

We need the very same thing in this dance of walking with God. We would like God to reveal His whole plan. We would love an outline of His plans, His timeline, and His ways so we know where we are going. We crave the details! An email from God would be so helpful—a little daily agenda to follow so we could know we are on His path.

But of course God doesn't work that way. He reveals one step of His plan at a time. But here's why that is good, even though at times it can feel kind of frustrating: He knows we would be overwhelmed if He threw the whole plan for our lives at us all at once. He knows that we would have trouble remembering the whole plan if He told us all of it. He knows that we might even talk ourselves out of His good plans if we knew them because they might seem impossible and daunting. So He reveals His plan for us one step of grace and love at a time. He shines just enough light for the particular step we are on.

God has a beautiful dance through life planned for you that His Spirit is leading you toward. Try to let go of the need to know the whole plan. Be free from the pressure to figure it all out. You don't have to. Just let Him lead you one step at a time.

Thank You, Lord, that You created a plan and purpose for not just my future,
but every single day of my life. Help me to trust You step by step
and day by day. Help me to release my worries about the future to You.

God is creating a beautiful life through
you one step and one day at a time.

STEP INTO YOUR DAY WITH JOY

The Lord your God is in your midst, a mighty One Who will save;
He will rejoice over you with gladness; He will quiet you
with His love; He will exult over you with loud singing.
Zephaniah 3:17

Know today that the God who made the stars and calls them by name sees you and knows you. He delights in leading you through this day and loves whispering encouragement into your heart. He has orchestrated your day with divine appointments and sprinkled it with glimpses of His love and presence. You are one loved daughter of the King, and He is guiding your every step. From the second your feet hit the floor in the morning to the moment you turn out the light at the end of the day, and even while you sleep, God is with you. He takes great delight in helping you through your day. He rejoices over you with singing—imagine that!

Remember to look on the bright side of things today. See the holy in the mundane. See the divine in the routine. See God in the everyday. Our hearts tend to bend toward a negative outlook, but you can dig for the good instead. Hunt for the treasures. Find the sweet moments. Notice the everyday gifts. When we focus on the negative things, our joy decreases. But when we look for the good, our joy increases. Look for the good today and step into your day with joy.

Lord, thank You for this day. Help me to see the bright side of things today:
the holy, the divine, You in my midst, the treasures, the sweet moments,
and the everyday gifts. Increase my joy as I look for You in my day.

Each day is filled with God's presence and gifts.
Today, take notice of the little ways God meets you in your day.

MAKE SPACE TO HEAR FROM GOD

I will take my stand at my watchpost and station myself
on the tower, and look out to see what He will say to me.

Habakkuk 2:1

Clear some space in your heart and mind today to hear from God. We have so much information and news, so many pictures and emails right at our fingertips that often it's difficult to tune it all out and still our hearts. Full calendars, to-do lists, and notifications on our phones pull at us and distract us from the Lord.

Make room for God today. Guard your heart from the things that are pulling you away from Him and intentionally seek Him.

God wants to step into the white spaces of your day and your heart and make Himself more known to you. He wants to direct your heart into special assignments that He has for you. He wants to speak to you, guide you, and whisper truth to your heart—but He needs room to do that.

Create space for yourself to hear from God. Turn off the phone if possible. Set emails and to-do lists aside for a while. Leave some white space on your calendar this week. Don't be so quick to fill up every day. And in the quiet, seek the One Who longs to comfort you, carry you, and calm your heart. He's in the quietness and stillness. He's in the busyness too, of course, but it's in the quietness and stillness that He wants to speak to you and encourage you. Station yourself in a position to hear from the Lord by clearing some space in your heart, your mind, and your schedule. You will be so glad you did.

Lord, You know the things that fill up my heart and my day to overflowing.
Today, help me to clear some space to be quiet and still before You.
I want to hear from You. I want to feel Your presence. So often I fill the
pauses in my day with more information, emails, and distractions. Instead,
help me to be still before You and trust You to meet me there in the quiet.

Don't be so quick to fill the white spaces of your day.
Instead, let God meet you in those moments.

EVERY DAY IS
A FRESH START

The steadfast love of the L<small>ORD</small> never ceases, His mercies never come
to an end; they are new every morning; great is Your faithfulness.

Lamentations 3:22-23

Every day is a fresh start. No matter what yesterday looked like, God showers us with His grace and love, again and again. We don't have to strive harder to live better today or prove ourselves to God in some way. No, we get to simply lean on His grace and trust His Spirit in us to lead, guide, and tend to our hearts throughout the steps of our day. Today, breathe in the fresh grace of God. He loves you so dearly. And He will guide you moment by moment.

We are all going to have days where we fall short, mess up, or regret how we handled a situation. That's part of growing and becoming more like Christ. He transforms us and sanctifies us through our struggles. And every morning we are greeted with the grace of God again and again. You cannot wear out God's grace! He is cheering you on day by day as you simply rely on Him and do your best. You are more resilient than you know, and every day that you lean on God's strength instead of your own, you grow stronger and stronger.

Lord, thank You for a fresh new day. Thank You for Your
unlimited grace. I long to reflect You in the way I live, but I know
that I will make mistakes. Thank You that You give me grace for
every new day. Thank You that You don't expect perfection from me.

Today is a fresh start. Remember that you're learning as
you go and there is unlimited grace for your journey.

PRESS ON IN FAITH

Submit yourselves therefore to God.
Resist the devil, and he will flee from you.

James 4:7

You have an enemy who loves nothing more than to discourage your heart. This enemy does not want you to flourish. He does not want you to do the things God is calling you to do. He does not want you to grow, know God, or walk in the callings God has placed on your life. He is working hard to discourage you daily, to distract you from the Lord, and to plant lies in your heart. So when you feel a sense of discouragement or you feel like your life or your calling doesn't matter, take note that the enemy may be lurking. He would love for you to quit. He would love for you to give up. He would love for you to turn your back on God.

God is stronger than the enemy. We serve the One Who has already overcome the enemy. And God loves to help you flourish. He loves it when you do the things He's calling you to do. He loves watching you grow, and He loves your desire to know Him better. Don't give up. Keep pressing into the Lord. He is for you, and He provides all that you need to overcome discouragement. Press on in faith. When you feel discouraged or like the enemy is lurking in your midst, take note. Look to the Lord and say a simple prayer: *Lord, I submit my heart to You.* Resist the enemy's taunts of discouragement, distraction, and deception by reminding yourself that God is greater.

The second you acknowledge the Lord's presence and power, the enemy runs. The devil has to flee. Stay strong when you are discouraged. The Lord is near.

Lord, help me to be aware of the enemy's tactics today, and
when I sense discouragement, help me to resist it with Your help.

We have an enemy who is lurking,
but we have a God who is more powerful!

NO REQUEST IS TOO SMALL

Why, even the hairs of your head are all numbered.
Fear not; you are of more value than many sparrows.

Luke 12:7

What are you praying for in this season? Remember that no request is too small or insignificant for God. Keep praying. Prayer is the pathway to experiencing God's peace. No perfect words are required; God just wants your honest heart.

Tell God what you need. Bring Him that thing that's on your heart today that feels really small in the grand scheme of things, that thing that feels so minute but is causing turmoil in your heart. That thing that you've tried taking into your own hands—you've tried to work it out on your own, you've tried to tackle it by yourself, but it's still not resolved.

Life is full of small moments, and they all link together to form a beautiful life. We need God for the small moments just as much as we need Him for the bigger challenges of life. It's in the small prayer requests that we learn to trust Him. We learn that He can handle anything and that He has ways of working things out that are better than our ways. God made us to need Him and lean on Him. You can stop carrying all those small things, and instead turn them over to the Lord in prayer.

- *Lord, I hand over this situation that I can't seem to resolve …*
- *Lord, please take care of this conundrum I find myself in today …*
- *Lord, what should I do in this situation … ?*
- *Lord, this thing is really getting under my skin. Please take control …*
- *Lord, You know I feel anxious about this today. Please calm my anxious heart …*

There will be moments in life when you're on your knees praying about huge trials and you need huge miracles. But most days, a bunch of small things will be on your plate. You can turn those small things over to God. He would love to take them off your plate and show you that He cares about everything that concerns your heart.

Lord, here are all the small things on my heart today.
Thank You that You care for me so personally.

The God who knows the number of hairs on your
head cares about every concern on your heart.

FAITH LEADS TO PEACE

For we walk by faith, not by sight.
2 Corinthians 5:7

I wish there were a perfect formula for discerning God's will. I wish He would send a weekly email to fill us in on His good plans for us. But instead, He asks us to have faith that He's leading even when we don't feel like He is.

He asks us to have faith that He is keeping us on His course for our life even when we feel like we are making a mess of things. He asks us to have faith that He will guide us even when we aren't sure where He is leading. Faith that He will provide us with the strength, energy, and divine power we need to do the things He is calling us to do. Faith that when we listen for His voice, He will speak.

When you feel that churning inside you, that unsettled restlessness because you aren't sure which way God wants you to turn or which step He wants you to take next, take a step toward Him. Sit with Him. Still your heart. Tell Him where your faith feels weak. Tell Him where you are having trouble discerning His voice. Wait on Him, and keep waiting until His peace slowly begins to permeate your heart. Faith in God will lead your heart to peace.

Lord, increase my faith. Help me to trust You every day to lead my life.
Help me to believe that You really are with me throughout my day.
Help me to choose to have faith in You instead of living in worry and fear.

Choose faith instead of worry. Choose faith instead of fear.

FOCUSING ON TRUTH

Whatever is true, whatever is noble, whatever is right,
whatever is pure, whatever is lovely, whatever is admirable—if
anything is excellent or praiseworthy—think on these things.

Philippians 4:8, NIV

Lies can mess with you, but they don't define you. Sweet one, you know how those lies that you believed about yourself in the past seem to sneak up on you at the oddest moments? The lies you've believed about yourself, your body, your life, your dreams, yes, they can mess with you, but they don't define you.

When the lies of the enemy try to suppress your joy, remember that you are known and seen and loved and held by the One Who created you. When you feel a lie creeping into your heart, remember who holds your heart. When you feel bogged down by a thought that isn't lovely, remember to point your heart back to all that is true, right, lovely, excellent, and praiseworthy.

Focus on truth today: You are loved by God. You are His daughter. He is in control of your life. You are lovely to Him. He's got precious plans for you. You don't have to be enough for Him. You're not too much for Him. He loves you just the way you are because He made you.

Lord, reveal the lies I have been believing and help me to focus on
Your truth. Thank You for setting my heart right again and again.

You're a daughter of Christ. No lie can squelch that truth.
What lies do you need to let go of today?

A RESCUE

To the roots of the mountains I sank down; the earth beneath barred me in forever. But You, Lord my God, brought my life up from the pit.

Jonah 2:6, NIV

God rescued Jonah from the depths of the ocean in quite a miraculous (and kind of funny) way. Jonah 1:17 (NIV) says, "Now the Lord provided a huge fish to swallow Jonah, and Jonah was in the belly of the fish three days and three nights." Jonah found himself in quite a situation—in the stomach of a whale! But Jonah celebrates God's deliverance while he sits in the belly of that giant fish. He thanks God for delivering him from the depths of the ocean and the engulfing waters even before the rescue. Thankfully, God does eventually help Jonah out of the fishy situation, but I marvel at the way Jonah praised God as he sat in the belly of the fish.

From our point of view, sitting in the belly of a giant fish looks more like a problem than a deliverance. But Jonah saw it differently. He saw his temporary abode as a rescue. He saw his situation as a shelter in the storm. Jonah saw the bright side of a very dark and perhaps smelly situation.

What if you looked at your circumstances today with a different perspective? What if you saw the bright side, like Jonah did? What if you considered that the difficult place God has you right now might be a place of rescue, deliverance, or shelter from the storm?

Sometimes we get so far ahead of what God is already doing right in our midst. We want to see the full rescue plan. We want to see everything worked out to completion. But if we look a little closer at our situation and dig for the goodness of God and the light in our circumstances, we might just find that God has already provided in incredible ways. He may still have more to do, but we may just be sitting in the belly of a giant fish on our way to full deliverance!

Lord, sometimes I am so focused on waiting for the answers to my prayer requests that I forget to see where You have already provided. Help me to be like Jonah today by looking at my circumstances with a different perspective. Help me to see the goodness and light that You have already provided. Thank You for the countless ways You have already rescued me, delivered me, and helped me.

Look around you today and notice the ways God has already provided. Be amazed at the many ways He has answered your prayers.

REMEMBER GOD'S FAITHFULNESS

Let us hold unswervingly to the hope we profess,
for He who promised is faithful.

Hebrews 10:23, NIV

Remembering God's faithfulness and pursuing love in the past gives us peace and calm for the present. God has pursued you your whole life and will never stop pursuing your heart. He Has brought you through trials in the past, and he will bring you through this trial too. God has a track record of faithfulness, and He will be faithful in your difficult season. He has carefully and tenderly guided your life in the past, and He will do the same now.

When you feel the tension and angst of your difficulties and trials this week, perhaps:

- Choose the porch instead of the anxiety of the news.
- Choose prayer instead of the newsfeed.
- Choose gratitude over focusing on the negative things.
- Choose to trust God instead of trying to control your circumstances.

We don't have to do all of the above in our own strength and might. The Holy Spirit gives us supernatural strength, peace, joy, endurance, and faith. Remember God's faithfulness over the course of your life. Hold on to hope. Always know that God is faithful.

Lord, thank You for Your faithfulness.
Grow me into a woman of strong faith.

Think of some ways God has been faithful to you over
the course of your life. May His faithfulness in the
past give you a deep sense of His nearness today.

HELD TOGETHER

He is before all things, and in Him all things hold together.
Colossians 1:17

You are held together by Christ. Your life, your family, and your circumstances are held together by Him. There's nothing He can't hold together. There's nothing too difficult for Him. There's nothing above Him. He's got you and all that concerns you. He cares so much about you, your day, and your life. He cares about all that is on your heart today.

So bring Him those cares as you go about your day. Imagine Him sitting next to you all day, helping you, counseling you, just being with you. He's so thrilled to walk alongside you. Listen and watch for Him as you bring Him your cares and concerns. Remind yourself throughout the day that God is in your midst. You are never alone because He is always with you.

**Lord, there are days when I feel like I am trying to hold my life
together by myself. I'm trying to fix things, change things,
and move things along. Help me to let go of control today and let
You be in full control. Thank You that You hold everything together.**

*May your day be bright and abundant as you remember that
Christ holds you and all that you care about together, dear sister.*

July

A HOPE-FILLED DAY

The hope of the righteous brings joy.
Proverbs 10:28

A little hope does wonders for our hearts. Dear daughter of Christ, you are named righteous in God's sight. He sees you as holy and pure through the eyes of Jesus. And so because of Jesus, you always have hope. You have hope when you feel like a mess. You have hope when you find yourself striving through life instead of trusting God with your future. You have hope when you're indecisive and you change your mind a million times. You have hope when you can't decide what you want to do with your life. You have hope on the bright and sunny days when you feel at peace with who you are, where God has you, and how you look and feel. And you have hope on the darker days when you question who you are and where God has you. You have hope on the brightest days and on the darkest days because you have a Savior who loves you when you're at your best and when you're at your worst.

Hope brings joy. Let me repeat that so the truth of it really sinks in as you sit on your back porch, perhaps a little weary from the ups and downs of life: Hope brings joy.

When you hope in the Lord, joy rises up in your heart.

When you hope in the Lord, joy takes over in your day.

When you hope in the Lord, joy is the lens through which you see your circumstances.

Choose hope in the Lord today. Because when you do, your joy will overflow.

Lord, I find myself riding a roller coaster of ups and downs through life,
and with each mountain and valley, I find my joy taking a hit. Would You
steady my joy by steadying my hope in You today? Thank You that You
love me no matter how I feel on a particular day. Your love is constant.

A hope-filled day is a joy-filled day.

GOD IS FULL OF SURPRISES

*Now to Him Who is able to do far more abundantly
than all that we ask or think …*

Ephesians 3:20

God is full of surprises. He loves to lift you up and delight your heart when you least expect it. Just when you think life has hit its prime or the best is behind you, God surprises you with more than you can imagine. Life only gets sweeter from here.

So when you feel those doubts about your circumstances, your prayer requests, or the dreams of your heart, bring those to the Lord in prayer. Give your heart the space to bring each concern to Him. When you feel stuck in a season where the future looks bleak, remember that God has far more abundance in store for you than you can even think to ask in prayer. When life feels a little dull, a little ho-hum, a little mundane, just hold on. When you least expect it, God will delight you. He knows when you're feeling a little stuck. He knows when you need a little boost.

God ultimately has the gift of heaven on earth in store for us. He has eternal joy and pleasure and love awaiting us. But in the meantime, He wants to delight us here in this earthly life. As we surrender to Him, trusting Him day by day, He will surprise us with good things.

God will never stop delighting your heart. He will never stop answering your prayers in ways that are better than you can imagine. Don't give up hope that life will get sweeter. God is a pursuing God, and He adores you so much. He will be there in life's storms, and He will never stop surprising you with His love, His miracles, His everyday wonders, and His goodness.

Lord, help me to trust You to surprise me in big ways and little ways.
Thank You for pursuing my heart. Help me to trust You for the sweet
surprises in life that I need, especially when life feels a little mundane.
Help me to trust You to do more than all I ask or image or think or pray.

*When you're not sure what to pray, trust God. When you're
not sure what's ahead, trust God. Then let Him surprise you.*

GOD WILL COME THROUGH

The Spirit of God was hovering over the face of the waters.
Genesis 1:2

God wants us to believe that He will come through in our circumstances. As women after God's heart, we are looking to Him and striving to keep believing that He will, yet again, come through for us. But of course, we have days when we're filled with doubt, fear, worry, and anxiety. We wonder, *God, will You come through, even in this?*

God has always been here. He is the uncreated One. He has always been and always will be hovering over our circumstances, our unknowns, our voids, and our dark places in life. Just like He hovered over the world before He even created it, He hovers over us in our daily lives.

The Spirit is hovering over you as you wait on answers to your prayers. He's hovering over you as you battle anxiety and fear and unrest. He's hovering over you as you look ahead to the future. He's hovering over you as you pray and seek Him and go about your day-to-day life in His grace. He's hovering over you this moment. And He's at work to bring the darkness to light again in your life and your circumstances.

God is faithful. He always has been and always will be.

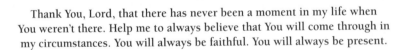

Thank You, Lord, that there has never been a moment in my life when You weren't there. Help me to always believe that You will come through in my circumstances. You will always be faithful. You will always be present.

Choose to believe God today for your impossible situations.

CELEBRATE

*They celebrate Your abundant goodness
and joyfully sing of Your righteousness.*

Psalm 145:7, NIV

The Fourth of July has become one of my favorite holidays to celebrate. It's a sweet time to be with family and to celebrate the freedom that we have in our country. It's a time to pause and remember the incredible heroes of the present and past who have done everything they can to secure our freedom. It's a time to feel the deep-down gratitude of living in a country where we can be free.

When I think of the Fourth, I think of swimming with my kids; my Dad's red truck in the neighborhood parade; my mom and grandmother wearing their star-shaped sunglasses and waving their flags with all the grandkids; watching fireworks on red, white, and blue patched quilts with my parents, siblings, and our tribes of kiddos; spending time at the lake, the sound of boats and water inviting me to slow my pace a bit. I can almost taste the fruit salad and the hot dogs with mustard, relish, and white onions. I think of juicy watermelon and sticky popsicle fingers. I think of hot Texas weather, but not minding a bit because the popsicles, watermelon, iced tea, and swimming keep us cool. I always love enjoying the back-porch rocking chairs and good company. July Fourth reminds me to celebrate our country.

Our country, while imperfect, is beautiful and good. And celebrating our political freedom reminds me to celebrate our freedom in Christ. Because of Him, we don't have to live perfectly. Because of Him, we don't have to earn our way to heaven. Because of Him, we don't have to do life alone. Because of Him, we are completely free from sin. Because of Him, we are counted righteous. Because of Him, we are forever a part of God's family. Our freedom in Christ is secure forever. July Fourth reminds me that it is good to celebrate. So today, celebrate our country, celebrate our faith, celebrate the ones you love, celebrate God, and celebrate life. Celebrate the ways God is working in your heart, your life, and your dreams. It is good to celebrate!

**Lord, thank You for our country, our freedom, family, and friends,
the delights of summer, and especially for our freedom in Christ.
Help me to soak in the summer days by celebrating all that I have in You.**

Take time to celebrate and appreciate all of God's good gifts.

July 5

GOD IS ALWAYS WORKING

*But they who wait for the L*ord *shall renew their strength.*

Isaiah 40:31

Are you in a season of waiting? In your waiting, God is working. In your waiting, God is present. In your waiting, seeds of faith are beginning to sprout as you entrust all your cares to God. In your waiting, you are growing more dependent on Jesus. As you water your heart with the truth of God's Word and His promises, your heart will deepen in faith, grow in grace, and bloom with hope.

What are you waiting for today?

- A prayer to be answered?
- A problem to be solved?
- An issue to be resolved?
- Your joy to return?
- Your faith to be rekindled?
- Your angst to dissolve?
- Your deepest heart questions to be answered?
- God's plans to be more clear?
- A decision to be made?
- Peace to fill your soul?
- A loved one to know the Lord?
- Your anxiety to be lifted?

God uses these seasons of waiting to draw you close to Him, to shape your character, and to reveal more of Himself to you. The things you wait on aren't necessarily the end goal; God is using the waiting to cultivate His relationship with you. It's in the waiting that we deepen our faith in God. It's in the waiting that He shapes our hearts. It's in the waiting that He reveals His power in our lives. It's in the waiting that we learn to trust Him.

So as you wait for the answers you long for, remember that God is always working in your waiting seasons, and that He hasn't left you as you wait. This waiting season is stretching your faith, but it will also deepen your love for Him as you realize that He really does hold your whole life in the palm of His hand.

Lord, You know the things I am waiting for. Give me Your peace in the waiting. Help me to trust You more fully and rest in Your timing.

If you're in a season of waiting, God is working to bring you the answers you need.

GOD KNOWS
WHAT YOU NEED

The LORD will guide you continually and satisfy your desire in
scorched places and make your bones strong; and you shall be like
a watered garden, like a spring of water, whose waters do not fail.

Isaiah 58:11

God knows what you need, who He designed you to be, where you need to go, and the purpose for your life. He has a special, unique plan for your life. So when questions come to your mind and threaten to make your mind and emotions swirl with anxiety, bring those questions to Him and let Him guide you to what He wants you to do. He has your best interest in mind, and His plan for your life is better than anything you could have planned or imagined.

It's so easy for us to plan our lives without checking in with our Maker. We stress and strategize over our future with good intentions to trust God with our lives, but without even realizing it we can slip into controlling our lives. We make our plans and decide on our futures and then bring that to God: *Okay, Lord, this is what I've decided to do moving forward. Please guide me in my plans.* Have you been there? Have you overanalyzed God's will for your life? You mean well, but perhaps have you slipped into making your own plans instead of seeking God's heart for you.

Sometimes the pressure to find God's will for our lives causes anxiety in our hearts because God's will can feel like a mystery. So we strive to live well and use our gifts and be the best version of ourselves that we can possibly be, but have you noticed that all the striving and pressure to find God's will leaves you exhausted? And what you thought was God's will actually doesn't feel right at all?

Dear sister, God knows what you need, and He knows His plans for your life. You can't mess up His plans for you. Actually, when you let go a little more and surrender to His plans and will for your life, your heart will feel more at ease. You can stop overanalyzing and strategizing. You can surrender, and He will do the rest.

Lord, I choose to let go of trying to control my life and plan my
future because it's quite exhausting. I want Your plans for my life.
As I let go of striving and planning, Lord, take over my life.
Thank You for relieving me of the pressure to be in control.

God will satisfy you and strengthen you, and you will blossom
into all that He's calling you to be—no striving required.

GOD IS UPHOLDING YOU

You are My servant, I have chosen you and not cast you off; fear not,
for I am with you; be not dismayed, for I am your God; I will strengthen you,
I will help you, I will uphold you with My righteous right hand.

Isaiah 41:9-10

Today, may you believe deep in your soul that you are chosen by God to be His beloved daughter. May you walk hand and hand with Him, trusting Him to guide your steps. May you joyfully serve Him today in the little things, making your tasks and assignments joy-filled as you believe that He is in all of it.

Today, release your fears to the One Who is always with you. Don't be discouraged or let your hope dwindle, but remember who holds your hand. When you find yourself thirsty in your soul, let that thirst point you to the One Who loves to fill you up. May you run to Him when you need refilling.

Today, may you remember that God holds you, your life, and this world together. May you trust Him with the future and be fully present in this beautiful day. May God strengthen your heart as you let Him be your helper. Remember that God is upholding you and loving you today.

Lord, keep my faith in You strong today. Help me to remember
how much You love me. Help me to run to You when
I feel thirsty and look to You when I need guidance.

Depend on the Lord. As you lean on Him, your heart will feel lighter,
your circumstances will seem brighter, and your joy will overflow.

GRACE AND REST
FOR YOUR HEART

Blessed is the one … whose delight is in the law of the LORD, and who meditates on His law day and night. That person is like a tree planted by streams of water, which yields its fruit in season and whose leaf does not wither—whatever they do prospers.

Psalm 1:1-3, NIV

God lavishes His blessings on you right in the middle of everyday life. Sometimes it's hard to feel His blessings when your world feels more broken than whole. But His blessings are shining down on you today.

And as you linger over God's Word and think on His truths and promises, your heart and soul breathe deeper. Your heart feels lighter. Your soul feels freer. When you lean into the Word and soak your soul in time with Jesus, you are like a flourishing tree planted by a refreshing stream of water, yielding fruit in season. You're not withering; instead, you're blooming.

So today, may your heart rest a little easier as you plant your heart in God's Word little by little. May you know that you are blessed as you look to Jesus.

Lord, deepen my roots in You as I look to Your Word.
Make me strong, like a tree planted by streams of water.

May you feel God's rest as you rest in Him.

BLESSING FOR YOUR DAY

You keep him in perfect peace whose mind is stayed on You,
because he trusts in You. Trust in the LORD forever,
for the LORD GOD is an everlasting rock.

Isaiah 26:3-4

May you walk through this day depending wholly on Jesus. May you look to Him when you're weary, praise Him when you sense His nearness, and run to Him when you need refilling.

May you believe that He hears your prayers, know that He sees you, and trust Him to speak into your heart. May you watch for Him during this day, believing that He's present and for you and with you step by step.

May you set aside distractions and tune your thoughts to Him. May you trust Him in a fresh way with your circumstances and concerns. May you see God at work today in the little things and the big things. May you feel His peace as you look to Him.

Lord, make me aware of Your beautiful presence today.

The Lord is with you in all you do today. His presence
is your shelter, your strength, and your perfect peace.

THE LORD SUSTAINS ME

The LORD sustained me.

Psalm 3:5

It is the Lord who sustains you through this day, this week, and this season. He is your strength, your song, and your sanctuary. In Him is the delight and joy you're looking for. In Him is the peace and abundance you crave. In Him is the rest and grace you're looking for. Today, may you keep looking to Him.

Look to Him instead of the news.
Look to Him instead of your fears.
Look to Him instead of feeding your worries.
Look to Him instead of filling up on things that don't satisfy.
Look to Him for hope.
Look to Him for peace.
Look to Him for joy.
Look to Him for miracles.

Lord, sustain my heart today as I walk through this day.
Help me to keep looking to You.

Trust the One Who is in control even when things
feel out of control in our world. In Him, hope is
always alive. Let Him sustain your heart today.

CHOOSING FAITH
OVER FEAR

In all circumstances take up the shield of faith, with which
you can extinguish all the flaming darts of the evil one.
Ephesians 6:16

Hang on to faith today, dear sister. In **all** circumstances, take up the shield of faith. We can choose faith over fear, faith over worry, and faith over uncertainty. I know that it's difficult to choose faith in trying circumstances. Our natural inclination is to fear, to worry, and to waver in uncertainty.

In whatever thing is on your heart and causing fear, worry, or uncertainty today, choose to have faith in the Lord. Choose faith by talking to God about it. You can be honest with Him because He knows all things.

> *Lord, this situation feels impossible.*
> *Lord, I'm weary of this struggle.*
> *Lord, the answer seems so far off.*

You can choose faith by asking God for faith. You don't have to have faith in your own strength and power.

> *Lord, increase my faith.*
> *Lord, fill me with faith even though this situation feels impossible.*
> *Lord, give me strength to choose faith over fear, worry, and uncertainty.*

Ask Him for faith. He longs to shower you with the faith you need. When we take up the shield of faith, the darts of the evil one are extinguished. All the darts of doubt, discouragement, and deception from the enemy are snuffed out as we choose faith.

Lord, help me to choose faith over fear, worry,
and uncertainty today. Boost my faith as I look to You.

Choose faith today when you're tempted to fret.
You will find that faith leads to peace.

HE IS WITH YOU ALL DAY

Your name and remembrance are the desire of our soul.
Isaiah 26:8

The Lord is with you throughout your whole day. Sometimes it's easy to box Him into our quiet time part of the day, when we have our Bible and journal and coffee in front of us. We close our Bible, dog-ear the page of our journal, finish the last sip of coffee, and then move on to conquer our day. But He wants our whole day to be quiet time! He wants to do our whole day with us. Remember the Lord today as you step out of your quiet time and step into your day. Don't leave Him on the back porch; invite Him into your day.

This makes me think of my sweet dog, Shaka. He sits at my feet in the mornings when I'm on my back porch as I sip my coffee and read my Bible. He's under my desk when I'm working at my computer. He sleeps nearby when I'm talking on the phone. The only time he steers clear of me is when I'm vacuuming! My point is that he's always there, even when I don't realize it. He seems to follow me around all day whether or not I pay attention to him. He is one faithful pup.

In the same way, God is always there. He's on your back porch as you sip your coffee and read your Bible, and He's near as you go throughout your entire day. He faithfully stays with you all day long. Look for Him, listen to Him, and reach out for Him all throughout your day. He's always there, dear sister.

**Lord, thank You for Your constant presence in my life.
Help me to look for You throughout my day today.**

God is with you in your everyday moments.

MAKING DECISIONS

But for You, O LORD, do I wait; it is You,
O Lord my God, Who will answer.

Psalm 38:15

When we have a decision to make or we are waiting on a prayer request to be answered, the waiting time can cause us to be so swelled up with anxiety that we forget to enjoy where we already are. God understands this. He knows that our waiting times can hang over us and weigh down our hearts. But God certainly doesn't want us to be so hung up on tomorrow that we miss the beauty of today.

Our job to *enjoy* the present. To not worry about tomorrow. To not agonize over future decisions. To pray—yes. But to also trust God in the waiting. To take no thought of the future. Let tomorrow be tomorrow. In the meantime, enjoy today.

God will guide you through any decision you have to make. He will listen to your prayers, and in due time, He will answer. For now, imagine taking that decision or prayer request and placing it in God's able hands. Let Him have it. He knows you would rather fiddle around with it, analyze it, and weigh it. He knows it's hard to let it go. He knows you're eager to have it all figured out. Hand it over anyway. And go enjoy this beautiful, good, lovely day. Go enjoy what is already answered. Go enjoy what is already decided. Go enjoy what God is already doing in your precious life. And when the time comes, He will bring the issues you're wondering about back up again and answer you in the way He sees fit. He will help you make your decisions. He will answer your prayer request. Let it all rest in His hands for now.

It's possible to have God's peace in the waiting. As you turn over the burdens of your heart to Him—and let them go—you will find rest.

Lord, help me not worry over future decisions.
Help me to stay present to this day and trust that when
the time comes to make a decision, You will guide me.

Be all in this day. Don't worry about what's ahead.

THERE IS ALWAYS HOPE

Rejoice in hope, be patient in tribulation, be constant in prayer.
Romans 12:12

Rejoice in hope today by celebrating the fact that you get to be in a close personal relationship with the Lord. Celebrate His gift of salvation and His constant presence in your life.

Be patient in trials—oh, that's challenging. Most times, when we are in the midst of a trial, we simply want out! We want the trial to end. We want resolutions and solutions. Romans 12:12 reminds us to be patient in the difficulties. Give God time and space to see it through. Trust His timing. Be present where you are because God is doing things in your heart and in your circumstances right in the midst of the trial.

And lastly, be constant in prayer. I love that! Pray throughout your whole day. Pray for the answers you need. Pray for God to move in your trials. You cannot over-pray! God will never tire of your petitions.

This is a prescription for peace: *rejoice in hope, be patient in tribulation, be constant in prayer.* When you feel anxious or stuck, overwhelmed, or weary, take a pause in your day and rejoice in hope—celebrate the hope you have in Jesus. Be patient in the trial. Take a moment to breathe, to slow down the rush to find answers or resolutions and just breathe. And pray. Pray when you need peace. Pray when you need answers. Pray when you need patience.

May you feel the love of God today in a fresh way and sense His presence in your life. Keep turning to Him even when He feels far away. He has never left you—not once. And He never will leave you. He's with you in the dark, in the light, in the shadows, in the night. He will never stop pursuing you. He will never stop helping you. Your miracle is coming—there is always hope.

**Lord, give me strength to rejoice. Give me patience in my trials.
And give me perseverance in prayer. Thank You for filling my life with hope.**

Rejoice, be patient, be constant in prayer. Repeat.

GUARDING YOUR MIND

Behold, I give you a wise and discerning mind.

1 Kings 3:12

Guard your mind today. Protect it from the overload of the world, the distractions of the day, and the worries of your circumstances. Guard your mind by scooting your heart up close to God. Make some space to retreat with Him. Clear some minutes for just being with Him. Guard your mind so that you can hear and feel God today.

What things are depleting you? What's getting inside your mind and darkening your faith or stirring up your anxiety?

The news?
Digital overload? (emails, the internet, texts, social media, images)
Movies or television shows?
A crowded calendar?
Constant connectivity to your phone?
Focusing on the mirror?

When you guard your mind, you'll find Jesus.
When you guard your mind, you'll hear His voice.
When you guard your mind, you'll experience more joy and deeper peace.
When you guard your mind, you'll live loved and fueled up by the Spirit.

**Lord, show me the things that are depleting me and stirring up
my anxiety. Help me to guard my mind today. Give me wisdom and
discernment so that I can make wise choices with what I allow into my mind.**

*Guard your mind today from the overload of the world,
and you will experience the reprieve of God's peace.*

A DANCE OF ABIDING

Abide in Me, and I in you. As the branch cannot bear fruit by itself,
unless it abides in the vine, neither can you, unless you abide in Me.

John 15:4

Maybe your soul is tired—tired from striving, performing, trying hard, and keeping up with all you have to do. Maybe you feel buried underneath the weight of life. Maybe you feel weary from trying so hard to keep everything together.

Sweet one, Christ invites us to a slower pace. He invites us into His lighter rhythms of grace, where we can find a rootedness to our life that flourishes whether we are in spring or winter. No matter what winds blow, no matter what storms come, no matter what debris flies at us, we can be steady in Christ and in step with His lighter rhythms of grace moment by moment. I know you feel like you're stuck in a pit of pressure, stress, expectations, and busyness. I know your heart and soul feel weighed down, and maybe you're wondering how in the world to break free.

Know today that you don't have to try harder. Instead, you can lean on the One Who created your heart. You can come honest before Him and tell Him what's going on in that beautiful heart and soul of yours, and then you can trust Him to help you learn this dance of abiding in Him. Abiding in Him is not a formula of steps, but a posture of the heart. It's trusting Him even when you don't understand what He's doing. It's staying in this present moment with God instead of striving and worrying about future moments.

And as you abide in Him, He will steady you. You will flourish, grow, blossom, and thrive as you abide in Christ.

Lord, show me what it looks like to abide in You.

You can let go of striving. You can let go of performing.
You can let go of the try-hard life.

REST, REPLENISH, RECOVER

*Keep your heart with all vigilance,
for from it flow the springs of life.*

Proverbs 4:23

Summer can be a time to rest, to replenish, and to grow. This summer give your heart time and space and room to grow closer to God. Use this season to recover from the busy year. Explore more of God—go on an adventure with Him in the pages of your Bible and take time to play and enjoy His creation. That heart of yours is so precious to God, and He needs you to protect it from unnecessary wear and tear. Keep space for God this summer.

Talk to Jesus as if He's you're very best friend. And then listen for His whispers through His Word and His Holy Spirit. Take time away from the news, the emails, the internet, and the phone, and give yourself some room to breathe. You've had a lot on your plate I imagine, so give yourself time to rest, replenish, and recover. Use the lazy days of summer to guard your heart from stress, because everything you do flows from your heart. What does your heart need today?

- Time in the Word?
- Space to pray?
- Permission to rest?
- The discipline to unplug?
- A break from the world?
- A place to enjoy God's creation?

Take care of your heart this summer. Your heart is like your command center, and when your heart is weary and stressed, it affects everything in your life. Guard your heart from the noise of the world and the influx of information. Take a breather. You will be so glad you did.

**Lord, help me to be careful to guard my heart by giving
myself time and space to rest, replenish, and recover.**

Let summer be a reset for your heart.

EYES ON JESUS

Our eyes look to the LORD our God.
Psalm 123:2

We can get so busy that if we're not careful, our eyes become more focused on our work, our world, and our circumstances than on Jesus. We can get so busy that we lose sight of Him. Add to that the busyness of everyday life, to-do lists, and the dings and pings of email notifications, and we can easily lose our way.

When our eyes are fixed on Jesus, our hearts stay in line with Him.
When our eyes are fixed on Jesus, we are free from the pull of the world.
When our eyes are fixed on Jesus, we focus on the right things.
When our eyes are fixed on Jesus, our hearts follow Him.
When our eyes are fixed on Jesus, we feel His peace.

Be careful where you're focusing. Keep your eyes on Jesus. From there, abundant life will follow.

Jesus, help me to keep my eyes firmly fixed on You.

*Check your focus throughout the day. When you find
yourself focusing more on your circumstances or
your worries than on Jesus, take a moment to refocus.
As you look to the Lord, your heart will feel at ease again.*

UNPLUG TO TRULY FLOURISH

My help comes from the LORD, Who made heaven and earth.

Psalm 121:2

Studies show that the more we unplug from screens, the better we sleep, the better we feel emotionally, the better we concentrate, and the more we are able to enjoy our lives. I also believe that the more we unplug, the more we will hear God and enjoy the life He's given us. I don't want us to look back in ten years and wish we had been more present to our lives. I don't want us to miss God's gifts right in front of us because we are looking through a screen.

Jesus is in the secret place of our hearts. He resides in us. We have constant access to His presence, and He wants to help us through life. But He needs us to make space for Him. Think of the beauty of a woman who has made room in her heart for God. This gal's life flourishes from a deeply-rooted relationship with God. As she leans on God, she grows and blossoms into the woman He wants her to be.

Keep pursuing God in a deeper way by making room in your heart for Him, because God wants more abundant life for you. He wants you to experience full life in Him. And as you keep your heart spacious for Him, He pours more joy, more peace, and more abundant life into you.

Lord, be my Helper. Empower me to keep my heart spacious for You.

Unplug from the noise and distractions,
and you will find more of God.

LET GOD BE YOUR REFUGE

You are my hiding place and my shield.
Psalm 119:114

Do you ever feel a burden to completely unplug from the technology that has made our lives more convenient, but overly connected? More convenient, but more stressed? More convenient, but moving at a faster pace than our hearts can keep up with?

Do you long to be more present with the people in your life?
Do you long to be less stressed and more peaceful?
Do you long to live at a slower pace?
Do you long to feel more connected with God?

The burden on your heart to unplug is beautiful. Your desire to make God your refuge is beautiful. And when you choose Him, He will be your hiding place and your shield from the world's enticements. He will guard your ways and honor your efforts to unplug. So keep going in His strength. Let Him be your refuge over and over again as you choose Him over the distractions.

It will be so worth it.

**Jesus, be my refuge and shield. Thank You for giving me
the desire to unplug in order to more deeply tune into You.**

*Listen to that nudge in your heart that longs
for peace from the noise. Turn off the phone.
Turn down the noise. And find God in the quiet.*

SWEETER THAN HONEY

How sweet are Your words to my taste,
sweeter than honey to my mouth!
Psalm 119:103

Nothing is sweeter to our hearts than the honey of God's Word. Nothing is sweeter than time spent in God's company. Of course, the world will try to convince us otherwise and our own hearts will question the value of God's Word. Meanwhile, the digital world will go on as usual—enticing us, drawing us in, and tempting us with its pings and whistles.

God and His Word are what our hearts are truly craving. Desire isn't a bad thing. In fact, God gave us desires. He gave us a desire in our hearts to want more of Him. The trouble is, often we try to feed our desires with the world's stuff. But it never satisfies, am I right?

We need to want God more than we want the world. When we let God's Word be our main thing, our phones, distractions, and the noise of the world become less of a thing.

God desires for us to live in His rhythms of grace, not caught up in the world's fast pace.

When we run to God over the world, we find everything we need. His company and His Word will become the sweetest thing to our hearts. The more we run to Him, the more we want to run to Him.

Maybe today spending time in God's Word feels more like duty than delight, more like a chore than a joy. Dear sister, we all feel that at one time or another. Ask the Lord to sweeten your love for His Word, and He will be faithful to do so.

God, make Your Word my delight—sweeter than honey.
Help me to choose You over the world every day.

Time in God's Word will refresh your soul.
You were made to need and crave the words of Scripture.

DELIGHT IN GOD'S WORD

If Your law had not been my delight,
I would have perished in my affliction.

Psalm 119:92

God's Word settles our hearts, helps us sort out our emotions, uplifts our hearts, and satisfies our longings. It strengthens our hearts, souls, and minds. When we make the Bible the delight of our lives, we thrive.

Every day, we have choices to make about what we will allow to shape us. We have endless options to turn to for comfort, guidance, and wisdom. But God's Word is the only thing that shapes us in a healthy way. And we desperately need it. It's not so much about sticking to our Bible reading plan or having a quiet time for a certain number of minutes, it's more about growing to love God's Word and to believe that His ways are best for us.

I honestly don't know where I would be without Jesus and His life-giving Word. My mind would feel chaotic, my soul would feel restless, and my heart would feel anxious all the time. I still feel those things sometimes, but when I choose to get God's Word into me, it settles me, sorts me out, sustains me, satisfies me, and strengthens me like nothing else in the world.

Don't allow technology, distractions, a full calendar, or busyness to steal your delight in God's Word. Don't let distractions interrupt you from studying God's Word. It is the very bread you need for your hungry heart and the water you need for your thirsty soul.

Jesus, Your Word is everything I need. Thank You that You use Your Word to shape me, satisfy me, and strengthen me. Teach me Your Word. Show me new and beautiful things within its pages. Give me fresh delight for Your sweet Word.

Today, when you feel anxious or unsettled,
head to the back porch and open your Bible.
Let God's Word be the soothing remedy to calm your soul.

STEPPING OFF THE TREADMILL OF LIFE

You have given me hope.
Psalm 119:49, NIV

We all need to pull over every once in a while. We need to step off the treadmill of life and rest. And in this day and age, that means we need to log off the internet. Tune out the newsfeed and rest from the digital world.

Our devices can distract us from God. They can deplete our energy and cause our souls to feel maxed out. Life can feel like a never-ending race at a breakneck speed, and our devices seem to rev up the pace even more. It's okay to step off the treadmill. In fact, stepping off the treadmill of life will keep our souls healthy. Living at a slower pace gives us room to breathe, space to think, and best of all, time to seek God.

Jesus offers us eternal hope, but He also offers us everyday hope for our everyday trials. He gladly helps us with anything that's burdening our hearts, including the desire to step off the treadmill of life.

We are a busy generation. Our lives are full, and we have an encyclopedia of information at our fingertips. And yet we are an anxious generation. Our devices and technology and the constant flow of information distract us from the Lord if we are not careful. Today, take note of your pace. Do you need a reprieve from all the noise and busyness?

Jesus, thank You that You are my hope. Thank You that
You are my Helper and Counselor, and that You care about
every detail of my life. Give me the strength to choose
You over the distractions and entanglements of this world.

Slow down. Breathe. Rest. Unplug.

TAKE CARE OF YOURSELF

But my eyes are toward You, O GOD, my Lord.
Psalm 141:8

What do you love to do? What are the things that bring you joy? **What's** *a hobby that you enjoy?*
What makes you come alive?
What makes you lose track of time?
What makes you feel joy?

You need to get back to doing those things. It is important to tap into the things we love to do. Those talents and interests are innately wired into us by God to give us a sense of joy and pleasure. They help us take care of ourselves and recharge. The things we love to do help us to enjoy life. They minimize our stress, give us reprieve from the daily grind, and infuse our hearts with joy. But so often the tyranny of the urgent can easily take over our days. We stop doing the things we love and enjoy.

I believe that the things we love to do help us feel closer to God because we are tapping into the way He wired us. Get back to the things that make you feel fully alive. Ask the Lord to show you the things you need to do in order to enjoy life, come fully alive, lose track of time, and feel the joy of the Lord.

Lord, You wired me in a specific way. Help me to take care
of myself by taking time to do the things I love. Thank You that
You use these things to delight my heart and lighten my load.

Take care of yourself today. Do the things that make you lose
track of time. God is handling your burdens, cares, and prayers.
Enjoy the things that God has wired you to love.

LET HIM PAVE THE WAY

Trust in the LORD with all your heart, and do not lean on your own understanding. In all your ways acknowledge Him, and He will make straight your paths. Be not wise in your own eyes; fear the LORD, and turn away from evil. It will be healing to your flesh and refreshment to your bones.

Proverbs 3:5-8

I tend to take situations into my own hands before I check in with the Lord. I wait until I am totally overwhelmed by life before I call on the Lord for help. I lean on my own understanding instead of acknowledging that true wisdom comes from God alone.

Jesus wants us to look to Him in everything. He knows the best way to walk through each and every situation we face in a day. He wants to be intimately involved in the details of our lives. So today, check in with God. Trust in Him and His ways instead of leaning on your own feelings, emotions, or ideas. He will guide you. He will let you know what to do in each situation you face. Trust Him and anticipate great joy as you watch your Savior work on your behalf!

Lord, I surrender to You. Help me to trust You with all my heart.

Let God pave the way through your day and your circumstances. Look to Him for the wisdom you need for this day. Trust Him to guide your path.

EVERYDAY WORSHIP

Let them praise His name with dancing,
making melody to Him with tambourine and lyre!

Psalm 149:3

Our everyday tasks can become worship with a simple shift in our perspective. Instead of seeing our tasks and routines as mundane or insignificant, we can remember that God is in our midst. We can worship Him whether we are sitting on our back porch spending time with Him, folding clothes in our laundry room, or sitting at a desk crunching numbers. And when we do our everyday tasks for the Lord, each one is infused with purpose and joy!

Today, turn your everyday tasks into worship. Turn on some worship music as you go about your day. Or pray and talk to God while you do your tasks. Choose to believe that the work you are doing has purpose. No task is holier than another. No part of your day is more spiritual than another. Praise God as you go about your day.

Dear Jesus, thank You for the tasks You've given me to do today.
Help me to have a spirit of praise and a joyful heart as I go about my day.
Help me to remember that whatever I am doing today can bring glory to
You and make the world around me more beautiful in big and small ways.

All that you do today has significance in God's eyes.
What feels mundane can become worship as you look
to the One Who fills your day with hope and purpose.

MORNING

Let the morning bring me word of your unfailing love,
for I have put my trust in You. Show me the way
I should go, for to you I entrust my soul.

Psalm 143:8, NIV

Jesus wants to set the tone for our day. Before we head out into our day, if we will pull over for a few moments of stillness and quiet, God will speak to our hearts, teach us His Word, and prepare us spiritually for the day ahead. Every morning God's unfailing love is there to greet us. Every morning we are given a fresh start to trust God with our day. Every morning we can look to God for guidance. And every morning, God lifts us up. His offer of renewal and refreshment never ends.

Whether you find a few quiet moments in the morning or another part of your day, know that pulling over for a reprieve with God will uplift your heart, renew your perspective, and empower you with His strength. His presence is your weapon for the day. His presence is your shield. It is where you will find your center, a sense of calm, and His strong and steady love.

If you're having trouble feeling like your time with God is effective, or maybe you're struggling to feel His presence, try something new. Perhaps take a walk with God, listening for His voice and tuning into His presence. Or turn on a worship song that speaks to your heart and uplifts your soul. Read through a favorite Psalm and allow the divine words of Scripture to wash over your heart. A few minutes of quietness and stillness with your Savior before your feet hit the ground running will lighten your heart for the day, stir your faith, and empower you with His strength. Find Him in the morning, even if for only a few minutes.

Lord, help me to start my day with You. Help me to soak in the
riches and blessings of Your Word. Prepare me for the events of
this day. Thank You that I can talk to You throughout the day.
And thank You for Your grace that covers me no matter what.

Those first few minutes of your day
can set the tone for your whole day.

HIDE IN HIM

You are a hiding place for me; You preserve me from trouble;
You surround me with shouts of deliverance.

Psalm 32:7

God wants to be your safe haven, your quiet sanctuary, and your reprieve from the world. He wants to be the One you run to, the place you go for rest, and the source you look to for strength. He wants to be your hiding place.

That's what time with God on your back porch is all about. It's a place to meet God, to be known by Him, and to know Him more and more. It's the place where you can fully be yourself. You can let down your guard. You don't have to perform, impress, or feel pressure here—it's just you and God.

So come often. It's the place where He delivers you again and again from your fears, your worries, your doubts, and your insecurities. It's the place where your human heart collides with His holy heart. You are loved here. Seen here. Heard here. Known here. Just come as you are to the hiding place of His presence. He will meet you here anytime. And when you head back into your day, He will be with you in your day, too. But the porch is always waiting, and the Lord is always ready to refill you and make you feel safe and loved and known again and again.

Lord, You know what I am facing today. Thank You that
I can hide in You; help me to remember to run to
You for comfort, guidance, wisdom, and strength.

You always have access to God. So every time you
need to know you are loved, seen, heard, and known,
hide in Him. There you will find everything you need.

TIME TO BLOSSOM

Even to your old age and gray hairs I am He,
I am He who will sustain you. I have made you and
I will carry you; I will sustain you and I will rescue you.

Isaiah 46:4, NIV

Do not be discouraged today. I know sometimes you feel like you are wilting instead of flourishing, struggling instead of thriving. Hold on, dear one. The Lord is doing something good in you and in your circumstances.

Imagine a rose bush that looks completely withered. Maybe it was scorched by the sun and never quite received enough water. It looks dry, thirsty, frail, and finished. I nearly threw away a rose bush that was in my backyard because it just did not look like it was going to flourish. But instead I began to water it more regularly and made sure it was getting enough sun. I didn't give up on it, even though it looked like it had no chance to blossom and thrive.

After a while, the rose bush started blooming beautifully—right when I thought it was completely finished. It began to flourish and thrive right when I thought it was on its last leg.

You are like that rose bush. You have buds and seeds that are waiting to sprout and bloom. I know some days you feel spiritually dry and emotionally spent, but there will come a time when you will blossom again. Trust in the Lord and trust that He has a plan for your life and for this particular season of your life. Even though you can't see any blossoms yet, God sees the bigger picture. God promises to sustain you. He made you, so He knows just what you need to blossom.

Lord, thank You for sustaining me,
carrying me, and rescuing me.

When I feel spiritually dry, help me to trust You
to bring my heart into full bloom again and again.

NEEDING HIS PEACE

Then they cried to the L<small>ORD</small> in their trouble, and He delivered them from their distress.
He brought them out of darkness and the shadow of death, and burst their bonds apart.
Let them thank the L<small>ORD</small> for His steadfast love, for His wondrous works to the
children of man! For He shatters the doors of bronze and cuts in two the bars of iron.

Psalm 107:13-16

Those days that are harder—perhaps a little darker or more stressful or gloomy— Jesus meets us. He delivers us out of darkness and distress. We can cry out to Him in our troubles, and He will bring us out of the darkness and break away our chains. Our chains may be the countless things that are stirring up our anxiety, the lies we find ourselves believing, or the taunts of the enemy. What are your chains today? What are the things binding you up and keep you from full joy? Jesus can break every one of them.

The Lord breaks down gates of bronze and cuts through bars of iron. He can break down our stress and any negative feelings or emotions. No feeling or attitude is too strong for Him to deal with. So when you are having one of those difficult days, cry out to Jesus, soak in His Word, and let Him soothe your heart. Be encouraged that Jesus can lift the darkness, break the chains, and restore your joy.

Lord, on those days that are harder, help me to come to You. Check my
heart and my attitude, for You know me better than anyone. Help me to
come to You to bring me back to joy, and help me to look around and thank
You for the blessings that are right in front of me but are foggy at the moment.

Turn to the Lord when you feel stuck in the dark
and when your heart needs peace. Trust Him
to deliver you from any and all distress.

QUIET MOMENTS

For He Himself is our peace.
Ephesians 2:14

As you walk through this day, take some quiet moments here and there to acknowl-edge God's presence in your life. Take some quiet moments to breathe, to rest, to just be. Like a cup of tea out on your back porch soothes your heart, Jesus' company can calm your nerves, your worries, your fears, and your restlessness.

How would it change your day if you had more of those quiet moments throughout your day?

A quiet moment to know deep in your heart that God is near.

A quiet moment to remember that God is with you.

A quiet moment to replace a lie you're believing with God's truth.

A quiet moment to turn a burden over to the Lord.

A quiet moment to reflect on the goodness of God.

What if we stop, pray, and let Jesus' peace wash over us before we tackle our next task or run those errands? It is easy to try to just push through the day, barely stopping for a breath. But we wind up feeling empty and exhausted by trying to do our day in our own strength. Take quiet moments through the day to enjoy His company, to feel His love, to know that He cares, and to remember that He is in control.

**Jesus, thank You for Your Holy Spirit in me that calms me, comforts me,
and enables me to do what I cannot do in my own strength.
Help me to remember to take quiet moments during the day to just
enjoy Your presence, feel Your love, and depend on Your strength.**

*Be intentional today about taking some
quiet moments to sit with the Lord.
Notice the difference it makes in your day.*

August

GOD IS ALWAYS NEAR

Seek the Lord and His strength; seek His presence continually!
1 Chronicles 16:11

Dear friend, what things feel out of your control today? Are you praying for a loved one's health? Are you concerned about your child thriving in school? Are you wondering if you're raising your kids right? Are you anxious about a dream you're trying to follow? Are you wondering how your circumstances are going to work out?

We tend to want to control our circumstances. We think if we could just control the outcome, we would feel better. Perhaps we think if we could just see the result we are waiting for, we would feel less anxious. But when we realize that God is fully in control of our lives and that He is always good, we will discover that it is a relief to surrender control of our lives to Him. There is relief in letting go of our circumstances and turning them over to God. There is rest in letting God handle our prayer requests and the things that make us anxious. There is goodness in letting God be God. There is peace in surrender.

Today, know that God wants to take full control of your circumstances. Know that while He is handling all that concerns you, He is always near. He never leaves you alone, dear friend. He is in all the things that feel out of your control. He knows how much you care about each thing that concerns you. He knows what burdens your heart. And He is at work in every care, concern, and burden. He wants to ease all your anxiety. He wants you to know today that you can surrender everything to His control. He wants you to know that He's always near and He's always ready to take on your every burden. Keep seeking the Lord. Keep looking to Him for strength. Keep seeking His presence continually.

Lord, thank You that You are always near—that You never leave me and You never abandon me to fend for myself. Lord, here are all the things that feel out of my control today. Take every care, concern, and burden of my heart and remind me that You are in control.

Surrendering control of our lives to God will unburden us from having to manage our lives. He wants to manage our lives. He wants us to depend on Him.

GOD IS PERSONAL

What man of you, having a hundred sheep, if he has lost one
of them, does not leave the ninety-nine in the open country,
and go after the one that is lost, until he finds it?

Luke 15:4

God is personal. He cares specifically for each individual person. Dear one, He cares so personally for *you*. God sees you. God knows you. God created you. And when you have those days where you feel a little lost, where your heart strays a bit from Him, or where you wander away from Him as you strive to find your way through the trials of life, He runs after you.

In Luke 15, Jesus tells the parable of the lost sheep. One sheep wanders off. Somehow he gets displaced and finds himself far away from all that is familiar and safe. He is separated from his flock, wandering all alone through unfamiliar territory. And what does the shepherd do? He leaves the ninety-nine other sheep to go after the one. He drops everything to find his beloved sheep. He pursues him. He finds him. And he brings him back home to safety.

God pursues you personally. He pursued you to bring you to a place of finding salvation in Him, and He pursues you day by day, bringing you to a place of experiencing His love and care. He loves you.

Lord, thank You for pursuing me. Let the truth of Your pursuing and
personal love and care wash over my heart today. Restore my sense of identity,
worth, and confidence as I remember that I am pursued and loved by You.

God goes after you, day after day. He will always pursue you.
He will always bring you back into the safe harbor of His presence.

GOD OVER GOOGLE

Answer me when I call, O God of my righteousness! You have given me relief when I was in distress. Be gracious to me and hear my prayer!

Psalm 4:1

The gift of the internet is that we can access any information that we could possibly need. The curse of the internet is that we can replace seeking God with Google. We can look to the internet for the answers we need instead of looking to God first. The internet is a blessing, but it cannot replace the personal care, love, and wisdom of God.

You can bring every question to God. You can bring every problem to Him. He has every answer you need. While clearly He may guide you to use the internet to find some of the answers you need, He cares more about the state of your heart than giving you all the answers. He cares more about your relationship with Him than how much you know. He wants to be your heavenly Daddy, the One you turn to and run to. He wants to help you in ways that only He can. He wants to give you hope for your circumstances, solutions to your problems, and real answers for every question of your heart.

God is here with you. He is present in your heart. He is weaving together a perfect plan for the trials you face and using each one to draw you closer to Him. He loves you and cares for you so deeply. You are not alone in the trials you face. He wants to give you unwavering peace today as you seek Him for relief from your distress. He wants to be the One you turn to for the answers you need. So run to Him today when you need an answer. Run to Him when you need wisdom. Run to Him when you find yourself needing a distraction. Then let Him surprise you with the sweetest answers.

**Lord, help me to run to You today for the answers I need.
When I find myself tempted to Google my way
through a problem, remind me to seek You first.**

You are saved by grace eternally, but you are also guided and led by God daily. The miracle of being in a relationship with Jesus is that You have constant access to the One Who has all the answers.

YOUR CONSTANT HOPE

*When the righteous cry for help, the LORD hears and
delivers them out of all their troubles. The LORD is near
to the brokenhearted and saves the crushed in spirit.*

Psalm 34:17-18

One thing I love about living in Texas is that we typically experience every season, and the weather changes quite a bit. Just last week, we were experiencing a cool breeze, a reprieve from the Texas summer heat. The sun was shining and the leaves were beginning to gently fall. We pulled out our light jackets, thankful for the refreshment of a little bit cooler weather. Then this week a cold front blew through, bringing a bitter-cold coolness to the air. Just when we thought we were settling in for fall, we are digging out our winter coats and hats. And I am fairly certain that this weekend is supposed to be back in the mid-sixties with sunshine. Texas weather keeps us on our toes for sure.

Just like God created the seasons, He made life to be experienced in seasons. Life brings us many changes. Just when we settle into one season, something shifts. But the common thread through all of life's ups, downs, and all arounds is our constant hope. When we're in a season where the sun is shining in our circumstances and the future looks bright—we're feeling joy in our hearts and peace in our souls—God is there, and He is our constant source of hope. And when we find ourselves in a season where the sun isn't shining—our circumstances seem impossible and the future looks bleak or we're feeling a sense of unrest and inner turmoil—God is there, and He is our constant source of hope.

God created life to be a mixture of the good and the hard, the light and the dark, the peace and the trials. But He is in all of it, and the hope He offers never expires. When you find yourself in a difficult season, remember that God is still there. Hold on a little longer, and before you know it, you will find yourself in a place of sunshine again.

Lord, thank You that You are my constant hope in any and every season.
You are the one constant in my life in an ever-changing world.
Keep my perspective hope-filled and bright no matter
what the weather of my circumstances looks like today.

God is your help and source of hope in every season of life.

BELIEVE IN MIRACLES

*Have faith in God. Truly, I say to you, whoever says to this mountain, "Be taken
up and thrown into the sea," and does not doubt in his heart, but believes that
what he says will come to pass, it will be done for him. Therefore I tell you,
whatever you ask in prayer, believe that you have received it, and it will be yours.*

Mark 11:22-24

God is doing miracles all around us, and He wants us to keep believing Him for
more miracles. It's easy and human to grow numb to the miraculous things God
is doing. Little things can seem more like coincidences than works of the Almighty.
But God is at work in our days, and when we look for His miracles, we see that our
lives are full of them.

Look at today as a miracle. Where God has you, how He's answered your prayers,
the people He has put in your life, the ways He has provided for you, the gift of
salvation—all miracles! Your day isn't full of coincidences; your day is full of divine
appointments. Your day isn't full of random happenings; your day is full of heaven-
sent workings of God. Have faith today that God is working miracles all around you.
And believe for the miracles you still need. What things have you stopped praying
about because you're skeptical that God will come through? What things have you
stopped praying about because they are impossible? What things have you stopped
praying about because they feel mundane? God wants to do miracles in everything
that you feel skeptical about. He wants to do miracles in your impossible situations.
He also wants to do miracles in the things that feel mundane.

See your day through the lens of faith. Watch for God's divine intervention today.
Believe that He's working miracles in your day. And bring Him every prayer request
where you need a miracle.

**Lord, increase my faith today. Help me to see the miracles You are doing
all around me, and help me to believe You for the miracles I am praying for.**

Keep praying for your miracle.

BE STRONG AND COURAGEOUS

Only be strong and very courageous.
Joshua 1:7

Sometimes I forget to be strong and courageous. Or maybe I forget that I have God in me **making** me strong and courageous. My natural tendency is to feel inadequate and weak. Overwhelmed and fearful. That's because doing hard things is hard. Working hard is hard. Being courageous is scary! Being uncomfortable and pushed outside my comfort zone makes me want to put my slippers on, curl up with a cup of tea, and watch a good movie with my husband. It's hard to be strong and courageous sometimes.

In Joshua 1, we find God commissioning Joshua for the battles ahead. God encourages him to be strong and courageous. But God doesn't leave it at that. He encourages Joshua to be strong and courageous because He will not leave Joshua alone: "Just as I was with Moses, so I will be with you. I will not leave you or forsake you" (Joshua 1:5). Joshua can be strong and courageous because His God is with Him. God's presence is the foundation of his strength and courage.

So it is with you. God is not calling you to find your strength in yourself. He's not calling you to be courageous because you have a strong will and a can-do spirit. No, He's calling you to be strong and courageous because you have God with you. You can be strong and courageous, like Joshua, because God is with you, and His presence is the foundation of your strength and courage.

So whatever feels hard in your life right now, whatever feels impossible, whatever is making you feel inadequate, weak, overwhelmed, or fearful, remember that you don't face it alone. God is with you. Choose today to do the hard things with strength and courage. You can do it because God is with you. As you fully trust in the Lord, He will strengthen you and build your courage.

**Lord, the things in front of me today feel hard.
Help me to remember that You are with me in everything.
Help me to be strong and courageous today.**

*Go into your day with the strength of the Lord. He will make
you strong and courageous as you trust Him with your day.*

THE GOD WHO SPLIT
THE RED SEA

For we have heard how the Lord *dried up*
the water of the Red Sea before you …

Joshua 2:10

Keep in mind today that your God is the same God who split the Red Sea for the Israelites. As you bring your prayer requests to Him and walk through your day with Him, remember that He is the same God who created a highway through the sea. He pushed aside the waves to make a road through the dark waters. He held the waves in place as His people trekked through the muddy depths of the ocean floor. He made a way through the sea for His people when it seemed like there was no way.

Whatever that thing is on your heart today that feels like a Red Sea—it feels impossible, there's no way around it, and the situation is hopeless—remember that the God you pray to is the One Who make impossible things possible. He is the One Who makes highways through life's unsolvable problems. He is the One Who pushes aside obstacles and makes roads through the darkness. He is the One Who holds back the darkness and makes a way for the light. He is the One Who helps you when there is no other way.

Bring that impossible thing to God today. I know it feels insurmountable. I know it looks like there will be no way through it or around it. And I know the answer you long for may be a ways off, or it may never seem to come in the way you hope. Dear one, hold on to the hope that your God is Joshua's God. Your God is Rahab's God. Your God is Moses' God. He's the same God who split the Red Sea, and He longs for you to believe Him for your own Red Sea moments.

Lord, help me to believe You for the things that feel impossible.
Help me to trust You to make a way when it feels like there is no way.
Help me to look to You for the help that I need.

Trust God to make a way where it feels like there is no way.

GIVE GOD ROOM TO WORK

When you come to the brink of the waters of the Jordan,
you shall stand still in the Jordan.

Joshua 3:8

We are quick to fix things. We kiss boo-boos, handle emails, come to the rescue, jump in and help, and resolve the issues. We jump into hard circumstances and daily stresses and try to handle them on our own. We put out a lot of little fires throughout our day until we run out of water.

When the Israelites came to the edge of the Red Sea, God ordered them to stand still. Instead of giving them an outline of the plan, He said *stand still*. Instead of expecting them to find a way on their own, He said *stand still*. Instead of leaving them on their own, He said *stand still*. Can you imagine how they felt in that moment when their enemies were close behind them and they stood in front of an endless ocean with no place to turn? And God calmly said, *stand still*. I know that if I had been one of the Israelites, I might have raised my hand and said something like, *But God, our enemies are right behind us! We don't have much time. I'm sure I can think of something! God, what about this? God, what if we tried something else? God, are You sure You're going to help us? God, standing still seems ridiculous! God, are You there?*

But God knew what He was doing; He was setting His people up for a miracle. He was about to show them how powerful He was. He was about to do something that they could not even fathom. But He needed them to just *stand still*.

What if today, when you feel yourself jumping into situations to handle things, to solve things, and to help things along, you gave God room to work? What if you let go of trying to control and handle and resolve the situation and just simply chose to *stand still*? I know it seems a little ridiculous. I know it seems easier to put the fires out by yourself. But I believe God wants to show us His power. He wants to help us in ways we haven't thought of yet. He wants to solve problems in ways that are better for us in the long run. He wants to handle our daily stresses and protect our hearts from unnecessary wear and tear. He wants to help. Today, *stand still* in those moments when you want to jump in and be quick to fix things. Give God room to work. I know He has miracles He wants to do in your life if you will just *stand still*.

Lord, help me to stand still instead of being so quick to fix things.

When you come to the brink of hard circumstances,
stand still and let God take over.

MORE THAN YOU CAN FATHOM

So these stones shall be to the people of Israel a memorial forever.
Joshua 4:7

The Lord told Joshua to have his people collect stones that would serve as memorials of remembrance. God wanted these stones to be reminders of how God delivered His people through the Red Sea. Reminders of His miracles. Reminders of His presence.

The daily stresses of life can cause us to forget that God is present and faithful. We can grow so focused on the hard things of life that our hope slowly dissipates, and we forget God. Our God is more powerful than we can imagine. He is more loving than we can fathom. He is more present than we can comprehend. He is more real than we can feel. But sometimes we forget!

That's why we need reminders of His goodness and love, so we can continue to believe Him and trust Him through life's challenges. As we remember His goodness, His love, and His faithfulness in our lives, we find strength in the times we need hope. We find perseverance in the times we need strength. And we find joy when life gives us cause for despair.

What are some ways you can keep God's goodness, presence, and faithfulness over the course of your life in the forefront of your heart?

Lord, thank You for Your faithfulness. Help me to remember all
the ways You have answered my prayers, comforted me in hard times,
and guided me through life. Help me to remember Your faithfulness.

*Remembering God's faithfulness in the
past will give you peace about the future.*

ON HOLY GROUND

Take off your sandals from your feet,
for the place where you are standing is holy.

Joshua 5:15

You are standing on holy ground today in all of your everyday moments. God isn't just inside the church walls. He isn't just on the mission trip. He isn't just in the moments when your Bible lays open on your lap. He's in all your moments.

Could that change of perspective be the catalyst for joy? When we see the everyday moments as holy—meaning we see God in our midst in everything we do and everywhere we go and in every interaction we have with others—our daily lives gain meaning and purpose. Instead of compartmentalizing our days into spiritual and practical, meaningful and mundane, holy and ordinary, we begin to see that God is more present than we realize.

The ground you're standing on today, the chair you're sitting in, the tasks you're doing, and the conversations you're having—all of it is holy, dear sister. God is in your midst every moment. Sometimes it just takes remembering. It just takes checking in with God. It just takes being aware of His presence. Remember today that as you go through this day, there is never a moment when you are not on holy ground.

Will you always feel God's presence? No. Will you sometimes wonder if He's really there? Absolutely. Will every task feel holy and meaningful? Probably not. But when you start to consider that every part of your day is holy because God is there with you, there will be a shift in your heart. You will see purpose in the mundane, joy in the small moments, and God's grace in the everyday. All of it matters. All of it is holy ground.

Lord, shift my perspective to see that everyday moments are holy.
Help me to seek Your presence all day long.

God is here with you in this very moment, and the next moment, and the
one after that. There is not a moment of your life when God is not with you.

THE LORD IS WITH YOU

So the LORD was with Joshua.
Joshua 6:27

Pop your name in today's verse: "So the Lord was with _____ (your name here)." As you go about your day, remember this simple truth: God is with you. Sometimes we forget. We go, go, go through our day, and we forget that we have a Helper.

We have so much to remember in a day, right? Dates, appointments, to-dos, tasks, kiddos to pick up from school, meals to make, etc. Our minds are full of our lists and our hearts grow weary from keeping up with it all.

Don't forget that God is with you. Don't forget that He wants to help you even in the most miniscule tasks of the day. Just as the Lord was with Joshua, the Lord is with you. Just as the Lord helped Joshua, the Lord wants to help you.

Here are some practical ways we can remember that God is with us:

- Pray about the things on your heart that come up throughout your day. This will keep your conversation with God going throughout your day.
- Set aside the things that distract you from God and from the present moment—turn the phone off for a while. Set aside the to-do list. Turn off the email notifications. Unplug.
- Find God in the quiet moments of your day. Take some time to check in with Him when you find a reprieve in your day.

Remember that God is with you today. I know it's simplistic. I know it's a truth you already know and that you've probably heard a thousand times. But remembering that God is with you will change your perspective, increase your joy, and relieve your heart from stress. He is with you. Don't forget!

Lord, I know You are with me, but today, help me to really remember it! Help me to be aware of Your presence all day long.

Push aside the distractions and seek God wholeheartedly throughout your day.

HOLY NUDGES

The LORD said to Joshua …
Joshua 7:10

Sometimes I skim quickly through Bible verses looking for the deeper meaning, the treasures hidden beneath the surface of the printed page. But oftentimes the treasure is right before my eyes—simple and direct. Simple and true.

The Lord said to Joshua … It's easy for me to miss the miracle of such a verse. The Lord talked to Joshua. He spoke directly to him. The God of the universe articulated spoken words to him. The Lord communicated with Joshua, and the Lord wants to communicate with you and me.

May this simple verse in Joshua encourage your heart today. The Lord is speaking over your life; He's communicating with you. Although we cannot hear His holy voice in an audible way like Joshua did, through the Holy Spirit, we can sense His holy nudges of direction and love. If we intentionally listen, we will learn to hear His guiding voice and notice His holy nudges. As we keep His Word front and center in our lives, as we slow our pace and tune into His presence, and as we sit on the back porch and listen for His voice—He will speak.

Sometimes I get so focused on wanting to hear what God has to say to me that I forget the miracle. I forget that it's a miracle that God communicates with His children. It's too lofty to fully comprehend. It's too amazing to understand. And, dear friend, I know that there may be times in our lives when we feel like God is silent. We can't hear His voice. We can't sense His holy nudges. What do we do then? I think we go back to the simple truth that God speaks to His children, and we trust that He will speak to us. We keep seeking Him when He seems silent. We keep seeking Him when we're not sure what His voice sounds like or feels like. We ask Him to help us hear His voice and sense His holy nudges.

Today, may you simply let the wonder that God speaks to His children soak into your heart.

**Lord, thank You that You communicate with us. Though we
cannot see You, You speak to our hearts and nudge us with guidance
and direction every day. Help me to decipher Your voice and Your holy
nudges from the noise of the world and the thoughts in my own mind.**

*May you experience extra joy in your day as you
remember that God speaks directly to your heart.*

RISE UP

Then the Lord said to Joshua, "Do not be afraid;
do not be discouraged.... You are to rise up ..."
Joshua 8:1,7, NIV

Is there something in your life right now that feels really hard? Something that feels impossible? Something that you feel totally and absolutely inadequate to handle?

Joshua was in the midst of an intense battle with his enemies—we're talking swords and fighting and everything I would want to run away from! Perhaps one thing God wants us to know from Joshua's battles is that God is more powerful than any enemy, struggle, or obstacle in our lives.

In the midst of the danger, the Lord calls Joshua to be brave. He reminds him not to live in fear and not to let discouragement stifle his confidence in the Lord. He commissions Joshua to rise up and to be courageous in the midst of the battle.

Dear friend, do not fear or be discouraged today. God is on your side. He's got you and He's got all that concerns you. You can rise up and rise above your circumstances, knowing that God is with you in your battles. Trust that God is guiding you and speaking to you. Know that He will help you in the things that feel hard and impossible. Remind yourself that He is in control and He is powerful. God leads you daily in victory, just like He led Joshua to victory. God fiercely battles for your heart every day.

You can rise up and walk through your day in confidence and persevere through your trials and storms with God's help, trusting Him for the restoration and healing and solutions you need.

Lord, sometimes my circumstances feel too hard and too overwhelming.
Thank You that You help me through every trial, struggle, and obstacle.
Thank You that because of You, I can face my battles with confidence.
Help me to face this day with courage, knowing You are constantly by my side.

There's nothing you face today that
God will not help you through.

TALK TO HIM

*At that time Joshua spoke to the LORD.... The sun stopped in the
midst of heaven and did not hurry to set for about a whole day.
There has been no day like it before or since, when the LORD
heeded the voice of a man, for the LORD fought for Israel.*

Joshua 10:12, 13-14

The Lord wants us to talk to Him. He wants us to bring Him our worries and concerns, our anxieties and our fears. He wants us to bring Him our whole hearts. He wants us to speak to Him through prayer and talk to Him like He's our closest friend. God speaks to us, and God wants us to speak to Him. It's a two-way conversation, a back-and-forth dance of communicating with our Father.

When Joshua spoke to the Lord, the Lord acted. The Lord answered his prayer for the sun to stand still! Can you even imagine? The sun took a pause due to one man's prayer. Let me say that again: God stopped the sun because His child prayed.

God wants to answer your prayers too. He wants to put things in motion in your life and the world around you. He wants to pause circumstances that feel unstoppable. He wants to move things forward on your behalf. He wants to take action in your life. He's listening for your prayers. So today, bring Him everything. Pray about everything. Ask Him to move in your life and your circumstances. He wants to amaze you with His movement in your life, and He wants to use your bold prayers to move His kingdom purposes forward in the world around you.

**Lord, remind me what a gift it is that not only do You speak to me,
but I get to speak to You. I get to talk to You like You're my
closest friend. You hear every prayer and every word that I pray.**

Your prayers move the heart of God.

YOUR FIERCE GOD

And Joshua captured all these kings and their land at one time,
because the LORD God of Israel fought for Israel.

Joshua 10:42

What is God trying to show us through the Old Testament battles and wars? Through such pain and darkness, battles and victories? One thing we can see through it all is that our God is fierce and strong. He is mighty and powerful, and He calls us to not be afraid or discouraged, but to let him be God of our lives. The Lord God of Israel, who fought for Israel, is the same Lord God who fights for you.

Dear friend, let God fight all your battles.

- The battle for your wholeness.
- The battle for your loved ones.
- The battle for your trials.
- The battle for the dreams God has laid on your heart.
- The battle for others to know Christ.
- The battle for you to daily walk with God.
- The battle to be strong and courageous.
- The battle to be a light in a dark world.

Your God is fierce and mighty. He's strong and holy. He's good and just. He's a warrior for your heart and your life and the world. Trust Him with your battles. Be strong and courageous because He is with you and resides in you.

Lord, thank You that You are my mighty God—the very same God Who
fought for Israel. You are the same God Who helped Joshua fight and
win his battles. Remind me to look to You when I feel afraid or worried.
Fill me with strength and courage as I let You fight my battles daily.

God is fighting your battles for you, so choose
strength and courage over worry and fear.

DEPENDENT ON GOD

Listen to My voice, and do all that I command you.
Jeremiah 11:4

Joshua of the Bible was a man who was dependent on God. He looked to God for guidance, and his success was directly related to his dependence on God. Over and over again, God spoke directly to Joshua. And over and over again, Joshua listened and obeyed. Joshua took his marching orders from God. And as Joshua followed God's plan for the battles he faced, he found success.

Like Joshua, God wants us to be dependent on Him. He wants us to listen to Him and trust Him enough to obey Him when He speaks and when He gives us direction. He wants us to see the gift of His caring presence in our lives. He wants us to follow His ways. He wants to help us be successful.

Invite God to lead your day and your life. Remember that He wants to help you and He wants you to be successful at whatever lies ahead of you. When you feel stuck in your circumstances or you're unsure of your next step, check in with the Lord. Ask Him to lead you and to show you His plan.

Joshua took steps of faith even though he couldn't see the whole plan. Look to the Lord today as you go about your day, and take small steps of obedience as He leads you. Tune into His Spirit inside you, and ask Him for direction for your day. He wants to be intimately involved in your life. He wants to be the One to direct your days. He wants you to depend on Him.

Lord, help me to hear Your voice. And help me to take the steps of faith
and obedience that You are asking me to take. Help me to trust Your
ways over my own. Help me to look to You for daily guidance.

Dependence on God leads to true success.

THERE REMAINS
YET VERY MUCH

*Now Joshua was old and advanced in years, and the LORD
said to him, "You are old and advanced in years,
and there remains yet very much land to possess."*

Joshua 13:1

God is never finished working through you to bring more of His light into this world. You're never in a season where God isn't using you to impact the world for Him. Season to season He uses you in different ways, but He never stops using you. You will always be part of His plan to bring His light to the world.

Most days, you won't know that God is using you. You will wonder if you're making a difference in the world. You won't see what God sees. You won't realize that you sweetly affected someone's life, day, or heart. You won't know you made a difference in someone by the way you smiled, the word you spoke, or the kindness you showed. All you know is that you're just trying to be a woman who walks with God.

Your walk with God will shine through your life. All the time spent pursuing God, getting to know Him, praying and listening for His voice, studying His Word, and walking with Him through life's ups and downs will overflow and impact others. Your intimacy with God will shape your heart and renew your mind. Your intimacy with God will be a blessing to the world in ways that you cannot fathom.

So on those days when you feel small, remember that God is using you for His purposes, and He always will. *There remains yet very much* work for Him to do through you and very much fruit to bear in your life.

**Lord, help me to live this day with joy, knowing that You are
working in ways that I cannot see. Help me to be a light for You.**

*Your assignment today might seem insignificant.
But remember that God is using you to bring
His light to the world in ways that you cannot see.*

TRUE WHOLENESS

I wholly followed the LORD my God.
Joshua 14:8

We live in a time and culture of division, distraction, and busyness. It's tricky to keep our eyes and hearts on the Lord when so much is pulling at us and vying for our attention. There is reprieve in choosing to wholly follow the Lord like Caleb did. When we push aside the entanglements of the world and wholly focus on the Lord, our hearts are less overwhelmed, stressed, and anxious. We find a sweet simplicity when we let go of the many distractions and keep our attention on God.

On a typical morning, I know you have a million little things vying for your attention. As you wake up and get going, you do your best to choose God above it all. Those first moments of the day truly set the tone for the entire day. But there is grace for the times when you lose focus. God knows that the pull of the world on your heart is fierce. He knows the enemy is doing everything he can to divide your attention, distract you from your relationship with Jesus, and busy you with an overwhelming number of things to keep up with. God knows the struggle to keep Him first and foremost is intense. But He keeps pursuing you. He keeps drawing you out to your back porch. He keeps sending you little notes from Him throughout the day just to let you know you're unconditionally loved: a Bible verse that speaks to you, a song that brings the good kind of tears to the corners of your eyes, a sense of joy bubbling up in your heart, a person who encourages you with just the words you need.

A woman who wholly follows the Lord is a woman who, by grace and in grace, keeps her attention and focus on the Lord. And as she does, she finds peace and reprieve, freedom and deep joy, rest and relief from the many things that threaten to divide and steal her peace. The choice to wholly follow the Lord is a choice to experience more of God and more of His peace.

Today, choose to wholly follow the Lord. Not by mustering up determination and strength of your own. Not by following a checklist. Choose to follow the Lord by leaning on His strength and embracing His grace. Keep your attention on Him today not out of duty, but out of delight and love for Him. As you keep your focus on Him and redirect your focus again and again, you will experience peace and joy.

Lord, help me to wholly follow You today by keeping my eyes and heart focused on You. Help me to lean on Your Spirit to help me follow You.

To wholly follow the Lord is to experience true wholeness.

GOD IS DETAILED AND SPECIFIC

The allotment for the tribe of the people of Judah according to their clans reached southward to the boundary of Edom, to the wilderness of Zin at the farthest south.

Joshua 15:1

In Joshua 15, God lays out his specific, detailed, and orderly boundaries for the people of Judah. He even includes the specific names of cities: "And the boundary goes up to Beth-hoglah and passes along north of Beth-arabah. And the boundary goes up to the stone of Bohan the son of Reuben. And the boundary goes up to Debir from the Valley of Achor, and so northward, turning toward Gilgal, which is opposite the ascent of Adummim, which is on the south side of the valley. And the boundary passes along to the waters of En-shemesh and ends at En-rogel" (Joshua 15:6-7). The details are mind-boggling!

God's Word is filled with specifics and details that can seem irrelevant. But God included these tiny details in His holy Word to remind us that He is God, and He cares about the specifics of our lives.

God sees you and knows you intimately. He knows the ins and outs of your day. He knows about the cares of your heart and the thoughts that trickle through your mind. He knows where you've been, and He knows where He's leading you. He's working and orchestrating seemingly minute details of your life together to move you forward in His plans for you. He knows whom you need to meet, where you need to go, and what needs to come together in your life. He's in control of all of it. Just like in Scripture, God continues to weave together the details of your life in ways that you cannot see. God is specific and detailed because He is sovereign over our lives and over this world. He has the power to shift things, move things forward, and orchestrate circumstances.

So when you feel like everything about your day is simply coincidence or good luck or even bad luck, remember that God is specific and detailed. His will and His ways are good. You can trust Him to orchestrate your life because He is interested and involved in every step of your journey.

> Lord, help me to remember that my life has Your fingerprints all over it. Thank You that You are orchestrating and moving in my life and in our world in ways that are mind-boggling!

The details of your life that seem like coincidence are no coincidence to God.

PROMISED LAND

How long will you put off going in to take possession of the land,
which the LORD, the God of your fathers, has given you?

Joshua 18:3

God always has a promised land ahead for you. In every situation that you face, there is always good ahead because you always have hope. And you always have hope because you always have Jesus.

Those circumstances in your life that feel impossible—God has a promised land ahead for you. Those circumstances in your life that feel complicated—God has a promised land ahead for you. Those circumstances that feel stressful—God has a promised land ahead for you. God always has good ahead for you.

So don't give up hope. Don't stop believing for the miracle you need. Don't stop praying for the help you need. Don't stop hoping for God to come through. Don't quit when things feel hard. Don't quit when it feels like you'll never get through your trial.

God has an ultimate promised land for His children: heaven. That would have been enough. But He also wants to bless you with a promised land in your earthly life. He wants to show you how real He is and how much He cares for you. Does this mean God will answer our prayers exactly the way we hope? Not necessarily. Does this mean we will never experience hurt or pain? No. Does this mean life will be easy? Not at all. But it means that we always have hope in our circumstances. God never leaves us to fend for ourselves.

Today, in whatever circumstances feel overwhelming or impossible, know that God is at work to bring you to His promised land of hope. Hang on, dear sister. Your promised land is coming.

Lord, thank You for always giving me hope in every situation I face.
Help me to always hang on to hope and never stop trusting You with everything.

Heaven is coming. Hope is already here.

YOU CAN'T MESS UP GOD'S PLANS

You make known to me the path of life.
Psalm 16:11

Do you ever find yourself agonizing over God's will for your life? Do you find yourself trying to figure out the future or figure out your life?

Sometimes in our efforts to follow God and follow His will, we get stuck. We overanalyze. We jump ahead. Or we are paralyzed with indecision. We're afraid we are going to mess up God's plans for our lives.

Dear sister, you cannot mess up God's plan for your life. He knows your heart. He knows you're doing your best to follow Him. You don't have to overthink. You don't have to stress and agonize over every decision. You should be prayerful, but you don't have to be paralyzed with fear that you're going to make a mistake. You can focus on your relationship with God and let go of directing your own footsteps. You can lean back instead of striving to control your circumstances. You can bring your heart to God when you're unsure about something and trust Him to clarify your heart. You can bring your heart to God when something feels confusing and trust Him to sort out those feelings. You can bring your heart to God when you feel overwhelmed with trying to decipher His path for your life and trust Him to lead you.

Trying to perfectly follow God's path for your life by overanalyzing and worrying about it will only leave you feeling stuck and overwhelmed. You can take the pressure off yourself to get His will right; He won't let you get it wrong. The important thing is that you're seeking Him. Could it be that when you let go a little more and let Him be God, following His will won't feel so complicated? Let go, dear friend. You cannot mess up God's plan for your life.

**Lord, help me to stop overanalyzing Your will
and instead lean back and trust You with my life.**

Lean back and trust God. He will do the rest.

PATHWAY TO BLESSING

Blessed is the man who walks not in the counsel of the wicked, nor stands in the way of sinners, nor sits in the seat of scoffers; but his delight is in the law of the LORD, and on his law he meditates day and night. He is like a tree planted by streams of water that yields its fruit in its season, and its leaf does not wither. In all that he does, he prospers.

Psalm 1:1-3

You are blessed when you look to God for counsel and delight in and meditate on His holy Word. When you are firmly rooted in God, you are a like a strong and thriving tree planted by a stream of flowing water, which yields fruit in season and never withers. God helps you prosper in your days as you look to Him. Your strength and sense of well-being come from Him.

God wants to be your Counselor. He wants His Word to be nourishment for your sweet soul. He wants to make you strong. He is producing fruit in your life that oftentimes you can't see, but as you look to Him and steady your heart in His Word, He will bear fruit throughout the seasons of your life. In some seasons you will not see any fruit around you, but there are holy happenings taking place behind the scenes of your life that God is working on.

So today, seek God's counsel. Trust Him to produce spiritual fruit in and through you. Meditate, linger over, and think on His Word. Let it nourish your soul today, for that is your pathway to blessing. Your heart will be blessed—meaning a sense of holy joy and happiness will take over your heart—as you look to God and His Word for the counsel you need. Your relationship with the Lord is what makes you strong, rooted, and fruitful.

Lord, I look to You for all that I need. Keep me rooted in Your Word and help me to remember to look to You for the counsel I need every day.

Let God's Word nourish, strengthen, counsel, and bless you today.

COME TO THE BACK PORCH

You have given me relief when I was in distress.

Psalm 4:1

Trust God today. Trust Him with that situation or circumstance that has been gnawing at you since you took your first sip of coffee this morning. Release the situation into His capable hands and give Him time to work it out. Don't take things into your own hands and try to "fix" the situation. Turn it over to the Lord and let Him handle it.

Keep coming out to the back porch when you feel anxious about your circumstances. Let the sunshine, gentle breeze, and back porch view be a reminder that God is in control. Let it be a reminder that He is good and that He is always working on your behalf. And let it be a reminder that you do not have to do life alone. You do not have to face hard circumstances alone. You do not have to come up with the right words to say. You do not have to fix things. You have a constant Helper, Friend, and Champion for your heart. You have God, and He has you.

Today, every time a situation or circumstance in your life tries to rob you of joy—every time it seeps into your thoughts and tries to mess with your heart—every time the enemy attempts to put the blame on you and make you feel guilty …

Come to the back porch and let the One who loves you so dearly and personally give you relief from your distress. He will do it again and again—as often as you need it. Let Him be your Comforter and your Counselor, your Great Physician and your Healer, your Miracle Worker and your closest Friend. Come to the back porch again and again to find the comfort you need for this day.

Lord, every time I feel anxiety rising up in my heart today, help me to come to the back porch for a refreshing refill of Your love, grace, and comfort.

God eases your stress, encourages your heart, and frees you from the entanglements of your hard circumstances. Rest in Him today.

LEAD ME, LORD

Lead me, O LORD.
Psalm 5:8

Life runs more smoothly when we let God lead our steps, but oh how hard it is in some moments to be led. When life heats up and emotions erupt, it's hard to let God lead. When we feel hurt, when anger rises up in our hearts, and when hard circumstances sideswipe us, it's hard to let God lead. But when we do take a quick pause in our hearts, saying, Lead me, Lord, life runs more smoothly. He calms our emotions, empowers us with His Spirit, and directs us with His guiding hand. Today, take those little pauses in your heart throughout the day to say, Lead me, Lord.

Before you respond to a critical comment—Lead me, Lord.
Before you type out a harsh email—Lead me, Lord.
Before you make a big decision—Lead me, Lord.
Before you answer the phone—Lead me, Lord.
Before you try to fix a situation—Lead me, Lord.
Before you let your emotions erupt—Lead me, Lord.
Before you try to say the right words—Lead me, Lord.
Before you tackle your to-do list—Lead me, Lord.

This is what it means to depend on and lean on Jesus. He wants to bear the weight of everything you face today. He wants to help you in absolutely everything. He wants to lead you with His Holy Spirit. When you let Him lead, you will feel His joy and peace and strength. You will see Him work in your life. You will bear the fruits of His Spirit in you—love, joy, peace, patience, kindness, goodness, faithfulness, gentleness, and self-control (Galatians 5:22-23). And while life certainly will not run perfectly, things will run more smoothly because you have His help. Your life will shine for Christ, His love will radiate through you, His Spirit will touch others' lives through you, and His peace will permeate your heart.

Lord, lead me today. Thank You for Your grace when I forget to let You lead. Remind me today to reach out to You for help in everything.

*Ask the Lord to lead you in everything today,
and prepare to be delighted by His goodness.*

ADMIT YOUR WEARINESS

I am weary.

Psalm 6:6

Refreshment in the Lord often comes the moment we admit, *I am weary.* What are the things that are making you weary today? Those are the very things the Lord wants to meet you in. He wants to help. He wants to relieve your weariness. He wants to show you His power. He wants to be your strength.

Too often, we keep running. We keep trying to control our circumstances and carry our burdens. Instead of admitting we are weary, we keep striving, and that wears us out. We were never meant to strive; we were always meant to lean on the Lord.

Today, name the circumstance, the person, the situation, the conflict, or the lie you're believing that is making you weary. Imagine holding that thing in your hands and then placing it in your Father's lap. And let it go. Release your grip. Turn it over to the Lord. It's in His hands now. He will take care of it. It's not your burden anymore.

When you admit your weariness to the Lord, you will find strength again. You will have peace in your heart. You will feel free from your burdens. Keep bringing Him your weariness, and you will find the refreshment you long for. You can stop running and striving.

Lord, I am weary. You know the things that burden my heart today.
Help me to turn them over to You. Help me to set them in Your lap and
release them into Your able and powerful hands. Thank You that I do not
have to do life on my own. Refresh my heart today as I bring You my burdens.

*Striving steals your peace. Admitting your
weariness to the Lord brings refreshment.*

DAUGHTER OF THE KING

*May you establish the righteous—you who
test the minds and hearts, O righteous God!*

Psalm 7:9

God knows your inner thoughts, and He knows every nook and cranny of your heart. As you look to Him daily, you can trust Him to grow you into a strong woman of faith. He wants to establish you as His loved, secure, and joyful child. He wants to be your stable footing, your strong anchor, and your fixed foundation.

God is using the trials you are walking through to draw you closer to His heart and to shape your heart to be more like His. He allows trials so that you need Him every day. As you take refuge in Him day after day, He transforms your heart to reflect Him in a dark world. Trials can shake us and make us question God. They can rock our confidence in Him. But dear daughter of Christ, they don't have to. Just remember that you are established in Christ.

You belong to Christ, and nothing can change that. There will be trials that rock you, shake you, confuse you, and hurt you, but your footing is stable, your anchor is strong, and your foundation is fixed in Christ. You cannot be shaken because the One who resides in you is strong and mighty, and He is for you. You have help in every trial, hope in every circumstance, and power in every debacle. You do not walk through these things alone. You have Jesus in you—shielding you from the enemy, fighting for your wholeness, and loving you with unconditional love and grace. He gives you peace, hope, and joy every day. You are established, rooted, grounded, and anchored in His love, and nothing can change that.

So today, when a trial comes, remember Whom you belong to and remember that He knows you personally and intimately. His help and power are accessible to you. Simply look to Him for the help and guidance you need. Trust Him to walk you through the trial, and know that nothing can shake you because you are established as a daughter of the King.

**Lord, You know the trials I face today. Remind me
that I am Your daughter, and that You are my anchor.**

You are established in Christ.

FLOURISH IN YOUR FAITH

You have established strength because of your foes,
to still the enemy and the avenger.

Psalm 8:2

There is a real enemy who does not want you to flourish. He does not want you to know that God has gifted you to bring light to a dark world. He wants you to be deceived. He wants you to walk through your day unaware of God's sweet presence, so He works hard to convince you that you can do life on your own. The enemy loves to make you feel guilty, confused, and disoriented. He loves to make you worry and fret and question God. He wants to water down your faith and keep you from believing God's promises.

But God is able to vanquish the enemy. He is more powerful than the avenger. When you feel like the enemy is sneaking lies into your heart, look to your faithful God. He wants you to flourish. He wants you to know and believe that He has indeed gifted you to bring light to a dark world for His glory. He wants you to be aware of His sweet presence in your life. He wants you to lean on Him, and He wants to help you through life. He does not condemn, confuse, or disorient you. He wants His truth to be your guiding light. He brings your heart peace instead of unrest, hope instead of angst, and joy instead of despair. He wants to build up your faith, and He wants you to believe Him for the everyday miracles you're praying for.

Let God sort out your anxious thoughts. Let Him help you flourish and live well. Let Him restore your joy. Let God remind you that nothing is impossible with Him. God can silence the voice of the enemy in your life. Give those thoughts of defeat over to the One who is mindful of you and cares for you. Don't let the voice of the enemy be louder than God's voice in your life. You are God's daughter, and He wants you to flourish in your faith.

Lord, I want to flourish in my faith, and I long to be aware of
Your sweet presence and mighty power in my life. Silence the voice
of the enemy in my ears and help me to be attuned to Your voice.

The enemy's voice is heavy and condemning.
God's voice is hope-filled, loving, and kind.

KEEP BELIEVING, KEEP PRAYING

I will give thanks to the LORD with my whole heart;
I will recount all of Your wonderful deeds.

Psalm 9:1

We are drawn to stories with good endings and movies with positive outcomes. We root for the impossible. We cheer for the underdog and sigh with satisfaction at fairy tales. We want the happy ending. We crave for good to defeat evil. But life wears us down. Sometimes we stop hoping for the good we long for. Sometimes we stop believing for the impossible. Life makes us question good endings, positive outcomes, wins, and possibilities. We feel like the underdog, and we stop cheering for fairy-tale stories. We feel the weight of evil winning.

Dear friend, you were wired to believe for impossible things. You were wired for hope, good endings, and positive outcomes. You were created to believe. Your love for a good ending is God's fingerprint on your heart. Your love for a good fairy tale points to God's bigger story for humanity. In the end, God wins. In the end, good defeats evil. In the end, we are gifted heaven—eternity with our Maker. Who could have written a more powerful and perfect story? Who could have conceived such an outcome, such a win? Who could have come up with a story like this? God wrote the story of salvation. He made a way for us to know Him and to live with Him forever. He made a way to cross out our sins with the cross of Jesus. He made a way for us to be in a personal relationship with Him.

Life will try to get you down and make you stop believing for miracles. But Scripture is full of the miracles of Jesus, recorded so that you and I would believe in His power for the miracles we need today. Who turned water into wine? Who multiplied bread and fish to feed thousands? Who raised people from the dead? Who parted the Red Sea? Who rose on the third day and defeated death?

Don't let your circumstances make your faith dull. Don't stop hoping for the good and believing for the impossible. Don't stop cheering for the underdog and being inspired by the fairy tales. You want the happy ending for a reason—because God wins in the end. Good defeats evil. And not just in the end. Here in this earthly life, God wants to do miracles right where you are. Keep believing. Keep praying.

Lord, You have written victory, goodness, and eternity on my heart. Help me to remember Your miracles of long ago and believe and pray for the miracles I long to see today.

Don't stop believing and praying for miracles.

PRAYER IS MORE THAN WE CAN FATHOM

O LORD, You hear the desire of the afflicted; You will strengthen their heart; You will incline Your ear.

Psalm 10:17

When you pray, remember to *believe* God will answer. It's easy to get into a rut in our prayer life—or stop praying altogether—because we stop believing. Remember today that God's timing is different than ours. When it feels like the answer will never come, keep praying. When it feels like God won't come through, keep praying. When it feels silly to keep praying, keep praying!

Take a moment today to look back over your prayer life. How has God answered your prayers in the past? How has He come through? He doesn't necessarily answer in the ways we wish He would or on the timetable we would prefer, but He knows our desires, strengthens our hearts, and inclines His ear to hear our prayers. And He always does what is best.

Prayer is more than getting what we want or need. It is communicating with Him, spending time with Him, loving Him, and acknowledging our need for Him. Prayer cultivates our relationship with God. He loves for us to pray for impossible things so that He can reveal His power in our lives. When we're not sure how to pray about a particular thing, He can lead us. And when He's leading our hearts, we can know that He will answer. Prayer is a two-way street. God wants to impress His truth on our hearts. He wants to speak to us; we just have to listen.

Today, pray like you believe God. Pray like He is going to answer in a way that is far better than you can imagine, because His ways are higher than our ways. Pray like He hears you, because He does. Pray like He's your heavenly Daddy, because He is. Ask Him to guide you as you pray so that your desires align with His, then watch for His answers. And in the meantime, keep praying.

Lord, I want to believe You for impossible things. I want to pray often and fervently. Increase my faith today as I pray and as I trust You to answer.

Pray. Believe. Listen. Watch for His answers. Repeat.

HOME FOR YOUR HEART

*"I will now arise," says the LORD, "I will place
him in the safety for which he longs."*

Psalm 12:5

God is your safe place. There are trying times when perhaps you feel misunderstood or you're not sure whom you can trust. You feel like you're not enough and too much all at the same time. You feel weak and imperfect, worried and incapable.

God takes you just as you are. You don't have to be more than you are. You don't have to be better or perfect. You don't have to be enough. You're not too much. You can be weak and imperfect, you can be struggling and incapable. God loves you as you are. He understands you like no one else, and He accepts you completely. You don't have to pretend with Him, just be yourself.

So come out to the back porch today just as you are. If your feelings are hurt, know that you are loved in His presence. If you feel misunderstood, know that He understands you completely. If you feel like you messed up, know that He is ready to help. If you feel alone, know that He's with you and loves you dearly. If you feel unseen and unknown, know that He sees you and knows you completely.

He loves you, dear sister. Just as you are. And when you allow yourself to be open and honest in His presence, your relationship with Him will only grow sweeter. You can lean on Him when you need strength, when you need the right words, when you feel unsure of yourself. Your weakness allows His strength to swoop in. He is your safe haven, and He always will be.

Lord, You are my safe place, my fortress, and my refuge.
Thank You for loving me and accepting me just as I am.
Help me to be my true self in Your presence.

God is home for your heart.

NOTHING CAN SEPARATE
YOU FROM HIS LOVE

"Who shall separate us from the love of Christ? Shall tribulation,
or distress, or persecution, or famine, or nakedness, or danger, or sword? ...
No, in all these things we are more than conquerors through Him who loved us.
For I am sure that neither death nor life, nor angels nor rulers, nor things present
nor things to come, nor powers, nor height nor depth, nor anything else in all
creation, will be able to separate us from the love of God in Christ Jesus our Lord."

Romans 8:35, 37-39

Nothing can separate you from the love of Christ. Nothing.
God has never left you. Even in your hardship, your pain, and your trials, He is with you. When you can't feel Him, He's still there. When the world feels like it's crumbling around you, He's by your side. When fear bubbles up in your heart, He's there to comfort you. A loss, trial, obstacle, or disappointment can't separate you from the love of Christ. Of course, that truth doesn't wash away the ache you feel or relieve the pain. But it helps to know you're not alone in your suffering. You don't walk through this life alone.

So today, when it feels like there's no hope for your trial to resolve, when it feels like the sun just isn't coming out in your circumstances,

Remember that NOTHING can separate you from the love of Christ. Nothing.

Lord, when You feel far away or my circumstances feel impossible
and heavy, remind me that nothing can separate me from Your love.

Hold on, dear sister. The Son is coming.
He's on a mission to bring light back into your heart and your life.

September

FEEL HIS PEACE AGAIN

But I have trusted in Your steadfast love; my heart shall rejoice in Your salvation.
I will sing to the LORD, because He has dealt bountifully with me.

Psalm 13:5-6

What are the little things that are distracting you from feeling God's peace today? Oftentimes, our thoughts regarding the little details of life can deplete our peace. These distractions can be kind of sneaky and drain our emotional and mental tanks in subtle ways. We get to the end of the day and wonder why we feel so tired. So what little things are on your mind today?

To-do list items?
Things that are coming up on your calendar?
Current world or national events?
Discontentment?
A hurtful comment?
A decision that needs to be made?
Negative thoughts?

Our thoughts take up emotional, mental, and physical energy. They can wear us out if we're not careful. But they don't have to. Scripture sets our hearts right again as we set our focus back on the Lord and rehearse truths like these:

God is with me.
God restores me.
God is gracious to me.
God is my refuge.
God is good.
God gives me His peace.
God is guiding my path.

When we walk in these truths, our energy is restored. Our hearts are lighter and more free. Our hearts sing again. When we linger over the beauty of salvation and the wonder of how God has so tenderly cared for us our entire lives, our thoughts scoot back in line and we feel renewed. Notice when your thoughts are stealing your peace, and simply take a few quiet moments on your back porch to realign your thoughts.

Lord, thank You for Your goodness and steadfast love,
Your salvation and care for me. Help me to turn my thoughts back to
You today and let go of the distracting and energy-sapping thoughts.
Restore my energy and refresh my soul like only You can do.

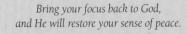

Bring your focus back to God,
and He will restore your sense of peace.

PRAY THROUGH
YOUR BURDENS

I have set the LORD always before me; because He is at my
right hand, I shall not be shaken. Therefore my heart is glad,
and my whole being rejoices; my flesh also dwells secure.

Psalm 16:8-9

You know those things on your mind that keep coming back up? Those burdens you can't quite shake? Those thoughts that keep knocking on the door of your mind? It's easy to assume that they will disappear on their own if we simply keep shrugging them off. But what if we considered those burdens as signals that we need to pray?

See your troubles as arrows pointing you to your Father's heart. View them as a green light to pray. God created us to be dependent on Him, and so every trouble, every burden, and every nagging thought is an invitation to step closer to Him, to bring Him our concerns, and to pray through them. I've found that every so often, my heart needs a good cleaning out. When my heart feels extra burdened or my mind feels cluttered with troubling thoughts, I know that I need to spend some time in prayer. And when I do take that time to pray, it's like the Lord resets my heart. He declutters my thoughts, lifts my burdens, and frees my heart from carrying such a heavy load.

I know you have burdens on your heart that you have been carrying, and I imagine they're feeling heavy today. I know you have a million thoughts coming at you at a million miles per hour. I know you long to feel settled in your soul and peaceful in your heart. Head to the back porch this week and take the time to pray through each burden. Perhaps grab a journal and a pen and list each and every concern, each and every nagging thought, and each and every thing that's weighing down your heart. Then simply pray about them. No fancy words required. No perfect prayer required. Pray through each one, and as you do, you will find that you feel a bit more steady, more joyful, and more whole. You are a daughter of Christ who dwells secure because the Lord is always with you. And you always have access to the One Who is your burden-bearer. He wants to release you from the pressure of carrying all these details of life on your own.

Lord, thank You that I can bring You each and every burden.
Help me to make time in my week to pray through my burdens.

Unload your burdens to God through prayer.

LOOK TO GOD FOR TRANSFORMATION

As for me, I shall behold Your face in righteousness;
when I awake, I shall be satisfied with Your likeness.

Psalm 17:15

Not only can you look to God for direction about your future, guidance in your decisions, strength for your everyday life, eternal salvation, and help for your circumstances, but you can also look to God to transform you into His likeness. You can look to God to transform your character—and that affects everything in your life.

When we rely on God to develop His fruits of the Spirit in us, we are set free from the prison of self-focus. We women often look to other things to bring us the peace, joy, satisfaction, and wholeness we are looking for. We look to vitamins, the right workout regimen, the right outfits, the right hairstyle, the right home, the right self-care routine, and the right number on the scale to give us the happiness we long for. None of those things will bring us the wholeness we crave. But when we look to Jesus for wholeness and satisfaction, He transforms us from the inside out. He brings forth our Mary-like qualities instead of our flesh-like qualities. He helps us maintain composure when our emotions want to erupt. He helps us to love when we want to lash out. He frees us from our own self-destructive ways. Christ offers us relief from the pursuit of vanity. Look to the Lord for freedom from self-focus and you will discover the joy of a God-focused life. Practically speaking, consider:

- Not checking the mirror as much.
- Putting the scale away.
- Taking a break from social media and picture-perfect magazines.
- Not comparing your outfit and appearance to others.

God wants to make you a light in this dark world. And as you look to Him to transform you on the inside, you will radiate with His light on the outside. You will draw others to Him with your gentle and quiet spirit. And you will enjoy the freedom of walking with and abiding in Christ.

Lord, thank You that I am free from having to transform myself.
Make me more like You. Free me from self-focus and vanity.
Make me a light for You as I look to You to transform my character.

You can rest from transforming yourself.

THE DARKNESS CANNOT TOUCH YOU

For it is You who light my lamp;
the LORD my God lightens my darkness.

Psalm 18:28

My young son was afraid to go to sleep by himself one night. He had seen an animated movie where the bad guy was a little creepy. I reminded him that though there is creepy stuff in this world, because of Jesus, the darkness cannot touch him. As I tucked him in bed, I could see the angst in his eyes as he tried to focus on reading his book. He was working so hard to be brave. He was internally fighting that creepy bad guy in his head, and I reminded him once again,

The darkness cannot touch you.

If you're in dark place today, or you're going through difficult circumstances, remember that because of Jesus, the darkness cannot touch you. Darkness cannot defeat you, destroy you, or deflate you. You always have hope because you always have Jesus. And Jesus is an expert at lighting your darkness. Talk to the Lord today about the things that feel dark in your life. Whether the darkness is coming from culture and the world or something more personal, tell God about it. There is power in saying it out loud; just like my young son admitted his fear, we can admit our fear to the Lord. When we do, we find comfort and strength. We are reminded of hope. And we are assured that we are children of the Light.

The enemy will try to make you feel like darkness is winning. But the darkness cannot touch you. The light of Jesus has overcome the darkness.

Lord, here are the things that feel dark in my life. Lighten my darkness.
Help me to remember that the darkness cannot touch me because of You.

God will always bring light to your darkness.

TRUE SECURITY

He made my feet like the feet of a deer
and set me secure on the heights.

Psalm 18:33

Who told you that you weren't enough? Who told you that you don't have what it takes? Who told you that you aren't beautiful and lovely? Who told you that you don't fit in? Who told you that you're unlovable?

Dear sister, insecurity wrecks our hearts. And I think we believe a lie that says that insecurity is our fault. That somehow we choose to be insecure. That maybe we like to feel bad about ourselves. Insecurity and doubt about who you are, how you look, and how others perceive you isn't your fault. We live in a culture that demands perfection, and perfection is an exhausting pursuit that only leads to insecurity. But you can find true security and wholeness in Jesus.

You are enough because you belong to Jesus. You are adequate and capable and strong because you belong to Jesus. You are beautiful and lovely because God made you. You belong to Him, and He loves you unconditionally. God wants to make you secure. He wants to establish you in God-confidence. He wants to help you shake off insecurities as you look to Him. Insecurity, dear daughter of Christ, is not your fault. Insecurity comes from a lifetime of believing the enemy's subtle lies.

Today, take some quiet moments on your back porch to pinpoint the lies you've been believing about yourself and the insecurities that have overtaken your heart. Bring them to the Lord and ask Him to free you from insecurity once and for all. Ask Him to set your heart secure in Him. He is your security and strong foundation. You can let go of society's pressure to be perfect because you are beautiful just as He made you, and He has beautiful plans for you. You can let go of striving to fit in with the world because you were never meant to fit in. You fit in God's heart. Let Him make you secure.

Lord, I bring You the lies I have been believing about myself.
Make me secure as I look to You instead of the world's standards.

True security is found in Christ.

LIKE A HOT CUP OF TEA

The law of the Lord is perfect, reviving the soul.
Psalm 19:7

I know you're weary from your journey at times. Perhaps you have been stuck in circumstances that do not seem like they are going to let up. You wonder if it's worth hoping for the outcome you're praying for. You're starting to feel hopeless and helpless. Your circumstances feel too heavy and too cumbersome. You're wondering where the light at the end of the tunnel is because right now, there seems to be none in sight.

Come back to God's Word today, dear sister. Grab your coffee or your steaming-hot mug of tea and come sit out on the porch with God. Crack open your Bible and remember God's promises. Let His Word soothe your heart, realign your perspective, and revive your soul. God is good. He is in control. He cares for you, and He cares for the circumstance that has your soul in knots today. He wants you to keep hoping. He wants you to keep praying. He wants you to keep believing that He will come through like He always does.

So rest your weary heart today. Let the back porch be your haven and let God's Word recharge you. You've been fighting a long battle. You've been praying and waiting and praying and waiting. You're a little weary, and that's okay, dear friend.

God is on His way. In the meantime, let His perfect Word revive your soul.

**Lord, You know I am a bit weary on some days. Soothe my heart,
realign my perspective, and revive my soul with Your perfect Word.
Help me hang on to Your precious promises today and always.**

*Drink in God's Word like a steaming-hot cup of tea.
His Word will revive your soul—He promises it will.*

YOUR HELP AND SUPPORT

May He send you help from the sanctuary and give you support from
Zion! … May He grant you your heart's desire and fulfill all your plans!

Psalm 20:2,4

God loves to help. He loves to grant you your heart's desires. So bring the desires of your heart to the Lord. Don't suppress them. Instead, pray about them. God wired you and formed you just as you are, and when you keep your gaze on Him and keep His Word before you, you can trust Him to guide the desires of your heart and then fulfill them.

Whatever desires are on your heart today, God wants to help fulfill them in your life. He wants you to lean on Him, to pray to Him, and to trust Him. He wants to help you navigate the obstacles in front of you. Yes, dear sister, even that thing in your life that feels impossible and outlandish. He wants you to remember that nothing is too difficult for Him.

So keep hoping. Keep dreaming. Be expectant for His help and His answers. Keep on believing for the things you're praying about. Tell Him what you need, what you're hoping for, what you're dreaming about. Talk to God about the desires of your heart. Surrender your plans to Him, and He will do the rest. You can lay your desires and your plans in His hands and trust Him to fulfill His good plans for your life.

Lord, thank You that I can talk to You about the desires of my heart.
Help me to keep my gaze on You and keep Your Word before me day by day.
Send me the help and support I need for the plans You have for me.

The desires of your heart can be arrows
pointing to God's plans for your life. Bring your
desires to Him and let Him direct your footsteps.

HEAR FROM GOD
IN THE QUIET

*You have given him his heart's desire and have not withheld
the request of his lips. For You meet him with rich blessings.*

Psalm 21:2-3

We are quick to feel guilty for wanting something good in our lives. We assume that our desires are selfish. We try to disconnect the desires of our hearts from the God of our hearts.

But God uses the desires of your heart to guide you into His good plans for your life. He uses your longings to draw you close to Him. And He uses them to lead you to ways you can be a blessing and a light to the world around you. So don't be so quick to dismiss those desires of your heart. There's something in them that could be a divine note from the Lord. There's something in them that could be God trying to get your attention. There's something in them that is pointing you to pray.

How do we decipher whether a desire of our heart is from God or if it's just something we've conjured up on our own? We quiet down our hearts and listen. If our hearts are crowded and the noise of the world is loud, it's difficult to hear God. He speaks in the quiet. He speaks when we get still. He speaks when we seek Him.

So take some time today to let your heart quiet down. Set aside the distractions. Shut down the phone for a while. Tune out the news. Ask the Lord to quiet your thoughts. And just listen for His still, small voice. Bring Him the desires of your heart and ask Him to speak to you about those things. Ask Him to clarify your desires. He may not answer right then; it might take some time. So take the time to listen to your Father today. He wants to give you the desires of your heart, and He wants to direct the desires of your heart. He will answer your prayers and bless you!

Lord, I give You the desires of my heart. Please shape my desires and guide me in my desires. But most of all, help me to listen for Your voice.

In the quietness and stillness, God speaks to your heart.

TURN TO THE LORD

Turn to the Lord.
Psalm 22:27

God knows that you long for answers to the prayers you lift up to Him. He knows you're waiting for Him to come through. He hears your prayers. And He knows that sometimes it's hard to believe He will come through. Remember today that the Lord is listening when you turn to Him in prayer. He is your Deliverer. He's the rescue you're looking for. And He satisfies your heart like nothing else. Turn to the Lord when your heart is thirsty or unsure or your faith feels small. It's so easy to turn to other things to numb our anxiety or to distract us from our troubles. But when we turn to the Lord, we find the peace and comfort we need.

When David turned to the Lord, he was honest with God. Earlier in Psalm 22, David cries out to God, "My God, my God, why have you forsaken me? Why are you so far from saving me, from the words of my groaning? O my God, I cry by day, but you do not answer, and by night, but I find no rest" (Psalm 22:1-2). Talk about honesty! I think it's difficult to be that honest with God. But look what happens next. David goes on, "Yet you are holy, enthroned on the praises of Israel. In you our fathers trusted; they trusted, and you delivered them. To you they cried and were rescued; in you they trusted and were not put to shame" (Psalm 22:3-5). David does a dance of honesty and praise. He's honest about his troubles. He doesn't hide his hurt, anger, or despair from God. But then he praises God. He remembers how God was faithful in the past. He pours out praise, and as he does, his spirits begin to lift. Back and forth David prays: honesty and praise, honesty and praise.

Honesty deepens our intimacy with God. When we're completely honest with Him, we are admitting our humanity; we are admitting our need for Him. And when we bring praise to our prayers, God lifts our spirits and reminds us of His love and faithfulness—that He is in control and He is good.

So today, pray honestly. It may feel difficult. It may surprise you how you really feel about some of the things in your life. But then bring in praise, remembering God's faithfulness in the past and throughout Scripture. This may take a while—it did for David. He went back and forth between honesty and praise until his emotions were settled and his faith was built up. But he kept at it, and he always found the strength to continue trusting the Lord.

Lord, help me to turn to You today. Thank You that I can
pray honest prayers, and that praise reminds me of Your
faithfulness and goodness. Strengthen my spirit as I pray.

Turn to the Lord. Pray honest prayers. Praise Him.

YOUR SHEPHERD

The LORD is my shepherd.
Psalm 23:1

One fall morning, as I sat in my car in a mall parking lot waiting for my son to finish up a rehearsal for his upcoming Christmas musical, I noticed a mom and her little toddler son playing nearby in the empty parking lot. The little boy was in fall heaven, playing with the leaves on the ground, crunching each one with his little feet. He had a stick in one hand, and he looked like he was in his own little world, perhaps fighting dragons with his stick sword or exploring a magical forest. He was busy playing, and his mom was busy keeping her eyes locked on her son.

Where he went, she went. Where he stayed, she stayed. She followed him from one pile of fall leaves to the next, keeping a close eye on him to make sure he was safe. She was like a mama duck watching out for her little duckling. She never let her little boy stray too far away from her. And when the little boy was tired from his fall adventure, he looked up to his mom and held his arms up to her. She lifted him up and swept him off into his car seat, perhaps for a good nap. His mom was his guide and protector, his shield and his shepherd.

God is your guide, protector, shield, and shepherd. Where you go, he goes. Where you stay, he stays. He's following you everywhere you go, keeping a close eye on you. He will never let you stray too far away from him. And when you're tired, weary from a hectic day or an exhausting season, He's there to swoop you up in His arms and give you rest. God is your Shepherd, always guiding, always leading, always protecting you. As you walk through this day, God is with you. He will never take His eyes off of you.

Lord, remind me that You are always with me.
Thank You that You never leave me.

GLADNESS OF HEART

*For our heart is glad in Him,
because we trust in His holy name.*

Psalm 33:21

When we are trusting in the Lord, our hearts are glad. On those days when you feel anxious and stressed, check in with Him and ask, Lord, am I trusting You? Salvation in Jesus is a onetime transaction, but trusting the Lord is an everyday decision.

It's not easy to trust the Lord when circumstances are difficult and crisis hits. We want to take control of our circumstances, and we want to get through our storms as quickly as possible. But when we remember the steadfast love of the Lord, when we remember that God is God, and when we remember that He is kind and good and faithful, we begin to trust Him again. And in the trusting, our hearts find gladness.

Trust is difficult because we are human. But trusting in the Lord leads to gladness of heart. You can trust God with that circumstance that is making you fearful today. You can trust Him with that circumstance that is making your heart anxious. You can trust Him with the thing that feels impossible. Turn those things over to the Lord. Ask the Him to help you trust Him. Remind yourself over and over again that He is trustworthy. It may take some time for your trust muscles to catch up with your words, but they will!

You can let go of controlling your circumstances and trust the Lord. You can let go of stressing and agonizing over your circumstances and trust the Lord. You can let go of your anxiety and fear and trust the Lord. He is holy, faithful, steadfast, good, and in control. When you need that sense of gladness again, trust in the Lord.

Lord, help me to trust You. Restore gladness to my heart as I trust in You.

Trust in the Lord and your heart will feel gladness.

IN DUE TIME

*Great is the LORD, Who delights
in the welfare of His servant!*
Psalm 35:27

One of my sons was performing in *The Lion King*. He was a cheetah, and his good friend was a zebra. As I was painting cheetah spots on my son's face and driving him to and from rehearsals, I found myself filled with mom worries. I was worried about each of my boys finding their place. I so desire for each of them to discover what they're good at and what they enjoy. I want them to feel a sense of belonging and a sense of joy in doing things they love, just like my little cheetah had found in the Lion King.

One fellow mom—the zebra's mom—sent me a note to remind me that God had good plans for each of my sons. She offered to pray for them to find their place and to find the things that God had gifted them to do. She shared that she had prayed those same prayers for her own children—that they would find something that suits their interests and their talents.

Her simple note reminded me to trust God with my children. She reminded me that God cares about my children even more than I do. I had let my worries and fears choke my faith. She reminded me to circle my concerns in prayer, trusting that in due time, God will reveal the path that is right for my children. She noted that waiting isn't easy. In fact, waiting is so hard! But it helps to know that God is always listening to us, always there for us, and surprises us when we least expect it.

This mom was a bright light in my moment of worry and angst. She directed me back to the Lord and reminded me that God delights in the welfare of His servants— His children! Circle your concerns in prayer. Know that He is listening. And trust that in due time, God will reveal His path for you. He will surprise you when you least expect it.

**Lord, thank You that You care so personally for me.
Thank You that I can bring every concern to You. Help me to keep
praying about my concerns, knowing that You are listening.**

*In due time, God will reveal His path for you
and your children. Trust Him and keep praying.*

ABUNDANT PEACE

But the meek shall inherit the land and
delight themselves in abundant peace.

Psalm 37:11

Abundant peace. That sounds heavenly, doesn't it? And that's exactly what God wants for you. Abundant peace. Full, deep, complete, and abundant peace. Throughout Psalm 37, David implores us,

> *Fret not yourself*
> *Trust in the Lord*
> *Delight yourself in the Lord*
> *Commit your way to the Lord*
> *Trust in Him, and He will act*
> *Be still before the Lord*

When our hearts are in a trusting stance, we can walk in abundant peace. When we incline our ear to Him, delight in Him, commit our way to Him, trust in Him, and are still before Him, we are filled with His abundant peace. Trusting in the Lord leads to great peace. It seems so simple, yet we often miss the connection. We cannot seem to stop worrying and fretting. We long for peace, but we cannot find it. Remember the words of the Psalmist when you find yourself lacking peace.

> *Fret not yourself*
> *Trust in the Lord*
> *Delight yourself in the Lord*
> *Commit your way to the Lord*
> *Trust in Him, and He will act*
> *Be still before the Lord*

God will give you abundant peace when you trust Him. I know it's not easy to trust Him sometimes. But you can trust Him. And He wants you to trust Him. He wants to pour His abundant peace into your heart today.

Lord, I long for abundant peace. Help me to trust You!

Trusting the Lord leads to abundant peace.

WAITING FOR HIS ANSWERS

But for You, O Lord, do I wait; it is You,
O Lord my God, who will answer.

Psalm 38:15

My back porch is covered in fall leaves this morning. With each gentle breeze, a few more orange and yellow leaves float to the ground. Times slows down a bit when I take time to notice the fall colors. I think God gave us seasons to let us know that time is indeed in His hands. The changes of fall, the coziness of winter, the first signs of growth in the spring, and the bright sunshine of summer remind us that God keeps things moving and that things take time.

God's answers to prayer take time. So don't give up praying. Your prayers are shifting things in the spiritual realm. Your prayers are powerful, even though at times you cannot see their fruit. Your prayers may take years to be answered—or perhaps an answer will come sooner than you think.

The waiting is difficult, but there is purpose in all your waiting. God's answers take time, just like the fall leaves take their time in changing colors and eventually falling to the ground. God's answers take time, but there is beauty along the way in the waiting.

Don't give up on God in the waiting. Your waiting is faith—faith that God will answer, that He is in control, that He is good, and that He can do impossible things. Waiting on God to answer our prayers keeps us leaning on Him. I think God likes it that way. So keep praying, and do not fret as you wait on God to answer. He will answer. He always does.

Lord, keep my faith strong as I wait on You for answers to my prayers.

Notice the beauty today in your season of waiting.

THE BLESSING OF
TRUSTING THE LORD

Blessed is the man who makes the Lord his trust.

Psalm 40:4

There is a theme of blessing and trust that runs through the Psalms. When we trust in the Lord, we are blessed. We're happy, content, glad, joyful, peaceful, and courageous. A divine contentment washes over our hearts as we turn our worries and concerns over to the Lord and trust Him.

It is good to remind ourselves to trust in the Lord because in those moments of stress, it feels so hard to trust Him. We easily forget the benefits of trusting Him. But Scripture reminds us again and again that trusting in the Lord is so good!

So keep Scripture before you today. When you feel your worries rising up, return to the back porch, grab your Bible, and read a Psalm. Consider setting a Bible on your kitchen counter to remind you to trust the Lord with your circumstances. Put a sticky note on your car's dashboard: Trust the Lord. There is blessing, joy, and peace on the other side of faith. And God wants that blessing for you. Take a look at Jesus' words in Matthew 10:29-31:

Are not two sparrows sold for a penny? And not one of them will fall to the ground apart from your Father. But even the hairs of your head are all numbered. Fear not, therefore; you are of more value than many sparrows.

God has you, and He has all of those things that are on your heart today as you cozy up on your back porch. He knows you down to the number of hairs on your head. You are always on His heart; therefore, you can trust Him with your life.

Lord, help me to remember to trust You.

Trust the Lord today. As you do, your heart will be blessed.

LET HIM BE IN CONTROL

I am God, your God.
Psalm 50:7

You can let go of driving and steering your life. It's a lot of pressure for a gal to be in control of all that. You can release the pressure and let God be fully in control. You don't have to make a great life; you can let God drive your life because He is God and He is good.

God wants to free you from the burden of control. He is the God of Moses, David, Joshua, and Mary. And He is *your* God. As you look to Him to lead your life, His divine attributes will shine through your story. You don't have to write your story—He will.

Being in control is exhausting and stressful. When everything feels like it's riding on your shoulders, you feel the stress of holding things together. But you were never meant to carry that stress. Instead, release your grip and rest.

You will feel more peace when you let God drive your life. You will feel more content when you let Him steer. You will feel more joy when you trust Him to be in control. You will feel delight when you keep in mind that God is powerful enough to care for you and your circumstances.

Your God is near and never leaves your side. Turn your cares over to Him today. Turn your life over to Him. And live free from the need to control, drive, and steer. He has an adventure for you, and He wants you to ride in the passenger seat and enjoy the journey.

**Lord, help me to release control of my life to You.
Help me to trust You and enjoy the journey.**

Trust God with your journey. Let Him be in control.

PEACE AND STILLNESS
ON THE BACK PORCH

Anxiety in a man's heart weighs him down,
but a good word makes him glad.
Proverbs 12:25

Anxiety is prevalent in our society, and you are not a failure for feeling anxious. Anxiety is likely not something you are intentionally choosing, but it's something that you can intentionally overcome. One step we can do to overcome anxiety is to first acknowledge its damage. Proverbs 12:25 states, "Anxiety in a man's heart weighs him down." Anxiety is a burden you were never meant to carry. It is a heavy and exhausting weight in your life that keeps you fearful and stuck. Anxiety overwhelms you and limits you. It is damaging and suffocating.

Not all anxiety is bad; God allows our bodies to feel anxious to keep us out of harm's way. But when anxiety is too loud in our lives, it becomes a heavy weight. The verse goes on, "but a good word makes him glad." Practically speaking, God's Word makes our hearts glad because it reminds us that He is in control. It reminds us that God loves us and cares for us. When we try to control our lives, our anxiety skyrockets. But when we release control to God, it dissipates. God doesn't want us to live in a constant state of worry and anxiety. He wants to take the full weight of anxiety off our shoulders, which in turn will ease our anxiety. There are some practical things we can do to ease our anxiety physically:

- Take some deep breaths. Deep breathing sends the message to our nervous system that everything is okay.
- Cope with anxiety in healthy ways by problem-solving with the Lord. Pinpoint what is causing your anxiety and brainstorm some things that would ease your anxiety.
- Replace lies with truth. Notice your negative thoughts and replace them with truth.
- Pray when anxiety hits. Come to the back porch again and again and find peace and stillness as you turn your anxiety over to the Lord.
- Ask for help. If your anxiety feels overwhelming and constant, don't be afraid to ask for help.

The Lord wants to ease your anxiety and give you a sense of gladness. When anxiety is blanketing you with a sense of overwhelm, it's time to bring it to the Lord.

Lord, thank You that I can bring You my anxiety
over and over again. Free me from anxiety's grip.

Anxiety loses its grip on your heart as you
release control of your life to the Lord.

PEN YOUR PRAYERS

Humble yourselves, therefore, under the mighty hand
of God so that at the proper time He may exalt you,
casting all your anxieties on Him, because He cares for you.

1 Peter 5:6-7

Our anxieties can grip our hearts and hold on tight. They would like to stick around and follow us all day long. To release our anxieties to God, we must be intentional and deliberate about giving them over to Him. They will not disappear on their own. They would rather make themselves at home in our hearts and stay put.

Today, deliberately release your anxieties to the Lord. Take a pause from the to-do list and the busy schedule and notice the anxieties swirling around in your heart. Be intentional about handing those anxieties over to the Lord. Consider praying with your pen—write your anxieties and the things that are nagging at your heart to the Lord in a journal. Penning your prayers is a great way to intentionally and deliberately turn your worries over to Him. Tell Him all that concerns you. And finally, release those cares to His care. You will find that as you write your prayers, your anxieties will loosen their grip on your heart. And you will have a record of God's faithfulness. You will see Him at work in your life as you remember how He faithfully answered your prayers and addressed your concerns.

Don't let your anxieties and cares keep swirling around in your heart. Put them on paper as a way to deliberately and intentionally release control of them to God. When you let God be in control, you will find His peace again.

Lord, thank You that I can rest from all my cares and anxieties by placing them deliberately and intentionally in Your hands. I release control of my worries today. I trust You to be in control. Thank You for Your faithfulness.

God delights in hearing from you through prayer,
and He delights in carrying your burdens.

THE GIFT OF WEAKNESS

And, apart from other things, there is the daily
pressure on me of my anxiety for all the churches.

2 Corinthians 11:28

It's good to remember that the characters of the Bible were human and flawed, imperfect and real. We get a glimpse into Paul's anxiety in 2 Corinthians. Paul, this man whom God used in such mighty ways to spread the gospel, felt the suffocating pressure of anxiety. His cares for the church caused turmoil in his heart.

What pressures are you facing today? Pressure from people? Pressure from a job? Pressure to be a good parent? Pressure to raise kids "the right way"? Pressure to look a certain way? Pressure is linked to anxiety. The pressure you are feeling is likely causing anxiety in your life. But look what Paul goes on to say:

"If I must boast, I will boast of the things that show my weakness. The God and Father of the Lord Jesus, he who is blessed forever, knows that I am not lying" (2 Corinthians 11:30-31).

Paul sees his weaknesses as a gift because they keep him dependent on the Lord. Paul realizes that the only way to face the pressure he feels is to turn to the Lord. The only way to be free from anxiety is to turn to the Lord. And without pressure and anxiety, Paul wouldn't necessarily realize his need for the Lord.

You and I are just as human and flawed, imperfect and real, as Paul was. We don't always handle the pressures of life with ease. We are naturally bogged down with anxiety. Could this be a gift in disguise? Like Paul, we can celebrate our weaknesses because they keep us dependent on the Lord. The beauty of being human is that we get to be God's daughters. We get to lean on Him. We get to trust Him. We get to look to Him. In all our imperfections, we have One Who is strong for us. He makes us strong in our weaknesses and gives us all we need to face our daily pressures and anxieties.

Lord, You know the pressures I feel in my life. You know
the anxieties that fill my mind. But You are my strong tower.
You are my fortress. Thank You that I can depend on You.

Don't be discouraged when you feel weak or when you
find yourself struggling with pressure and anxiety. Instead,
ponder the gift of being dependent on the steadfast love of Jesus.

TRADE IN PRESSURE FOR PEACE

Only let each person lead the life that the Lord has assigned to him, and to which God has called him.

1 Corinthians 7:17

There is so much pressure from the world to conform, to blend in, to do what everybody else is doing, and to follow the ways of culture. This pressure only causes more anxiety in our hearts. Paul's encouragement here in 1 Corinthians 7:17 is to focus on leading the life God has called you to and let go of the pressure to conform. Resisting that pressure to conform will alleviate some of our anxiety. Take a look at Isaiah 35:4. "Say to those who have an anxious heart, 'Be strong; fear not!'"

God understands your anxiety, and He understands the pressure to conform to the world. He's calling you to lead the life He assigned to you, and doing so will release you from the pressure from the world that wants to mold you and shape you. Society and culture would love for you to blend in and go with the flow of the current trends and values of the world. But God wants you to follow His path for your life. He's calling you to be strong and not live in fear. He wants you to see that He is here, leading and tending your life. As you look to Him, your life will look different from the world. You will be a light in the darkness. You can be yourself instead of conforming to society's mold. As you follow God and His beautiful plan for your life—which, by the way, is more beautiful than you can think, dream, or imagine (Ephesians 3:20)—you will feel more and more free from the pressure to conform to the world's ideals.

Choose to let go of fear and to trust that the Lord is tending your life. Remember that when you feel pressure and anxiety building up, you can return to the throne of grace over and over again. You can release all the pressure you've felt into the Lord's caring and loving arms. You can trade in pressure for His peace.

Lord, help me to lead the life You have assigned to me and called me to. Help me to see the beauty of being different and the gift of following You.

God is shining through your beautiful life.

GOD CAN HANDLE YOUR ANXIETY

As for me, Daniel, my spirit within me was anxious.
Daniel 7:15

Here we see another biblical hero admitting to feeling anxious. It's good to see that the great heroes of our faith felt anxious just like we do. Jesus addressed anxiety as He preached and taught His disciples:

- *"Do not be anxious about your life."* (Matthew 6:25)
- *"Do not be anxious about tomorrow, for tomorrow will be anxious for itself. Sufficient for the day is its own trouble."* (Matthew 6:34)
- *"Do not be anxious how you are to speak or what you are to say, for what you are to say will be given to you in that hour. For it is not you who speak, but the Spirit of your Father speaking through you."* (Matthew 10:19)

Because we are human, we all get anxious at times. But God provides ways to step out of anxiety and to bring our worried hearts to Him. He commands us to not be fearful, but to instead bring our anxiety to Him, depend on Him, and let Him be in control. He does not want us to be anxious about our future. Instead, He wants us to trust Him day by day.

Dear sister, God can handle your anxiety, your needs, and your life! In fact, He wants to handle it all so that you don't have to. Because He is in control, you don't have to worry about your life anymore. You can turn things over to Him. He loves you so much, and He does not want you to carry the burden of controlling your life because control only leads to more anxiety.

Help me to release control of my life and my future to You, Lord. Thank You that I can put the whole weight of my worry and anxiety on Your shoulders. Help me to let go of anxiety.

We can admit, like Daniel did, our anxious thoughts. And like Daniel, we can overcome our stresses, fears, and worries with God's help.

TRUST LEADS TO PEACE

*Which of you by being anxious can
add a single hour to his span of life?*

Luke 12:25

Anxiety is disruptive to our lives. It steals our peace, weakens our faith, and interferes with our daily lives. It is destructive. But as we all know, anxiety is tricky to let go of; it returns again and again. Remember Paul's words: "The Lord is at hand; do no not be anxious about anything, but in everything by prayer and supplication with thanksgiving let your request be made known to God. And the peace of God, which surpasses all understanding, will guard your hearts and your minds in Christ Jesus" (Philippians 4:5-7).

How can we stop worrying about all that burdens our hearts? We can pray about *everything.* As we trust God with our prayer requests, we experience His peace in return. The word *guard* in verse 7 of Philippians 4 refers to soldiers guarding a city gate from inside the gate. So picture this, dear sister. As you entrust your prayer requests to God, His peace will stand guard within the walls of your heart and mind like a soldier stands guard at a gate. Right in the midst of your trials, He will surround your heart with peace as you trust in Him. Sometimes we need to talk our hearts into trusting Him!

Lord, I trust You (even though I'm feeling anxious).

Lord, I trust You (even though my circumstances feel impossible).

Lord, I trust You (even though I cannot see what You're doing).

Keep turning your anxieties into prayers. Keep looking to God for the peace you need. Keep declaring your trust in the Lord even when there are a million reasons to stay anxious. He promises to turn your anxiety into peace as you trust in Him. God cares for you, and He wants to take on each and every burden you carry.

Lord, help me to trust You.

When you trust God, His peace guards your heart and mind.

RETURN TO HIM

You will be delivered by returning and resting;
your strength will lie in quiet confidence.

Isaiah 30:15, CSB

There is peace and joy waiting for you when you return to the Lord. Our walk with the Lord is filled with obstacles, trials, bumps, U-turns, and wandering off only to be being found again. The Lord welcomes us back every time we stray too far away. He invites us to return to Him every day and any time. Your back-porch moments are really about returning to the Lord. You return to Him for perspective, for strength, for guidance, for satisfaction, and for His company. And it is in returning to the Lord that you will find rest, strength, and confidence.

As you quiet your heart before God, entrust your worries and concerns to Him, and spend time filling your mind with His Word, His peace wells up in your heart. Returning to the Lord releases your anxiety, shifts your perspective, and comforts your soul. It reminds you that He fights for you every day. "The Lord will fight for you, and you have only to be silent" (Exodus 14:14). You can be still in His presence and entrust every care to Him. You can trust Him to fight for the things that concern your heart.

It's possible to live free from fear and anxiety by returning to God again and again. When fear and anxiety rise up in your heart, return to the Lord. Return as often as you like! He's waiting. He's there. He wants you to live with His peace and joy, His rest and strength. And when you return to Him, a quiet confidence will form in your heart. It will be a confidence that comes from knowing:

- God fights for you.
- God carries your burdens, cares, and anxieties.
- God is your rest.
- God is your peace.
- God is your strength.

Keep returning to God. Run back to Him whenever you feel fearful or anxious about *anything*. As you return to Him, allow Him to return your heart to quietness and rest.

Lord, help me to return to You again and again throughout my day.

Run to God with each and every burden,
concern, and care. Find rest in His presence.

WONDERS AND MIRACLES

Who is like You, O Lord, among the gods? Who is like You,
majestic in holiness, awesome in glorious deeds, doing wonders?

Exodus 15:11

Remembering what God has done in the Bible, throughout history, and in your own life strengthens your faith. Remembering His wonders, might, and miracles builds your faith for the wonders and miracles you are praying for in your life.

What are you praying for today? Your God is mighty and miraculous. He is full of wonders today, just as He was throughout Scripture. Keep believing Him for the miracles you are praying for, and allow His Word to stir up your faith:

- "You are the God who works wonders." (Psalm 77:14)
- "… who alone does wondrous things." (Psalm 72:18)
- "I will remember your wonders of old." (Psalm 77:11)
- "Remember the wondrous works that he has done, his miracles." (Psalm 105:5)

God is mightier than you can fathom. He is more miraculous than you can imagine. Believe for what feels impossible in your life. When you remember His wondrous ways, your worries lose their power over your heart. God is still doing miracles, and He wants to do miracles in your life. Remember today that your God, the one and only God, is miraculous and full of wonders.

Lord, help me to remember how powerful, mighty,
and miraculous You are. Help me to look to You for the miracles
I long for. Help me to believe that You still do miracles.

God can make a way when there is no way.
God can do a miracle when things feel impossible.
God can do wonders when we trust Him.

HILLS AND VALLEYS

*Every valley shall be lifted up, ... the uneven ground
shall become level, and the rough places a plain.*

Isaiah 40:4

Life is full of hills and valleys. It's good to remember that the terrain will not always look the same. There will be ups and downs, good days and bad days, smooth sailing and storms. But through it all, you have the Lord as your guide.

He will take the valleys you're walking through and lift you up out of them in due time. He will make the uneven ground level again. He will make the rough places smooth. It's what He does. He is taking you on an adventure through life, and He is with you every step of the way. God has surprises for you around every corner. He has delights and goodness placed along your path. And He never lets go when the terrain gets a little more rough—He will walk you through the rough places. He will never let go of your hand, and you will come out on the other side with jewels of wisdom and a deeper love for your ever-watching and ever-loving heavenly Father.

So when you're struggling through a valley, remember to turn to the Lord. Ask for His divine help and intervention. Pray through the valley; don't go it alone. Keep holding His hand, trusting Him to help you find your way through. Name the valleys you're walking through today and remind yourself to trust God step by step. He wants you to always have hope and peace, even through the tough terrain of life.

**Lord, help me to stay strong in the valleys of life by keeping
my hand in Yours. Help me to never lose hope. Help me to live
without fear. Help me to believe that my prayers reach Your ears.**

*God is with you through all of life's hills and valleys, ups and downs,
good days and bad days, storms and smooth sailing days.*

CHOOSE FAITH

*For we are powerless against this great horde that is coming at us.
We do not know what to do, but our eyes are on You.*

2 Chronicles 20:12

Choose faith today. When those little worries pop up in your mind, choose faith. When you catch yourself overanalyzing your future, choose faith. When you find yourself wrapped up in noise and clamor of the world, choose faith.

It's often easier to keep worrying and overanalyzing. We get stuck in patterns of overthinking, and we grow comfortable in that place. But God wants us to move to a place of faith in Him. When we focus on Him instead of lingering over our worries, and choose faith instead of fear, we feel His peace. When we feel powerless in our circumstances and stricken with worry, we can look to God.

To rejoice in the Lord always (Philippians 4:4) is a wild step of obedience to the Lord. It's saying, *Lord, I release control to You. I trust You to do what I cannot do. I trust Your will, Your ways, and Your timing.* When you submit your heart to God, you are trusting Him with everything. And that's just the place He wants you to be. Choosing to rejoice in the Lord, to look to Him in faith, sets you on the path toward contentment and peace.

Nothing can ruffle your spirit when you choose to rejoice in the Lord. Nothing can shake you when you keep your eyes on Him. Nothing can rock you when you choose to have faith. God wants you to trust Him with everything that concerns you. Rejoice in the Lord. Look to Him. Choose faith.

**Lord, may today be a fresh start in choosing to have faith in
You every day and in every circumstance. Help me to stop
carrying my own burdens and instead release each one to You.**

*Take a giant step of faith today by choosing to rejoice
in the Lord and trust Him with your circumstances.*

HIS PURSUING LOVE

I led them with cords of kindness, with the bands of love,
and I became to them as One Who eases the yoke on their jaws,
and I bent down to them and fed them.

Hosea 11:4

In Christ, you will find the wholeness you long for. Fellowship with Him makes your heart right. We can be going about our lives at a fast pace, kind of leaving God in our quiet time spot on the back porch, and at some point we realize we are exhausted from running and striving through life. We are trying to find the answers we need, to solve the problems that need solving, and to fix the things in life that need fixing.

But everything we need is found in His presence. How easily we forget that, but God offers us His grace and love again and again. And when we come running back to Him, He kindly and lovingly makes our hearts right again. He restores our wholeness, calms our angst, and blesses us with the joy of His presence. That whole time we were running and striving, He was chasing us down with His kindness and love. He is leaning in our direction and drawing us back to Him.

Dear sister, God will get your attention when you're wandering, running, or striving. Out of love, He pursues you again and again. He reminds you that His presence is where you will find everything you need.

Your moments with God on the back porch are your time to come running back to Him every day for all that you need. It's your time to meditate on His life-giving Word and to bring your focus back to Him. He will renew and refresh your perspective like nothing else.

Lord, thank You for Your pursuing love and that in Your
presence I find wholeness. You make my heart right again.

Fellowship with Jesus makes your
heart right, whole, free, and content.

STRONG, STEADY, & UNSHAKABLE

God is in the midst of her; she shall not be moved.

Psalm 46:5

God is in your midst; therefore you cannot be shaken. You cannot be moved. There will be days when your faith feels strong, your hope in God feels fully alive, and your joy is complete. And there will be days when your faith feels wobbly, your hope in Him seems strained, and your joy is drained. Through all of it, God is in your midst.

He is your anchor and fortress. He is your strong tower and guiding light. He will always hold you together. He will always direct you toward hope and light. He will always watch over your life. And He will always refresh your perspective when you feel discouraged.

Keep meeting the Lord in the quiet stillness of the back porch. Keep praying prayers of honesty. Keep trusting Him for the impossible situations you face. Keep believing that He can part waters, create streams in deserts, and perform miracles in your life. When you feel shaky at times, as we all do, remember that He is the One Who provides stability for your heart. Remember that it is He who makes you immoveable.

Jeremiah 24:7 (NIV) says, "I will give them a heart to know me, that I am the LORD. They will be my people, and I will be their God, for they will return to me with all their heart." God has given you a heart to know Him. That desire in you for more of God, more of His presence, and more of His love is a God-given desire. Your desire to be close to Him is from Him. Your desire to be strong in the face of adversity by leaning on the Lord is God-given. That desire gives you the strongest foundation for your life. You are His daughter, and He is your God. As you follow Him day by day, listening for the Spirit's whispers and looking to Him, you will be unmoved in the midst of trials.

Lord, thank You that You are always in my midst.
You never leave me—not for a second. Help me to
keep my mind and heart on You as I navigate life.

God makes you strong, steady, and unshakable.

KEEP GOING

Their hands will get too weak for the work, and it will not
be completed. But I prayed, "Now strengthen my hands."
Nehemiah 6:9, NIV

Our trials teach us to be resilient. We learn to keep going and to stand back up when we've fallen. We learn to keep praying and to keep having faith. We learn that the things we are praying for take time. And we learn to trust the process.

When you feel too weak for the assignment God has put in front of you, ask the Lord to strengthen you. When you feel too tired to do the work God has called you to do, ask Him to strengthen you. When you feel like giving up, throwing in the towel, or giving up on God, ask Him to strengthen you. Hold on, dear sister, God will get you through your storm.

Faith is this interesting dance of holding on and letting go. We hold on by continuing in our race of faith. We hold on by not giving up on God. We hold on by being faithful to keep praying and to keep trusting God. And at the same time, we let go. We let go by surrendering our lives to God. We let go by letting God be in control. We let go by trusting God's ways and His timing. It takes resiliency to do both.

You're growing stronger day by day, dear sister. As you look to God, trusting Him with everything, your faith is stretching, your hope is growing, and God's love is radiating through you. Keep walking in faith. Keep trusting in Him. Keep exercising your muscles of resiliency. Don't give up when things are hard. Look to the Lord for strength.

Lord, strengthen me for the work You've set before me,
for the race I have been called to, and for the journey of faith.

Choose to keep going. Choose to keep
trusting God. Choose to keep praying.

GOD-MOMENTS

Be quiet, for this day is holy.
Nehemiah 8:11

This day is special. It's a holy day! Every day is a special and holy day because it is a gift from the Lord. It's easy to live future-minded, but today, try to stay present right here in this day. There are jewels to be discovered, treasures that will unfold, and delights that may surprise you. Watch for God in this day.

God can use the smallest of details and the most ordinary things in big ways. He is orchestrating your life behind the scenes, setting the stage for His goodness and love to follow you. He's at work this very moment in ways that you cannot see.

He may show up in your child's smile. He may show up in a friend's words of encouragement. He may show up in the birds as they sip from a fountain. He may show up in the sunset. He may show up in a text from a loved one. He may show up in a delightful meal. He may show up in a moment of gratitude. He may show up on the back porch as you sip your tea. But He will show up in this day. He will delight you with His presence if you will get still enough to see. He will comfort you with His love and guard your heart with His peace.

Your days are filled with God moments, but noticing them requires seeing things differently. Ask the Lord to help you see Him in your day and prepare to be amazed at all the little ways He shows up.

**Lord, wake me up to Your presence in this day.
Help me to see all the little delights of my day as God moments.**

God is in all the everyday things.

October

DEAR
OVERWHELMED HEART

He raises up the needy out of affliction.
Psalm 107:41

Most times when we feel overwhelmed, we think we are doing something wrong. I know when I have felt that sense of overwhelm in my life, guilt washes over me. I feel guilty for not being able to handle what's on my plate. I'm hard on myself for not being able to keep it all together and stay strong.

But my overwhelmed heart is trying to tell me something. And here's what I want to remember the next time my heart feels overwhelmed:

Dear overwhelmed heart, you don't have to carry your burdens by yourself. Don't be hard on yourself for feeling overwhelmed. Look at it this way: God designed your body, your brain, your emotions, your heart, your nervous system, and your soul perfectly. And He created your body to tell you when it's pushing too hard. He made a way for your heart to put on emergency brakes and to tell you that you are striving too much and taking on too much. Don't see the feeling of overwhelm as a fault, see it as a gift.

Dear overwhelmed heart, your body is telling you something needs to change because you're not functioning in a way that is healthy.

- Perhaps you are taking on too much. Are there some things that you can scoot off your plate?
- Perhaps you are taking in too much. Are there some things you can turn down or tune out for a while?
- Perhaps you are moving too fast. Are there ways you can slow down your pace?

Acknowledge the things that are overwhelming you and acknowledge that you need the Lord. He will gladly lift you up and out of that sense of overwhelm. Remember that that sense of overwhelm is actually a gift that God is using to help you function in a healthier way. Dear overwhelmed heart, God will lift you up again.

❧

**Lord, I always thought that the feeling of overwhelm was my fault.
I always thought that I am too weak or inadequate to carry my burdens.
Thank You that You designed my body in a way that protects me from
stress and anxiety. Show me, Lord, what needs to change today.**

*Bring the Lord your affliction and your need.
Let Him take over from there.*

ALWAYS COVERED IN GRACE

You then, my child, be strengthened
by the grace that is in Christ Jesus.
2 Timothy 2:1

There are days when we can't seem to find one spare moment to sit down and spend time with God. The phone keeps ringing, a crisis hits, a loved one is sick, or some details of our day need our full attention. Dear friend, it's okay. You are always covered in grace. The enemy will try to make you feel guilty for not spending time with the Lord. But the Lord sees you through the lens of grace.

On those days that feel more like a sprint, you are always covered in grace. You're doing your best to juggle the things that need your attention, and you're doing great! When life heats up and your day is particularly busy, know that God is still there. He's doing your day with you. He will be there when you find some quiet moments to sit with Him, and He will be there when you don't have a free moment. Oftentimes, when life's stormier days hit, the thing we most need to know deep in our hearts is that He's there. Plain and simple, He's there.

Keep trying to be intentional about sitting down with the Lord and tuning into Him, but on those days when life is moving fast and you're just trying to keep up, remember that there is always grace. God is not keeping a log of your quiet times. He's not upset with you for your busyness. He's not disappointed that you didn't have time to pray. God knows you're doing the best you can. He knows you're trying to put Him first. He knows you're trying to be intentional about spending time with Him, and He will help you find those quiet moments. But when you simply can't find the time in your day, know that He has never stopped watching over you. He has never stopped guiding you with His Spirit. He has never stopped holding you in the palm of His hand. Wherever you go, He goes. He loves you, and there is nothing that will change that. Let His grace strengthen you today, dear one.

Lord, on the days when my circumstances are pulling at me
and I don't have a chance to sit down and spend time with You,
help me keep in mind that that doesn't change the way You
feel for me. Thank You for Your sweet grace and constant love.

On the days when you feel like you are running
at full speed and you can't seem to slow down
to tune into God, let God's grace carry you.

TAKE REFUGE IN THE LORD

Blessed are all who take refuge in Him.
Psalm 2:12

When the noise and clamor of the world feel like they're closing in on you, when the trials around you feel like they're distracting you from true peace of mind, and when your heart feels worried, dear sister, take refuge in the Lord. He is like a safe harbor, shielding you in the rain and the storm. He's your lighthouse in life's storms, your fortress in your trials, and your haven in any turmoil. How can we make the Lord our refuge?

- Take a step toward Him whenever you feel a negative emotion creeping into your heart.
- Draw near to Him when life is hard, and draw near to Him when life is good.
- Return to Him again and again throughout the course of your day.
- Let your hope and your faith rest on Him, not on other things.
- When you feel worried, run to Him.

God longs for you to take refuge in Him because He can provide the peace, comfort, rest, and joy that you need. When you take refuge in the Lord, you are blessed with His presence, His peace, and His help. Running to the Lord as your refuge blesses you, dear sister. Our human nature wants to pull away from God when we feel a negative emotion. We want to handle our problems on our own or to find refuge elsewhere. But the only true refuge is God.

Today, bring the Lord anything that is bothering your heart, mind, and soul. Run to Him as your refuge. He is your haven and fortress, your shield and comfort, your light and your hope. When the Lord is your refuge, you will feel His peace, you will trust God more, and your heart will be full of joy.

Lord, help me to run to You as my refuge always. In those moments today when I need a reprieve from life's storms, help me to choose You.

Life can be stormy, but you always have a Refuge.

LIFTER OF MY HEAD

But You, O Lord, are a shield about me, my glory, and the lifter of my head.
I cried aloud to the Lord, and He answered me from His holy hill.

Psalm 3:3-4

I know there are days when you feel alone, hurt, or stuck in hard circumstances. Perhaps you've been on the receiving end of hurtful words, and you feel slighted. Dear sister, Jesus knows how your heart hurts. You don't have to explain it all to Him, justify yourself, or hide how you feel. Jesus knows. He knows you, and He knows the heart behind the hurtful words. You can rest in Him today.

Kindness and love go farther than we can imagine. Take the hurt you feel today and let it be a reminder to make others feel loved. Let the hurt be motivation to go the extra mile, to show kindness, and to bring light to someone's day in unexpected ways.

Beware of the enemy's taunts when you feel hurt. He may whisper things like, *You're a mess. It's all your fault. You're not a good Christian.* Resist his taunts and lies. And listen to the Father's whispers, which sound more like,

- *You are loved no matter what.*
- *I can heal your hurt.*
- *You're covered in grace.*
- *There's nothing you can do to make me love you less.*
- *I will heal your broken places.*
- *You're not a mess, you're my beautiful daughter.*

God is the lifter of your head, the One Who bears your burdens, dries your tears, and comforts your heart. He is the shield around you, the One Who protects you from the enemy's lies, the harsh words of others, and the world's critiques. You can cry out to Jesus today, and He will answer you. When you feel hurt, bring that hurt to the Lord. And just be held by Him awhile. Just be held.

Lord, You know how I feel hurt and slighted. I bring that hurt to You.
Thank You that You love me unconditionally and completely.

Lay down your hurt at Jesus' feet and let Him heal your heart.

BE MY CONFIDENCE

I can do all things through Him Who strengthens me.
Philippians 4:13

Confidence is something we grow into, but many of us struggle with it for years, perhaps decades, before we fully become comfortable in our own skin My husband will often say, "You're beautiful." And I will reply, "I am?" Or if he says, "I'm so proud of you," my response is typically, "You are?" He gives me an exasperated smile as if he's thinking, "Please believe me!"

We can be so hard on ourselves. I think that somewhere along the line in our Christian walks, we may have gotten the idea that believing in ourselves is a selfish thing. Or that having confidence is not humble. In our effort to be fully dependent on God, we sacrifice our confidence in ourselves.

The world shouts the message to just believe in ourselves and we can achieve anything, but the best way to do that is to remain dependent on Christ.

If you've lost your sense of confidence, your belief in yourself, or you're struggling to feel good about who God has made you to be, hold up! Instead, daughter of Christ, hear this:

Believe in yourself. Not in the world's way of depending completely on your own strength, but believing God has empowered you to do great things. Believe you are beautiful because God designed you. Believe you can do hard things. Believe you can achieve wonderful things with God's help. Don't be so hard on yourself. Don't let your insecurities win. You can do all things through Christ who strengthens you! Believe it today!

Lord, help me to believe in myself. Be my confidence and empower me with Your Spirit to do things I never thought I could do.

When you catch yourself being hard on yourself, reverse course and remember that with Christ you can do anything.

WHEN IT'S HARD TO HEAR GOD

Speak, God. I'm … ready to listen.
1 Samuel 3:9 MSG

When God's direction in your life seems foggy, it's easy to get discouraged. You may be asking God questions like,

Lord, where do I go from here?

Lord, what do you want me to do in this situation?

Lord, where are you?

When God feels far away and it seems as if His directing presence has left us, it's easy to feel a little lost. It's like our GPS stopped working all of a sudden. We are not sure what our next steps should be. Perhaps we thought we were on the right path, and then God closes a door.

When you feel like you've lost your way a bit, pull over for a rest stop. Take some time to reorient yourself on God's path for you by taking some time to listen. Often we want God to speak as soon as we send up a prayer request. We want His answers as quickly as possible. But He has us wait because waiting inspires us to trust Him. Bring your heart to the Lord, tell Him just what is concerning you, and tell Him that you're feeling lost. He wants you to come to Him. That angst inside you is a sign that you need Him. He will use the very thing that's causing unrest in your heart to bring you closer to Him.

So bring Him your questions. Be specific. Ask Him for direction. He will guide you. It may take some time, but when you're intentional about listening and watching for His direction, He will gladly give it.

Lord, I have felt a bit lost lately, unsure of my next steps.
Give me the direction I need and help me to be patient as I wait on You.

Sometimes feeling lost is the first step to finding where God wants to lead you.

YOUR STRENGTH AND SURE FOUNDATION

Lord, be gracious to us; we long for You.
Be our strength every morning, our salvation in time of distress.
Isaiah 33:2, NIV

The Lord is your strength for this day. He knows what keeps you awake at night. He knows what things make you toss and turn in your sleep. He knows what you are anxious about and what you are anticipating. He knows what's causing stress in your heart. Call on Him in your distress. Tell Him what's going on in your heart, emotions, and thoughts.

Perhaps ask Him, *Lord, what do I need from You today?* Do you need comfort, hope, guidance, peace, rest, joy, help, or simply His company?

The Lord provides everything you need. He will be your strength every morning, and as you turn over your burdens to Him each day, your sleep will be peaceful and restful. Check in with your heart today. Instead of wishing away your emotions, notice them. And let your emotions point you to God. It's good to need Him. In fact, we were made to need God. Isaiah 33:6 (NIV) goes on to say, "He will be the sure foundation for your times, a rich store of salvation and wisdom and knowledge; the fear of the LORD is the key to this treasure."

God is your strength and your sure foundation. He's a rich store of wisdom and knowledge. He is everything you need for this day, this week, this month, this year, and eternity. He's the treasure you've been looking for. He's everything. You are His daughter, and He is forever your heavenly Daddy.

Lord, be my strength today. Help me to lean on You for all that I need.

God is your strength, your sure foundation,
and your heavenly Daddy.

THE POWER OF REST

I will make peace your governor and well-being your ruler.
Isaiah 60:17, NIV

God gave us a desire to rest, to unwind, and to relax. And He gave us a desire to feel peaceful, satisfied, joyful, and free. Are you getting enough rest? What's keeping you from resting today? What's keeping you from feeling peaceful, satisfied, joyful, and free? God wants peace to govern your heart and well-being to be the theme of your soul. Find some ways to take care of your heart and to give it the rest it truly needs.

Can you unplug today?
Can you shut down your phone?
Can you read instead of scrolling?
Can you do something good for your soul?
Can you enjoy God's creation?

Our little choices pay big dividends in our sense of rest and peace. Be careful to not let our fast-paced, technological age steal your rest and peace. Step away from the screens and dive into things that are good for your soul. Get outside, dig in the garden, freshen up the back porch, cook a good meal, take a long walk. Make space in your heart and your life for your relationship with God. Don't let emails squeeze out time with God. Don't let the phone distract you from the Word. Don't let screens keep you from seeking God.

You will find the deepest peace, satisfaction, joy, and freedom as you push the world aside and let your soul breathe. Spiritually speaking, peace is our governor because Christ is our King. Well-being is our ruler because God is in control. But if we're not careful to protect our hearts and minds from the noise and clamor of the world, we will lose that sense of peace, rest, and well-being. There is power in resting. Good rest will rejuvenate you spiritually, emotionally, physically, and mentally. So today, guard your heart, give yourself room to breathe, make space to draw close to the Lord, and truly let yourself rest.

Lord, show me how I can care for my soul today. Show me how to truly rest.

Don't underestimate the power of rest.

REMEMBER THE DREAM GOD PUT ON YOUR HEART

Yet in spite of this word you did not believe the LORD your God,
Who went before you in the way to seek you out a place to pitch your tents,
in fire by night and in the cloud by day, to show you by what way you should go.

Deuteronomy 1:32-33

Is there a dream God has put on your heart that sometimes you kind of forget about or dismiss because it's too out there, too hard, or maybe just feels silly? What's the passion, the stirring, the vision, the dream that God has put into your heart? The Israelites had a dream of a promised land, and in spite of the word God gave them that this was a dream He put in their hearts, they kind of stopped believing it. They gave up and forgot that the living God had given them a promise. They were so focused on the obstacles, the problems, and the details of daily life that they forgot the dream that had their hearts pounding with giddiness.

We get excited about a dream God has put on our hearts, and then it grows forgettable as we become entrenched in daily life. We lay aside the dream and assume it's too impossible or maybe that it was just a silly notion in our heads. Like the Israelites, we doubt. We stop believing. We question. We analyze. We lose focus. We lose excitement. But I believe God wants us to stay stirred up inside for the dream He has put in our hearts.

Today, I want to encourage you to remember the dream God has put in your heart. Let your heart dance a bit as you remember what God has done in your life and what you feel He is leading you to do. Some days it will feel like the tiniest baby steps toward your dream. Some dreams will take a decade. Others might take a lifetime. But don't give up, and don't forget that small, obscure, unseen work matters. Because when we forget about the dreams God puts in our hearts, we lose a little light in us. We lose a little pep in our step. Remember the dream God put in your heart and let it light up your heart.

Lord, remind me of the dreams You have put on my heart
and help me, in faith, to trust You with each one.

Continue to dream with God in each season of your life.

YOUR DREAMING JOURNEY

The hope of the righteous brings joy.
Proverbs 10:28

The dreams we dream don't happen instantly. Instead, God walks us step by step, day by day, and even moment by moment. It's in the process that He cultivates our relationship with Him. Dreaming, then, becomes more about our relationship with the One Who formed us than about the dream itself.

Discouragement, fatigue, weariness, and doubts can slip in and steal the joy out of the dreaming process. One second we are believing God for the impossible, expectant, full of joy, and full of life. The next, discouragement settles in. Maybe the day-to-day starts to feel a little mundane or we lose the zest we originally had for the dream God put on our hearts. We lose a little bit of our joy, and ever so subtly, ever so discreetly, our dreaming hearts stop dreaming. And a gal who stops dreaming with her God loses a bit of her joy and zeal. She needs to remember that the dreams of her heart were planted in her by her Maker.

God knows, sees, and hears every prayer request of your heart, every grace-filled goal of your heart, every desire for change, every desire to live well and in step with God, every step of surrender, every habit you want to change, and every hope for a miracle. God sees all of your heart, your life, and your daily steps of faith. And He wants you to remember that He is with you in all your dreaming steps.

**Lord, help me to look to You as I navigate
the dreams You have put in my heart.**

*God sees you and knows your dreaming heart.
Keep dreaming with Him.*

FASHIONED BY GOD

He fashions their hearts individually; He considers all their works.
Psalm 33:15, NKJV

Your heart is fashioned by God. That means you have been specially formed for precious works that only you can do. Since before you were born, He's known you and He's known about all those dreams on your heart and His plan for your life.

The word *fashions* is *yatsar* in Hebrew. This word refers to a potter's work of molding, shaping, and forming something for a specific purpose. The object is formed for a reason, and it will have a specific function. When God conceived you in His mind, He assigned you a purpose. And so when He formed you in the womb, He specifically molded, shaped, and formed you with that purpose in mind. He knew who you would become. He knew the works you would do. He knew the people you would touch. And He formed you with just the right ingredients so that you could walk in His purposes for you. He gave you the gifts, personality, experiences, and skills to walk in His beautiful purposes, which were handmade just for you.

God made you, dear sister, on purpose. You didn't wind up here on earth by accident. You aren't a body of cells just finding her way in the world. No, you were made on purpose and fashioned by God. Everything about you is from God. And when you look to Him to guide you in walking in those purposes for your life, you will come fully alive. You will be doing what you are made to do. And your life will shine for Him. Don't put too much pressure on yourself to find your God-given purpose, because He will reveal it in due time. Your whole life is full of purpose, and as you walk hand in hand with God, He will reveal more and more the purposes He has for you.

Lord, when doubts creep into my heart about who I am,
remind me that I was fashioned by You. And help me to see
others in the same light. We are all made on purpose by You.

You were molded, shaped, and formed on purpose.

YOUR UNIQUE ASSIGNMENTS

For we are His workmanship, created in Christ Jesus for good works,
which God prepared beforehand, that we should walk in them.
Ephesians 2:10

One day I was browsing in a clothing store. Fall was in the air, and I was on the hunt for a good cozy sweater or two. As I moseyed around the store, a tall, elegantly dressed gal was working behind the counter. She looked kind, and I could tell she had a sweet spirit. She was busy checking customers out at the counter, folding clothes, and greeting each person warmly. She had such joy in her work. Her work wasn't fancy. She certainly didn't get much praise for it. And I imagine not every customer was particularly friendly. But she had a strength, a joy, and a sense of purpose about her that intrigued me. She was all in for the assignment God had given her that day. And she was doing that assignment with an incredibly joyful attitude. You would have thought she was working at the finest clothing store in New York City by the way she worked. I found my items and checked out. And I went home inspired.

God can use the simplest things to inspire us. I went home that day with a desire to go about my unique assignments with joy and purpose, to go all in right where God has me—even if the scenery feels a little unseen and unnoticed by the world. I wanted to be a light by being thankful where God had me and to trust Him to guide me in the work He had for me. Perhaps God will use you today in a similar way to inspire others.

Your assignments are unique to you. God specifically formed you for them, and no one else can do the specific things God is leading you to do. He is walking you step by step toward the good works He has made just for you. You don't have to worry that you will be late to find His assignments for you or that you'll totally miss something. He's your Guide, your Navigator, and your Anchor. Don't get caught up in looking at the world too much, wishing you could do something else or be someone else. Today, go all in right where God has you. Even if it's simple and unseen, you are a light! Enjoy where God has you and trust Him to lead you to the unique assignments He has for you.

Lord, help me to embrace my calling. Help me to go all in and
do the work You have set before me with joy and purpose.

You never know how God will use you to inspire others.

DELIGHT AND SAVOR

Every good gift and every perfect gift is from above,
coming down from the Father of lights.

James 1:17

We were created to feel God's pleasure, to delight in and savor His gifts, to enjoy life and soak in God's sweet blessings. Think of the delight on a child's face when she unwraps a present. She is delighted as she discovers the gift inside, picked out just for her. In the same way, God wants to delight you every day. He wants you to enjoy unwrapping the gift of each new day. He wants you to enjoy life, and He wants you to sense His pleasure.

As we get older and we have more and more responsibilities on our plate, I think we sometimes shove delight and pleasure away a bit. Life becomes a to-do list instead of a joy, or drudgery instead of delight. But God can bring that little girl in you back to life. He can stir up your delight and passion, your joy and exuberance.

Watch the sunset, get lost in a good book, and notice the little ways God reveals Himself to you throughout your day. Laugh with your loved ones, enjoy simple pleasures, and soak in the beauty of God's creation all around you. Do the things that make you feel fully alive. Push away the distractions and emails, and dive deep into something you love. The things that you love are instilled in your heart by God. The things that bring you delight are God's ways of loving you. Take pleasure in the little beautiful things of life, and you will find your joy overflowing.

Lord, help me to see the little gifts around me as direct gifts from You.
Help me to take time to get lost in the things that bring delight and joy.

See every little gift as a gift from your Father,
a direct blessing from Him, and a heavenly delight.

HARVEST IS COMING

*Let us not become weary in doing good, for at the proper
time we will reap a harvest if we do not give up.*

Galatians 6:9, NIV

Spiritual growth, prayer, and seeing the fruit of walking with the Lord takes time. We want to see the fruit instantaneously, but God likes to work in seasons. Whether you are working toward fulfilling a dream God has laid on your heart or you're praying for a miracle, whether you're doing the hard work of raising kiddos or you're wondering if your life will show any fruit, don't let yourself become weary in doing good. Don't give up, don't give in, and don't quit. A harvest is coming.

God holds time. He keeps the stars in place. And He holds your life in His hands. He knows what He is doing in your life. He can see the good that is coming. So keep trusting Him. Keep praying. And keep walking with Him. He has a harvest for you.

Our little family recently sat on our back porch one chilly Texas fall night. We squeezed together on a wicker sofa, willing it to hold us all up. We bundled up in furry blankets and watched the flickering flames of our little fire. The moon was bright and the stars were more visible than they typically are on a Texas night. We spotted a constellation and marveled at the night sky. I pondered in my heart how the God of the stars can see us and guide us. Just like He holds the stars in place, He holds us. And just like there is a galaxy beyond what we can see in the stars, there is a harvest of good in our lives that we cannot see yet.

Dear sister, your harvest is coming. God can see the harvest that's beyond your sight. Keep doing the good before you. Keep pressing forward. God will bring a harvest in due time.

**Lord, help me to keep doing good and not grow weary.
When I grow weary, help me to remember that a harvest is coming.**

Keep walking with the Lord and trust His timing.

DON'T LET FEAR HOLD YOU BACK

Fear not, little flock, for it is your Father's
good pleasure to give you the kingdom.

Luke 12:32

A sweet friend of mine and fellow dog mom was contemplating getting a puppy. Now if you've ever owned a puppy, you know what you are signing up for when you get one. Lots of cuteness, potty training, middle-of-the night potty breaks, potential damage to furniture, shoes, socks, and the like, lots of following the puppy around to make sure it doesn't get into trouble, and did I mention lots of cuteness? It takes time, energy, and persistence to raise a pup. It would actually be a lot easier to skip all that hassle, but the rewards of a sweet family dog outweigh the few months of puppy training (usually).

My friend's husband had already picked out the puppy's name and gender, and he was in love with the idea of having a puppy. My friend was not so sure. Her life was comfortable, and she really didn't want to have this cute little puppy invade her schedule, her sleep, and her sanity! But as we talked, she told me that she was listening to a sermon about how fear holds us back in so many ways. And she realized that the real reason she was not sure she wanted to get a puppy was fear.

In what area of your life is fear holding you back? Fear keeps us from faith. It paralyzes us with indecision. In fact, even just a little bit of fear can wreak havoc on our hearts and keep us from experiencing the joy and peace that God offers. God has so much in store for you; don't let fear hold you back from experiencing it. Imagine what it would feel like to live without fear. To parent without fear. To create without fear. To dream without fear. To walk through your day without fear. When you truly set your fears down and trust God, you will find that you enjoy life more. God doesn't want you to live in fear anymore. Let today be the beginning of a fearless life.

Lord, I hand my fears over to You. Fear wears me
out and keeps me from experiencing Your best for me.
Help me to trust You and truly release my fears to You.

Hand your fears over to God. He can handle them.
Then walk in the joy of faith.

FULL OF GRACE, LOVE, AND MERCY

The LORD is gracious and merciful, slow to anger and abounding in steadfast love.
The LORD is good to all, and His mercy is over all that He has made.

Psalm 145:8-9

When we were little girls, we typically lived without fear and worry. We danced through our days with joy. We delighted in the smallest things. But as we grow older and become more aware of the broken world we live in, it's easy to lose some of that delight. We begin to see that there's a battle between good and evil going on right around us, and it dampens our joy. Perhaps we even begin to question God's goodness or feel like He is out to get us. So we strive to be good Christians, somehow hoping that if we're good enough, we will avoid pain or hardship.

Dear sister, that little girl is still in there. And she wants to burst out from your heart and live with joy, delight, and faith. She wants to believe that God is good and that He's not out to get her. She wants to delight in the little pleasures of life and be free to enjoy all the things God has set before her. She wants to be free from fear, worry, and anxiety, to live abundantly and freely.

When we live with the perception that God is somehow mean and angry and out to get us, we live in constant fear and anxiety. Let's settle this once and for all: God is gracious and merciful. He is slow to anger and abounding in steadfast love, as it says in Psalm 145. He is good to all (including you), and His mercy is over all that He has made (including you).

You can rest from worrying that God is going to hurt you or abandon you. You can rest from fearing that God is out to get you. Dear one, don't let the world and culture jade your view of who God is. He wants you to know that He is full of grace and compassion. There's nothing you can do to change His love for you. He will never stop pursuing your heart. So you can have that little girl heart again. Live free from fear, worry, and anxiety. Dance through your day with joy. Delight in the little things again. Your heavenly Daddy is taking care of you. He's watching over you, and you can trust Him.

Lord, help me to see You for who You really are.

God is good, kind, merciful, and loving.
Release your fears to Him and live free.

UNCONDITIONALLY LOVED

For the mountains may depart and the hills be removed,
but My steadfast love shall not depart from you.

Isaiah 54:10

We tend to be so hard on ourselves when we make a mistake, when we say the wrong thing, or when we feel like we have really messed up. God gave you and me a conscience, and so we feel it deeply when we've sinned. But we are unconditionally loved by God.

God doesn't expect perfection from you. He doesn't expect you to never mess up in life. He knows that you're doing your best, and He's there to embrace you the moment you trip up. He will set you back on your feet again and again.

We learn from our mistakes and from our sin. That's how we grow and change and transform. God's steadfast love will never depart from you as you walk with Him day by day. Even on the days when you feel like you've really messed up. Even on the days you just feel like a mess. Even on the days when you're caught up in worry and fear. And even on the days when you feel like you could have handled a situation differently. He's your Counselor and Helper, your Friend and your Father. He's not going anywhere.

Don't be so hard on yourself when you mess up or when you feel like a mess. Your weaknesses keep you dependent on Him. So admit your weaknesses to Him. Confess your mess-ups. But remember His grace and love toward you—don't forget that part! You are loved unconditionally and saved by grace.

Jesus, thank You that You died to set me free from my sin. Remind me
that You see me through the lens of grace, and help me to embrace
Your grace and forgiveness and not be so hard on myself when I mess up.

Jesus paved the way to grace and unconditional love.

REST, MY CHILD

And on the seventh day God finished His work that He had done,
and He rested on the seventh day from all His work that He had done.

Genesis 2:2

God rested. There are days when perhaps you just really need a nap. And God wants you to rest when you need rest. As women, if we stop for a rest we somehow feel like we've failed. We push through fatigue instead of giving in to it.

When God created this beautiful world we live in, He worked hard for six days. He used every ounce of energy and creativity to splash color across our world, to create the most interesting animals and sea creatures, and to imagine and bring forth a world too beautiful for words. When He rested on the seventh day, He showed us the value of rest. Do you wonder what God did on that rest day? I imagine He enjoyed His creation. Maybe He watched the squirrels play or the birds float through the air. Maybe He simply enjoyed the scenery. What we know for sure is that He rested from working, creating, and producing. If God rested, how much more should we?

You work so hard, day in and day out. Perhaps you don't even realize how much energy you are using in a day. The next time you feel that fatigue set in, listen to what your body is telling you. Your body is telling you that you need to rest.

Rest does wonders for our bodies, our health, our energy, our minds, and our mood. Instead of fighting through fatigue, give in. Put your feet up. Enjoy a cup of tea on your back porch and soak in the scenery. Rest from doing, working, creating, producing, and striving. Take a breather. God wants you to rest. In fact, God needs you to rest so you can do all the things He has created you to do. You will function better when you're rested.

Lord, thank You for the reminder to rest when I feel tired.
Help me to listen to my body and get the rest I need.

Good rest will refresh your heart,
strengthen your body, and lift your mood.

LIVE FREE

Live as people who are free.
1 Peter 2:16

You can live above fear, worry, and anxiety when you continuously look to the Lord. When you keep your eyes on Him and your heart in sync with His Word, you will be strengthened by His presence and His promises. Break free from fear by praying through your fears. Break free from worry by turning each one over to the Lord. Break free from anxiety by trusting God.

God has set you free from sin. He's made a way for you to be in a relationship with Him, and He is holding a place in heaven for you because of His beautiful grace. Your eternity is secure. And your life on earth is secure because He is in control. So you can let go of your fears, worries, and anxieties. You can live free. God wants you to enjoy your life and enjoy Him. He wants to use you to make an impact for His kingdom. Your faith trickles out into the world and makes a difference in people's lives. When you live free, you inspire others to do the same.

I have a sweet friend who radiates joy. When she walks into the room, her smile makes you smile. She never complains. When I ask her how she's doing and how life is going, she consistently replies, "It's so good!" She's the kind of person who always sees the good in every situation and trusts that things will work out. She doesn't seem to worry or fret about her children. Instead, she trusts the Lord through the process of raising them. It seems like her default mood is joy. She inspires me to see the glass as half full instead of half empty and to have faith instead of fear. She inspires me to rejoice instead of giving in to negativity. Her joyful spirit lifts my spirit in a second.

I know her joy comes from the Lord. I know she continuously turns her fears, worries, and anxiety over to Him. And the result is sunshine in her heart! Let God make over your heart so that joy is your default. This doesn't mean that fear, worry, and anxiety will never knock at your door, but it simply means that the joy of the Lord is your anchor. With His help, you can see the good in every situation, assume the best, believe things will work out, release worry, fear, and fretting, and trust the Lord.

**Lord, help me to live free from fear, worry, and anxiety by
trusting You and keeping Your Word close to my heart.**

Live free and trust God. Joy will become your default mood.

CHOOSE FAITH, SEEK HIM

But seek first the kingdom of God.
Matthew 6:33

When we put God first, everything else falls into place. It's easy to take matters into our own hands before we consult with God. It's easy to make decisions before we check in with Him, and only turn to God as a last resort. But when we seek Him first, peace invades our soul.

But seek first the kingdom of God. These are Jesus' words, and they are tucked into his message about choosing to not be anxious:

But if God so clothes the grass of the field, which today is alive and tomorrow is thrown into the oven, will he not much more clothe you, O you of little faith? Therefore do not be anxious, saying, "What shall we eat?" or "What shall we wear?" For the Gentiles seek after all these things, and your heavenly Father knows that you need them all. But seek first the kingdom of God and his righteousness, and all these things will be added to you. Therefore do not be anxious about tomorrow, for tomorrow will be anxious for itself. Sufficient for the day is its own trouble. (Matthew 6:30-34)

Jesus addresses anxiety quite often because He knows how anxiety can dominate our lives. He knows it's hard to let things go. He knows that anxiety is stubborn. He knows that being human makes us vulnerable to anxiety. But Jesus connects anxiety to faith and to seeking Him first. He offers a remedy to help us live free from anxiety: seek Him first.

So when anxiety hits—and it will—don't let it weaken your faith in God. Choose to trust the Lord with your circumstances. And seek God first, before you try to take matters into your own hands, before you make a decision, and before you turn to anything else. Turn to Him first and foremost. As you turn to Him and choose faith, your anxiety will ease. Take each day as it comes, choosing faith and choosing to seek God first.

**Lord, help me to choose faith and to choose
to seek You first right in the midst of anxiety.**

*You are not weak for feeling anxious. You are God's
daughter, and He is your constant source of peace.*

WALK WITH GOD

For we walk by faith, not by sight.
2 Corinthians 5:7

Our relationship with God is often referred to as our walk with God. Throughout Scripture, we see this reference to walking again and again.
- "Walk in all His ways." (Deuteronomy 10:12)
- "I will walk before the Lord." (Psalm 116:9)
- "This is the way, walk in it." (Isaiah 30:21)
- "Walk in newness of life." (Romans 6:4)
- "Walk not according to the flesh." (Romans 8:4)
- "Walk by the Spirit." (Galatians 5:16)
- "Walk as children of light." (Ephesians 5:8)
- "Walk in the light, as he is in the light." (1 John 1:7)

God uses our most basic ability—walking—to give us a picture of what it looks like to be in relationship with Him. When my husband and I take walks together, each one looks different. Some days the weather is just right—not too hot and not too cool. The sun is shining. We can talk about light things. We can laugh together, or we can not say a word. Either way, we are comfortable in each other's company. Other days, the sky is darker. There's a chill in the air, so we dress in layers. We have harder conversations. We share our worries and talk through our anxieties. We work through things. But in both instances, we walk side by side. We share our hearts and encourage each other. When one is down, the other lifts them up, and vice versa. Some days our walks are brisk, and some days we just need a stroll.

God wants to walk through life with you. Each day will look different from the one before. Some days your world will be full of sunshine. God is there for you when things are good; He wants to share in your delights and walk with you through the joys. He wants to laugh with you and share in the goodness. Other days, your circumstances will feel bleak. You'll feel more vulnerable to life's storms. On those days, He wants you to know that you can share your worries with Him. He wants you to talk through your anxieties so He can help you work through them. In both instances, He walks by your side. He wants to encourage you and lift you up every day.

Lord, thank You that You walk with me through this life. May I always see the beauty of walking with You, and may I lean on You on good days and hard days.

God is your constant walking partner.

LEANING ON HIS POWER

… being strengthened with all power, according to His glorious might …
Colossians 1:11

God gives you the power to do the things that feel impossible. You don't have to do life in your own strength. You don't have to muscle your way through your day. He wants to empower you with the same power that raised Jesus from the dead, that turned water to wine, and that healed the blind.

How do we access His power? How do we lean on His power instead of our own willpower? I think it starts when we admit our weakness and our dependence on Him. His power takes over the minute we acknowledge that we cannot do what is before us. When we admit that we don't have the strength to do our day on our own, He gives us His supernatural power.

When you feel weak, ask God to help you rely on His power. Ask Him to strengthen you. Admit that you need His help. So often His power can feel mysterious, and we easily dismiss it. We operate in our own strength and forget that He's there to help. But prayer helps us access God's power. Simple prayers admitting our need for Him open up the gateway to His strength.

When you ask for God's help, you are trusting Him and proclaiming that He is God. When you ask for His help, you are worshiping Him. So ask for His power today. Ask Him to help you do what feels impossible. Ask Him to be your muscle and strength. Ask Him to empower your life.

**Lord, I cannot keep striving through life. I need You.
Strengthen me with Your power and help me to lean on You.**

Lean on God's power in you.

DON'T BE DISCOURAGED

*For whatever was written in former days was written for
our instruction, that through endurance and through
the encouragement of the Scriptures we might have hope.*

Romans 15:4

Scripture is your source for encouragement. Some days discouragement slips into your heart. It depletes your hope and saps your joy. The enemy loves to come up with ways to discourage you and to keep you in that place of discouragement. But God is the God of endurance and encouragement (Romans 15:5). He will always renew you with His Word. There you will find page after page of encouragement for your heart and life. There you can be reminded that He comes through for His people, and your hope will be restored.

So when discouragement slips into your heart, come back to God and His Word. Drink in the comforts of Scripture. Refocus your mind on His promises. Choose to endure by choosing to look to God's Word.

The Bible was penned so that you and I can have something tangible to hold onto in our walk with God. It gives us hope, guides our lives, and shows us who God is. When we keep turning to it, we find the strength we need for the day. We find the perspective we need for our circumstances. We are reminded that God is with us in our storms and that He is good.

Keep Scripture close when you feel discouraged. Run to God. He will refresh and encourage you with His holy Word again and again.

**Lord, thank You that I can run to Your Word
for encouragement. Help me to do just that.**

God's Word is the remedy for your discouragement.

DON'T LET DOUBT WIN

Why are you troubled, and why do doubts arise in your hearts?
Luke 24:38

Maybe God has called you to a challenge, and you're starting to doubt His call. Or maybe you are walking through one of life's storms, and you are starting to doubt that He will see you through. Or maybe your season of life has been especially difficult, and you're starting to doubt that God even exists.

Jesus' disciples had doubts too. In Luke 24, after Jesus has risen from the grave, he appears to his disciples and says, "See my hands and my feet, that it is I myself. Touch me, and see. For a spirit does not have flesh and bones as you see that I have" (Luke 24:39).

They were sure they had seen a ghost! They couldn't believe what they were seeing—Jesus walking and talking to them after all He had endured on the cross. The story continues: "And when he had said this, he showed them his hands and his feet. And while they still disbelieved for joy and were marveling, he said to them, 'Have you anything here to eat?'"(Luke 24:40-41).

Even the disciples who walked, talked, and lived side by side with Jesus had trouble believing Him. Their human minds could not comprehend Him. He was otherworldly and too good to be true.

Dear sister, I know that your doubts hold you back, get in the way, and cause inner turmoil in your heart. Doubts are normal. You're human. It's difficult to comprehend God, Jesus, and the Holy Spirit. It does at times all seem too good to be true. But that's where faith comes in! The gospel is true. God is real. Eternity with God is not a fairy tale. Being in a relationship with God is not a fantasy. Your God will give you strength for your challenges. He will help you walk through life's storms. When doubts creep in, remember that the disciples struggled to have faith too. Choose to believe instead of doubt. Choose faith instead of fear. Your doubts will dissipate as you keep believing.

Lord, it's difficult when doubts creep into my heart.
Don't let my doubts win today. Help me to choose faith.
Help me to believe You're really with me.

Don't let doubts rise up in your heart. Choose to believe God.

BE COURAGEOUS

Take courage.
Acts 23:11

It takes courage to be a woman of faith and prayer, but God will supply you with the courage you need to keep walking with Him and trusting in Him. When God wants to use you—and He does—He will ask you to step out in courage. To trust Him when things feel impossible. To pray when you need a miracle. To have faith in Him when you feel discouraged. To be a light in a dark world. To love when it's hard. To show grace when you've been hurt. To be brave when you would rather not step out. To keep believing in Him when it feels lonely.

Faith takes courage. Prayer takes courage. Being in a relationship with the Living God whom you cannot touch and feel and see takes courage. You are a courageous woman!

When I was a little girl, there was an obstacle at my summer camp called the faith pole. My stomach turns upside down just thinking about it. We would gear up in a harness and helmet, attach ourselves to the rappelling rope, and begin a long climb straight up an incredibly tall telephone pole. Even though we were all strapped in with a harness, the climb was scary! We knew that if we fell, the harness would catch us, but the climb still took incredible courage. When it was my turn, I made it up the pole fairly quickly. For me, the scary part was standing on the pole and then eventually leaping off the pole and attempting to catch a trapeze. As I held on for dear life at the top, I could feel the pole ever so slightly swaying right and left. My heart beating in my chest, I carefully placed two feet on the top of the pole, held my arms out horizontally, and took a deep breath. My camp counselors cheered me on from the safety of the ground while I worked up the courage to jump. It seemed a lot easier to climb back down. And it seemed a lot more sane to cry for help. But after a lot of contemplating, I finally took the leap. The leap was the hardest part, but the feeling of floating through the air in the safety of my harness felt magical. When my feet finally hit the ground, I realized it wasn't so scary after all. And I realized that if I had backed out in fear, I never would have experienced the joy of floating through the air.

On the other side of courage, there's joy. On the other side of courage, you will realize that things weren't so bad. On the other side of courage, you will see that God was with you all along. God has adventures waiting for you. Step out in courage.

Lord, help me to be courageous.

Be a woman of courage as you trust God,
keep praying, and take leaps of faith.

LET HIM SORT OUT YOUR HEART

He put a new song in my mouth, a song of praise to our God.
Psalm 40:3

Sometimes our hearts feel tangled up inside like a knot. We can't seem to shake off our worries, but we can't quite put our finger on what is causing our angst. We try and figure ourselves out. We backtrack mentally through our day and try to pinpoint the beginning of the knot.

God knows what's bothering us, and He loves to help us sort out the knots in our hearts. As we return to Him, He slowly and perfectly sorts our hearts out. As we bring Him our honest thoughts and worries and concerns, He unravels our angst and brings us back to a place of peace.

Before the knot of stress in your heart gets too big, go to the Lord and ask Him to untangle your heart. He will show you what's going on inside you. He will mend the places that feel hurt. He will ease the stress that feels too heavy. He will direct your footsteps in your circumstances. Don't just let the knot of stress sit there in your heart. Instead, bring it to the Lord.

The back porch is the perfect spot to return to the Lord. He will comfort you with His presence, strengthen you with His Word, and bring you the rest your heart longs for. And He will put a new song in your mouth. You will go from stress to peace, angst to rest, and turmoil to joy. He loves to sort out your heart. Run to Him, and He will gladly return peace to your heart.

**Lord, help me to run to You when my heart feels tangled
up in knots. Thank You that You always sort me out.**

*God knows you so well, and He knows
just how to sort out your heart.*

RUNAWAY THOUGHTS

*Search me, O God, and know my heart! Try me and
know my thoughts! And see if there is any grievous
way in me, and lead me in the way everlasting!*

Psalm 139:23-24

Our thoughts can affect everything about our day. And if we're not careful to be aware of them, they can become runaway thoughts that take us toward discouragement and negativity. If we don't renew our minds in God daily, our thoughts will naturally go south and pick up momentum like a runaway train. If we don't check our thinking and notice what we're believing, we'll start to doubt God, doubt ourselves, and fall into the enemy's traps.

Thankfully, we can live by the Spirit. We can ask God to help us think His thoughts. We can ask Him to help us keep His Word front and center in our minds.

God knows your thoughts. He knows them all! And when you look to Him to reshape your thoughts, He gladly will.

Science shows us that our brains can create new pathways as we think new thoughts. Gratitude is an excellent way to train our brains to think good thoughts. It takes intentionality. It's easier to dwell on the negative, isn't it? But when we catch ourselves in a thinking trap and readjust our perspective with God's truth, we carve a new pathway in our brains. And the more we do that, the more our thoughts line up with God's truth. When our thoughts line up with God's truth, our mood is more positive, our hearts are more content, and our stress is lower. It's a battle to keep our thoughts from running down the track of the enemy's lies and the messages of culture. But God is in the fight with us. He wants to help us, and He wants to lead us in the way everlasting. He wants to fill our minds with His peace, love, joy, and gratitude.

Lord, show me what thoughts need to go.
Show me the lies I'm believing, and renew my mind.

God wants to completely renew your mind with His Word.

GRACE IS HERE

It is good for the heart to be strengthened by grace.
Hebrews 13:9

When we realize the wondrous and lavish grace we have been given by God, we find strength from within to walk through our days in faith. Grace is:

- Knowing we are loved despite our mistakes.
- Being saved when we were still sinners.
- Being loved unconditionally.
- God making a way to Himself through Jesus.
- Knowing God and being known by Him.
- God's power working in us.

There's nothing you can do that will change God's love and grace toward you. When you feel like you messed up, God is still there. When you feel like you said the wrong thing, God is still there. When you feel far away from God, He is still there. When you forget about God, He is still there. When you sin, God is still there. He will never leave you. He will never stop guiding your life.

You don't have to earn God's grace and favor and love—you already have it. You don't have to impress Him or perform for Him; you're enough as you are. His grace will follow you your whole life. He will be your strength from day to day. As you lean into His grace, you can walk through any obstacle and overcome any challenge. You can look to Him for direction and lean on Him for all that you need.

**Lord, thank You for Your grace and unconditional love.
May Your grace be evident in my life.**

Grace is here. And it's here to stay.

SECURE IN CHRIST

He entered once for all into the holy places,
not by means of the blood of goats and calves but by means
of His own blood, thus securing an eternal redemption.

Hebrews 9:12

Your salvation in Christ is secure. Life is full of changes and transitions, but your salvation does not change. When you sin, your salvation is secure. When you feel like you failed, your salvation is secure. When you feel unsure that God will come through in your circumstances, your salvation is secure. God's love for you never changes, and His gift of salvation stands secure.

In life, we crave security. We want certainty. That's why we don't particularly like change and transitions. Christ wants to be your total security, your rock, and your fortress. As you walk through life and experience change, He wants you to know that He will never change.

So as you walk through this day, remember that Jesus secured your salvation with His blood. And in securing your salvation, He secured your relationship with Him. It will grow deeper and sweeter through the years as you look to Him and get to know Him better and better. He will be there through all of life's changes and transitions.

Your circumstances, finances, dreams, relationships, and the world we live in will never give you the sense of security you crave. Only a relationship with Jesus can give you the true security you need. And when you trust that your eternity is secure, you are free to enjoy this life. Life is your journey of walking with the One Who secures your eternity, who lavishes you with grace, and who died so that you could live abundantly and eternally with Him.

Lord, thank You for Your gift of eternal salvation.
May I rest my security completely in You.

You are secure in Christ.

LEAN ON THE LORD

*[They] will lean on the L*ORD.
Isaiah 10:20

The people of Israel learned to lean on the Lord. They learned that when they leaned on Him, they were prosperous. They functioned better. Life worked better. Like the Israelites, when we lean and depend on God, we are prosperous, we function better, and life works better. You were not meant to do life alone. You have a Helper, and He loves it when you lean on Him.

As you step into a new day, be intentional about leaning on the Lord. Invite Him into your day from the moment you wake up. Tell Him you desire to depend on Him today. Check in with Him throughout your day. Notice His presence. Listen for His gentle, quiet whispers. When an obstacle comes across your path, lean on the Lord by bringing that obstacle to Him in prayer. Ask Him for wisdom and discernment, and He will gladly give it to you. In the quiet moments of your day, thank Him for always being by your side.

Lean on God when you're not sure what to do in a situation. Lean on Him when you need comfort. Lean on Him when you need joy. Lean on Him all the time.

When you lean on God, He shows up in your day. He's been there all along, but when you intentionally turn to Him and rely on Him, He reveals Himself to you more clearly. God is right here with you in this day, and He is inviting you to completely lean on Him.

Lord, help me to lean on You throughout my day.

Leaning on the Lord makes life work better.

A LITTLE LIGHT MAKES A BIG DIFFERENCE

The light shines in the darkness,
and the darkness has not overcome it.

John 1:5

You never know how God will use you to bring a little light to someone's path. And you never know how God will use another person to bring a little light to your path. God uses His children as light in the darkness.

The world is dark, and life can be hard at times. Our journeys and circumstances can make us weary, and we can feel alone. We never know what people are really going through when we cross their paths. We never know what hardships they face. Yet God knows it all, and He uses us as His instruments of light.

When we choose to show kindness and love, we shine the light of Christ—most times, without even realizing it. A smile, a compliment, a kind word, or a gentle act of kindness can make a bigger difference in the world than we can comprehend. A phone call can be light in someone's day. A kind note can be a light in someone's day. A smile, a text message, a voice mail, a hug—the little things make a difference. They bring light and cultivate hope.

You may meet someone today who is desperately lonely, but your kind word cheers their soul. You may meet someone today who is hurt, but your gentle smile helps them feel seen. You may meet someone today who is discouraged, but your gentle gesture gives them hope. You may not say a Bible verse or give a sermon, but your life shines for Jesus in the simple things. And God uses the simple things to bring light to the whole world.

Lord, help me to be a light in the darkness.
Live through me so that I touch others with Your love.

Just a little light goes a long way.

SANCTUARY

Praise the LORD! Praise God in His sanctuary;
praise Him in His mighty heavens!

Psalm 150:1

In the Old Testament, God's presence could only be encountered in His holy sanctuary within the Temple. And only the high priests, after going through incredibly detailed ceremonies, could enter. There was no access to the presence of God for ordinary people. But through Jesus, God made a way for us to not only enter His presence, but to have complete access to Him at any time. And not just access—relationship. We became His sanctuary. We became the place where He resides.

Let the gift of having God living in you stir up worship in your soul. Sometimes I think the Psalms were written to give us words when we have no words. They point us to God, and they remind us of the incredible gift of our relationship with Him. So today, whether you're feeling thankful or gratitude feels hard, let the words of the psalmist fill in the gaps in your heart:

Praise him for his mighty deeds; praise him according to his excellent greatness!
Praise him with trumpet sound; praise him with lute and harp!
Praise him with tambourine and dance; praise him with strings and pipe!
Praise him with sounding cymbals; praise him with loud clashing cymbals!
Let everything that has breath praise the LORD! Praise the LORD! (Psalm 150:2-6)

You have complete access to God. He lives in you. There's never a moment when you cannot connect with Him. Praise God today for making a way for you to know Him and to be known by Him so personally.

Lord, thank You for the gift of Your presence in my life.
Thank You that I have access to You. Thank You that You live in me.

Praising God changes our perspective,
restores our joy, and renews our faith in the
One Who made a way for us to know Him.

TAKE A MOMENT

Sing to the LORD with thanksgiving.
Psalm 147:7

Starting the day with thanksgiving can make a huge difference in our day. It can start us off on the right foot and set the tone for the whole day. Thanksgiving to God can help us immediately feel connected to Him. But oftentimes thanksgiving is hard, especially when we're in a difficult season.

Our natural inclination in life is to focus on what's not right in our lives. To focus on what else we need and want. To focus on prayers yet to be answered. But when we give thanks to God for what's right, what we already have, and how God has already met so many of our needs, and we focus on praising Him for the answers He *has* answered, our hearts swell with gratitude. And gratitude leads to contentment. And contentment is so good for the soul. Contentment gives us a sense of peace and well-being, and it makes us feel settled inside.

Even in a difficult season, we can grow in gratitude, praise, and thanksgiving. The more we practice thanksgiving, the easier it gets. So today, just take one baby step. Take a moment to thank God for one thing.

The breath in your lungs.

The stars in the sky.

A warm bed.

A home.

The child in your life.

The warm coffee in your mug.

The coziness of your back porch.

Just name one thing. Typically, once we get started thanking God, thanksgiving overflows. So consider starting a list of things you're grateful for, and each day, take a moment to write down one more thing. As you begin to praise God each day for the little things, your perspective will change, your heart will lighten, and your soul will find more joy.

Lord, I have so much to be thankful for, but sometimes it's hard to be thankful in hard moments. Thank You that You understand me and that You love me no matter what. Help me to take a moment each day to cultivate thanksgiving and gratitude in my life. Thank You most of all for the gift of Yourself.

Just one moment of gratitude can change your outlook.

RELEASE PERFECTION

*My grace is sufficient for you,
for My power is made perfect in weakness.*
2 Corinthians 12:9

Perfectionism can be a trap that holds us back in life. It can keep us from trying new things, from stepping out in faith, and from being who God called us to be. If we fall into the trap of thinking that something has to be perfect, we can get stuck. On top of that, perfectionism often increases our anxiety.

Our culture doesn't help. We see picture-perfect images, picture-perfect homes, and picture-perfect lives in the movies we watch, the media we take in, and the magazines we peruse. Dear friend, God isn't calling you to be perfect. You can release the quest for perfection. You can be yourself. You can look like you, you can dress like you, you can wear your hair like you, and you can decorate your home like you. You don't have to live up to society's perfect standards. You don't have to measure up to culture's measuring stick. When you release yourself from the expectation of perfection, your anxiety will decrease, and you will find the freedom to do and be all that God has created you to do and be without feeling like you have to measure up.

Perfectionism and comparison are close cousins. Oftentimes where one is, the other is. When we're comparing, we feel like we don't measure up. It's an exhausting cycle.

Jesus can set you free from all of that. If perfectionism has been holding you back from trying something new, from stepping out in faith, and from being who God is calling you to be, today is a great day to release perfectionism and walk in grace. So let yourself be imperfect. Don't let perfectionism hold you back any longer.

Lord, show me where I am aiming for perfection and putting
too much pressure on myself. Help me to release perfectionism
and comparison today and enjoy who You made me to be.

Releasing perfection releases peace.

WHEN YOU FEEL UNSURE OF YOURSELF

You were running well. Who hindered you from obeying the truth?
This persuasion is not from Him who calls you.

Galatians 5:7-8

My sons and I like to start watching Christmas movies as early as possible. So typically, the week of Thanksgiving we are beginning our Christmas movie marathon.

We watched one recently about a brother and sister duo who wound up saving Christmas. It had been a difficult year for these kiddos, and the brother in particular had lost his confidence. He was down, hurt, and struggling to find joy. He was not really in the mood for Christmas. Well, they found themselves in a real pickle when they caught Santa coming down their chimney. Their Christmas adventure included meeting the reindeer and the elves, as well as helping Santa deliver presents across the world. At the very end of the movie, Santa asked the brother to drive his sleigh through the sky and across the world! The brother looked at Santa wide-eyed and said that he couldn't drive the sleigh. Santa put his arm around the boy and reminded him that he and the boy's parents believed in him and that he needed to believe in himself. It's a classic movie moment of triumph when the boy sits up a little taller, takes the reins of the sleigh, and takes on the task in front of him. He just needed a little boost in his confidence, and off they flew into the sky, saving Christmas for children across the world.

Have you lost your confidence? You were running so well, as it says in Galatians. Who hindered you? God wants you to be confident. He believes in you. He knows you can do the things He has set before you. He has given you everything you need for success. When you feel unsure of yourself, look to Him for the courage you need and He will build up your confidence again. The enemy will try to make you feel inferior and inadequate, but God is your confidence. You are strong because of Him.

Lord, I sometimes lose my confidence. When I'm unsure of myself, help me to look to You for the confidence I need.

God believes in you. He's cheering you on!

ABBA FATHER

For you did not receive the spirit of slavery to fall back into fear,
but you have received the Spirit of adoption as sons,
by whom we cry, "Abba! Father!"

Romans 8:15

You are God's little girl. Even though you're all grown up, you will always be His little girl, in whom He delights. I know that some days you're hard on yourself. You think you should be stronger by now. You think you should be able to handle trials better. You think you should be full of joy all the time. You think you should be able to have more faith. And yet you find yourself still struggling with the same old things, stuck in the same cycles. Right when you feel like you're making progress in your spiritual life, you feel like you trip over your own two feet.

Daughter of God, remember that you're human, you're growing, and you're transforming. The process can be messy, but God sees you through the lens of grace. Your weaknesses are where He meets you with His power. Your struggles and trials are where He comforts you and strengthens you. You are adopted eternally by His grace; You are His daughter, and you always will be.

So when the road is bumpy, call out to your Abba Father. Your heavenly Daddy will always come running to help you. He will carry you through your trials and help you overcome your struggles. He will transform you day by day according to His grace. Don't be so hard on yourself; your Father sees you, loves you, and cares for you.

Lord, help me to remember that I am adopted as Your daughter.
Help me to give myself grace and not be so hard on myself.
Thank You that You are my Abba Father.

You are God's adopted daughter, always and forever.

YOUR KEEPER

The Lord is your keeper; the Lord is your shade on your right hand.
Psalm 121:5

There will be days when you feel disappointed. Maybe your prayer request seems to have been unheard, your circumstances seem too daunting, or someone has let you down. Sometimes a sense of overwhelm clashes with your day. There's much to do and not enough time in the day to get it all finished. Add in the news of the day, and your joy becomes jaded. Perhaps you're trying hard to focus on the good things the Lord is doing, but some days your burdens feel extra heavy.

Surrender these cares, disappointments, and overwhelming circumstances to the Lord. Ask Him to restore your soul today. Ask Him to show you the good that you cannot see. Give Him your burdens again and again. Surrender everything to the Lord, and you will know His peace.

God cares about the burdens on your heart, and He will use each one to draw you close to Him. Remember that He is working in all your circumstances. He hears all your prayers, and He will use every disappointment and overwhelming trial for good.

Thank Him for the good you can see even as you keep asking God to orchestrate miracles in your life. Ask Him to help you believe His truths and promises and to remember that He is your Healer and Deliverer. Keep praying, and keep bringing every burden to the Lord. He is your keeper and your shade from the heat of life.

**Lord, I hand You every disappointment, every overwhelming circumstance,
and every prayer request. Help me to trust You to watch over me,
to guide me, and to take care of the things that concern me.**

*Surrender every disappointment, every overwhelming
circumstance, and every care to the Lord.*

QUIET YOUR HEART

Today, if you hear His voice, do not harden your hearts.
Psalm 95:7-8

Pray, but also listen for God's voice. He wants to speak to you. He wants to shower you with His truth and remind you of His promises. He wants to calm your anxious heart with His loving words.

Make room to hear God's voice. While His voice is not audible to the human ear, it's discernable by the human heart. You will know it when you hear it, and the more you listen, the more you will be able to recognize His gentle whispers. It takes faith to believe when you've heard Him speak to your heart. He speaks in whispers. He doesn't shout from the rooftops; He doesn't make a big production of speaking to you. He's subtle and quiet, sometimes so soft that it's easy to dismiss Him.

So pray. Bring Him all your prayer requests and pray about everything, but don't forget to listen, too. That's harder. It takes discipline to quiet your heart and mind and to simply listen for His still, small voice. But He wants you to hear Him, and when you make time and space to listen, He will speak. Don't harden your heart when you think you heard His voice. Instead, trust that He is speaking to you.

Lord, help me to listen for Your voice.
Help me to know when it's You speaking to my heart.

Quiet your heart, pray, and listen.

BE FAITHFUL IN THE SMALL THINGS

Therefore, my beloved brothers, be steadfast,
immovable, always abounding in the work of the Lord,
knowing that in the Lord your labor is not in vain.

1 Corinthians 15:58

Be faithful in the small things. God has more planned for you than you can think, dream, or imagine. He's guiding your dreaming heart. Even if you are in a season where your dreams feel like they are on hold, trust God and know that the small things in front of you are important; they are part of the picture of how He's leading you.

Keep being faithful in the small things because the small things matter. I know you wonder sometimes how the small things will add up. Will they be worth the time and effort? Will the work you are doing now pay off one day?

Dear sister, be steadfast and immovable in your faith. Keep doing the work of the Lord. Keep walking with Him. Keep praying. Keep loving Him with all your heart. Whatever work He has put in front of you will not be in vain. The labor, the faithfulness in the small things, will produce fruit. I know you can't see it now, though you wish you could. But God can see it! He is in the small things.

Lord, help me to be steadfast and immovable in my faith.
Help me to abound in the work You have put in front of me,
knowing that it's not in vain. Thank You that You are with me
in the small things, and that You know my dreaming heart.

Your faithfulness in the small things will bear fruit.

A SIMPLE FOCUS
FOR YOUR DAY

You who seek God, let your hearts revive.

Psalm 69:32

If we don't intentionally turn our focus to the Lord, countless things will steal our focus. Emails, text messages, news, to-do lists, phone calls, appointments—so many things need our attention. But when we choose a single-minded focus for the day—the Lord—all of that other stuff will seem less important and less appealing.

Don't let surface distractions steal your focus on God. Be deliberate about choosing daily to focus on Him. That focus will simplify your day because it will prioritize your relationship with Him above everything else.

God is personal, and He wants to help you throughout your whole day. Ask Him to help you keep a single-minded focus on Him today. From there, He will help you walk through your day in His rhythms of grace. He will guide your day, direct your heart, and flood your mind with peace. Put Him first from the moment you wake up, and then again when your trials and circumstances call for your attention—when the emails and the phone ding and ping for you, when the to-do list is calling and the many things in a day pull at you. As you refocus your mind, you will sense His presence with you. Ask for His help in all the things before you. He will help you handle your day with grace. He will root your heart in His peace.

Lord, there is so much to do in a day!
Help me to keep a simple focus on You today.
Thank You that You are so personal and loving.
Thank You for caring about my day-to-day life.

The details of your everyday life matter to God.
He wants to be Your main focus, and when He is, you will have
supernatural energy for all the things that need your attention.

PREACH TO YOUR HEART

For truly, I say to you, if you have faith like a grain of mustard seed,
you will say to this mountain, "Move from here to there,"
and it will move, and nothing will be impossible for you.

Matthew 17:20

When the mountain in front of you seems too big, pray about it. Jesus said we just need a little faith. There is no mountain—no obstacle, impossibility, trial, circumstance, or prayer request—that is too big for God to move. The trouble is, we have a hard time believing Him. We have a hard time having faith when confronted by the mountain in front of us. But Jesus says you just need to have a tiny grain of faith.

We recently went through a difficult season as a family. I remember feeling like our circumstances were completely immovable. The mountain in front of us was too looming, too large, and impossible to move. It was hard to have faith that God would come through. In those days, I had to preach God's truth to my own heart and pray for faith:

Jesus, help me to believe.
Help me to choose faith.
Help me to keep praying.
Lord, You can heal.
You can restore.
I surrender to You.
You can do all things.
Nothing is too hard for you.

Over and over again, I had to remind myself to choose faith, to believe, to keep praying, and to trust God for a miracle. It took time for my heart to catch up with my faith, but over time, I began to believe that God would come through like He always does. And He did. And He will do the same for you. Preach to your own heart if you have to. Write down the truths you know that you need to believe. It may take some time for your heart to catch up with your mind, but it will. Over time, your faith will grow. All it takes is a mustard seed of faith, and your mountain will move.

Lord, increase my faith that You can move the mountain that is in front of me.

God will come through—He always does.

TENDER STRENGTHENING

For the sake of Christ, then, I am content with weaknesses,
insults, hardships, persecutions, and calamities.
For when I am weak, then I am strong.

2 Corinthians 12:10

Oftentimes, it's in our weakest moments that God speaks the loudest. When we feel rejected or hurt, overwhelmed or fatigued, and we're honest about where we are, God meets us. When we come to the end of ourselves, God picks us up and holds us close. When we admit we're weary, He comes to us with His strength.

What Paul says here in 1 Corinthians is a big statement. We can read it and wonder if he was some kind of super Christian. How could he be content with weaknesses, insults, hardships, persecutions, and calamities? I imagine that over time Paul learned that those were the moments when he had to lean on the Lord the most, and as He deeply and desperately leaned on the Lord, His fellowship with the Lord must have grown sweeter.

I know you can't see it right now, but your weakest moments are your strongest moments. In the difficult days, God is speaking. He's strengthening you. He's loving you. He's making you stronger for the next trial. It's in your weak moments that you will draw closer to Him. You will lean on Him like you never have before. And you will come out of those weak moments stronger in your faith.

Lord, thank You that You are there in my weak moments.
Help me to see those moments as opportunities to
draw closer to You and to hear directly from You.

A tender strengthening happens in your weak moments.
The Lord is holding you and loving you,
letting you know that He never left you.

DIGITAL DETOX

But You, O Lord, do not be far off!
O You my help, come quickly to my aid!
Psalm 22:19

Be sure to take some time each day for a digital detox. Set the phone aside for a while so your mind and heart can fully and truly rest. You will hear God's still, small voice better. You will have space to think and process, rest and recharge. You will be refreshed!

Our phones are a blessing, but they can sometimes overwhelm our minds and hearts. Don't get lured in too much by the phone. Be intentional about using it wisely and not letting it control your day. I notice that when I check my phone first thing in the morning, it sets me off to a rocky start. Suddenly, after reading through my email, it feels absolutely urgent that I pay for this thing or run this errand or fill out that form—and it's only 7 a.m.! The urgency steals my morning peace and makes me feel frantic.

Sometimes the only interesting thing in my purse while I sit in the carpool line to pick up my kids from school is my phone. But scrolling through it just leaves me feeling exhausted, and I would be better off using that time to pray or talk to a friend.

The phone really does deplete us at times, so we must be diligent about taking breaks from it. Take a break from the phone today and fill that time with seeking God. Ask Him to replace your phone time with His presence and to meet you in the quiet. He will gladly meet you in the quietness.

Lord, help me to seek You first today. Give me the strength
to set the phone aside and to wade deeply into Your presence.

Meet God in the quiet of your day and
you will feel His peace in a deeper way.

THE BEST IS YET TO COME

Why are you cast down, O my soul, and why
are you in turmoil within me? Hope in God;
for I shall again praise Him, my salvation and my God.

Psalm 43:5

No matter your age, your season, or your stage of life, the best really is yet to come. Recently I was feeling a little sad about my three sons growing up so quickly before my eyes. It all seemed to be happening faster than I could soak it in. I felt a little twinge of ache in my heart for time to slow down. A sweet friend who has grown children listened as I expressed my concerns, and she encouraged me that the best really is yet to come. She told me about how she treasures her relationships with her adult children and encouraged me that life got even sweeter as they grew. Her words of encouragement were just what I needed to hear.

The best really is yet to come. God doesn't stop pursuing you and loving you. He always has good things and sweet surprises around the corner. Don't think that the best is behind you. No, God still has more for you. Eternally speaking, the very best is yet to come! Heaven will be more than we can imagine. But also, the best is yet to come in your life. I know it's hard to imagine or fathom, but let your hopes rise up. God has sweet surprises in store for you. Your relationship with Him will only grow sweeter and stronger as you journey along through life with Him.

Remember, too, that you never know the power of an encouraging word for a friend, family member, or stranger. The smallest encouragement can change someone's day. So today, be encouraged that the best really is yet to come. And pass on words of encouragement to a friend. You never know how you might change someone's day.

Lord, give me fresh hope and perspective as I walk with You each day.
Help me to trust You with the seasons of my life,
knowing that the best is yet to come.

Your relationship with God will grow
sweeter and sweeter over the years.

PRAY LIKE DAVID

O God, hear my prayer; give ear to the words of my mouth.
Psalm 54:2

When you feel uncertain about the steps you should take or unsure if you're hearing God correctly, lean in closer to Him. He will gladly guide you as you listen in. He will help you. You can trust Him to sort out your uncertainties.

David prayed to the Lord in good times and in hard times. He went back and forth between prayer and praise. He knew that there was never a time or a circumstance when he didn't need God. And when he struggled to believe God would come through, he prayed some more. Later in Psalm 54, David goes on:

Behold, God is my helper; the Lord is the upholder of my life…. I will give thanks to your name, O LORD, for it is good. For he has delivered me from every trouble, and my eye has looked in triumph on my enemies. (Psalm 54:4, 6-7)

God is your Helper and the upholder of your life. When life feels hard, He holds you in His hands. When it feels like it's falling apart, He keeps you in His grasp. When you're afraid, He embraces you. When you're uncertain and unsure, He upholds you. He will deliver you from *every* trouble.

Follow David's example and keep praying and praising God through every trouble. He will make your steps certain. He will help you hear His voice. He will deliver you again and again.

**Lord, help me to turn to You in prayer again
and again, trusting You to uphold my life.**

A NEW, PEACEFUL PATH

In all your ways acknowledge Him,
and He will make straight your paths.

Proverbs 3:6

Believe today that you are divinely guided by God. As you acknowledge His presence in your life and seek Him for direction, He will guide you in the right paths.

Sometimes we are afraid that we will make a wrong turn or take a wrong step in our journey through life. But when God is your guide, you cannot take a wrong a step because He will use every step for His purposes. You don't have to worry about getting it all right. You can take the pressure off yourself to figure out your future. You can stop worrying about finding God's purpose for your life. He has your future, and He will bring purpose to your life as you seek Him. You don't have to chase your purpose; He will unfold it day by day.

I think we usually sense when we're veering off God's path for us. His Spirit guides us and gives us discernment so that we stay on His good path for our lives. So listen to His Spirit and trust His promptings in your heart. You can let go of trying so hard to stay on the right path, and instead trust that by His Spirit, He will keep you on His right path for you. As you trust Him with your steps, a new and peaceful path will open before you. It's a path of faith, of love, of grace, of joy, and of purpose. Instead of stressing over finding God's perfect purpose for your life, you can enjoy walking with Him.

Lord, I look to You for guidance. Help me to trust
that You are guiding me. Keep me on Your path for my life
and help me to listen to Your Spirit as I walk with You.

Let God navigate your journey through
life as you enjoy His company.

PRAYER AND WAITING

*Wait for the LORD; be strong, and let your
heart take courage; wait for the LORD!*

Psalm 27:14

Prayer involves waiting on the Lord for an answer. Prayer and waiting go hand and hand. And oftentimes, waiting is really hard. It stretches our faith. It can cause us to feel anxious and discouraged. But when we choose to wait in faith, when we choose to be strong in the waiting, when we choose to courageously trust God, our waiting produces joy.

Our pastor once talked about how there is a precious depth to those who wait on God in prayer. You can see their humility when you look in their eyes. You can see that they have spent time in prayer just by the way they quietly trust God and wait on Him. They have a calm essence about them. They're trusting God in their waiting, and they're not giving up on prayer.

Acts 2:42 gives us a glimpse into the apostles' prayer lives: "And they devoted themselves to the apostles' teaching and the fellowship, to the breaking of bread and the prayers." The apostles *devoted* themselves to prayer before they went out. We can follow their example by devoting ourselves to prayer. Keep praying and waiting on the Lord with strength and courage. The waiting may feel more difficult than the praying. The waiting is what really tests our faith. Stay devoted and committed to prayer even when an answer feels far off or impossible. Because look what happened in Acts 2:43: "And awe came upon every soul, and many wonders and signs were being done through the apostles." There's no telling what God will do when you pray. Keep praying. Keep waiting on the Lord. Let your heart take courage and stay strong.

**Lord, help me to trust You in the waiting.
Help me to devote myself to prayer.**

*The Lord will do wonders in your
life as you pray and wait on Him.*

PRAYER FILLS
YOU BACK UP

Continue steadfastly in prayer,
being watchful in it with thanksgiving.

Colossians 4:2

On those days when you feel like you have run out of gas, remember that prayer can fill you back up. We tend to think that prayer will exhaust us more, and that taking the time to pray will interrupt our day. But prayer will calm your soul, lighten your burdens, and energize your heart!

When my car is low on gasoline, it makes me feel stressed and uneasy. When I am driving around with a near-empty tank, it's difficult to focus on anything else. I can try and beat the gas gauge, but that only adds to my stress. If I don't get to a gas station quickly, I will be asking for trouble! But the times when I acknowledge my car needs a fill-up and go on and pull over, I avoid a lot of unnecessary stress.

When our hearts feel like they are running out of gas, we would be wise to pull over to pray. Too often, we keep going and never stop. Our stress continues to build until we are completely depleted. But we can access God's peace for our hearts by pulling over to pray, and praying will actually fill us back up. As we pour out our concerns before God, He fills us with His peace. As we offer Him our empty tanks, He refuels us just like gasoline refuels the car. He's our power source, and we need to pull over often to refuel.

Lord, thank You that prayer fills me up with Your peace.
Help me to make prayer a priority. Help me to
return to prayer the moment I begin to feel empty.

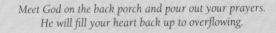

Meet God on the back porch and pour out your prayers.
He will fill your heart back up to overflowing.

LITTLE GIRL, ARISE

Do not fear, only believe.
Mark 5:36

In Mark 5, Jesus overhears that a man's daughter has passed away. Jesus tells the man, "Do not fear, only believe." When Jesus enters the house of the little girl, he passes family and friends who are upset and weeping. He says to them, "Why are you making a commotion and weeping? The child is not dead but sleeping." The people actually laughed at him. But he went to the precious child and, "Taking her by the hand he said to her, 'Talitha cumi,' which means, 'Little girl, I say to you, arise.' And immediately the girl got up and began walking, … and they were immediately overcome with amazement" (Mark 5:39, 41-42).

God wants you to believe that He can do miracles in your life. He does not want you to live in fear. He wants you to believe Him. Just like He held that sweet little girl's hand and called her *little girl*, He's holding your hand today too. You are His little girl, and He wants you to rise up in faith, trusting Him with all your cares and prayers. He wants to amaze you.

Trust God to do the miracles you long for. Trust Him to do more than You can fathom. Trust Him to take care of you because you are and forever will be His little girl.

Lord, help me to always believe that You can do miracles.
Help me to rise up in faith and keep praying.

Jesus is inviting you to believe Him for
the everyday miracles you are praying for.

YOUR STEADY ROCK

There is none holy like the LORD: for there is
none besides You; there is no rock like our God.

1 Samuel 2:2

It's challenging to keep our emotions steady when our circumstances are rocky. But with the Lord's help, we can stay steady in the Lord. He's our Rock.

When you feel your emotions welling up inside, remember your Rock. Remember that the Lord will keep you strong in the face of difficult circumstances.

Hannah of the Bible made prayer her go-to resource for rock-solid strength. Hannah's heart was sad. First Samuel 1:10 says, "She was deeply distressed and prayed to the Lord and wept bitterly." But she kept returning to the Lord in prayer: "She continued praying before the LORD … I have been pouring out my soul before the LORD" (1 Samuel 1:12, 15). Until one day her prayers were answered. Eli encouraged Hannah, "'Go in peace, and the God of Israel grant your petition that you have made to him.' … Then the woman went her way and ate, and her face was no longer sad" (1 Samuel 1:17-18). In due time, Hannah's prayers for a son were answered. Her prayers then became praise.

When you are deeply distressed, keep turning to the Lord in prayer. If there is a burden on your heart, bring it to the Lord. Pour out your soul to Him—He's listening. Then, like Hannah, go in peace, knowing that the Lord has heard your petitions. And in due time, God will answer. Then your prayers will become praise.

Hannah inspires me because she continuously turned to the Lord in her distress. She looked to God as her Rock, and she found peace through prayer. God wants to be *our* steady Rock too.

Lord, thank You that You are my steady Rock. Thank You that I can bring
You my raw emotions. Thank You for keeping my heart steady when
I am faced with rocky circumstances. Help me to be faithful in prayer,
like Hannah was. And help me to wait in peace for Your answers.

God's answers are on the way. Rest in His good timing.

THANKSGIVING BLESSINGS

Trust in the LORD and do what is good; dwell in the land and live securely. Take delight in the LORD, and He will give you your heart's desires. Commit your way to the LORD; trust in Him, and He will act.

Psalm 37:3-5, CSB

During this Thanksgiving season, enjoy a pause from your everyday routine and savor the gift of family and friends. Know deep in your heart that the God of this earth is keeping watch over you. Believe deep in your soul that He is tenderly guiding your life. Rest in His care, be rejuvenated by His love, and be restored by His constant company. Reflect on how God has been working in your heart, transforming you to lean completely on Him throughout the dance of life.

May sweet memories, good blessings, and remembering God's faithfulness stir up your gratitude and make your heart deeply joyful. Enjoy a day to rest and savor all the good blessings of your God. Every good and perfect gift is from Him, so hug your loved ones tight, laugh with them, and enjoy their company. Keep leaning on the Lord. Keep cultivating your sweet relationship with Him. May you feel the blessings of God today, and may you feel His presence over your life. He has you. He loves you. He's with you always.

Your relationship with God is growing, changing, and deepening. You are on a journey with the One Who made you and dreamed you up. He delights in helping you navigate this life day by day and moment by moment. Today, rest from the hustle and bustle, the toiling and striving, and take some time to look around at all the beautiful blessings around you. Take a moment to look to the One Who daily showers You with His blessings.

**Lord, thank You for Your constant blessings in my life.
Help me to see the joys and gifts all around me.**

Gratitude will lead to deeper joy and peace.

EVERYDAY FAITH

No unbelief made him waver concerning the promise of God,
but he grew strong in his faith as he gave glory to God, fully
convinced that God was able to do what He had promised.

Romans 4:20-21

One of the great heroes of our faith is Abraham. God told Abraham and his wife, Sarah, that they would have as many descendants as the stars in the sky when Abraham and Sarah were in their nineties and had never had children. This proclamation from the Lord that He would create an entire race through them seemed impossible. Yet they believed. In Romans 4:19, it says that Abraham "did not weaken in faith." Instead, "he grew strong in his faith as he gave glory to God, fully convinced that God was able to do what he had promised" (Romans 4:20-21). His faith was "counted to him as righteousness" (Romans 4:22).

The passage goes on to say, "But the words 'it was counted to him' were not written for his sake alone, but for ours also. It will be counted to us who believe in him who raised from the dead Jesus our Lord, who was delivered up for our trespasses and raised for our justification" (Romans 4:23-25). In the same way that Abraham's faith was counted to him as righteousness, our faith in God who raised Jesus from the dead makes us righteous children of God!

Paul ties this all in a bow in the next chapter: "Therefore, since we have been justified by faith, we have peace with God through our Lord Jesus Christ. Through him we have also obtained access by faith into this grace in which we stand, and we rejoice in hope of the glory of God" (Romans 5:1-2). Justified by faith. Peace with God through Jesus. Access by faith into grace.

You may have believed for your salvation, which of course is the most important step of faith. But I think sometimes the more difficult step of faith is believing God in our everyday walks with Him. Believing Him for the prayers we are praying, the miracles we are hoping for, the guidance we long for, and the everyday help we need. Everyday faith is opportunity after opportunity to believe God. Take Abraham's lead and choose to grow strong in your faith. Give God the glory by choosing to believe Him today. Be fully convinced that He is able to fulfill His promises. Ask God to give you faith like Abraham.

Lord, help me to believe You every day. Help me to grow strong in my faith and trust You to do what only You can do. Grow my everyday faith!

Believe God today!

HIS PRESENCE
NEVER LEAVES YOU

Where shall I go from Your Spirit? Or where shall I flee from Your presence?
If I ascend to heaven, You are there! If I make my bed in Sheol, You are there!
If I take the wings of the morning and dwell in the uttermost parts of the sea, even there
Your hand shall lead me, and Your right hand shall hold me.

Psalm 139:7-10

Whatever you do today and wherever you go, God's presence will never leave you—not for a second. From the moment you wake to the moment you hit the pillow tonight, and every moment in between, His Spirit is with you. He's with you here in this moment on the back porch. And He will be with you when you get up and go about your day. He's with you in everything you do—caring for your children, washing the dishes, driving in the car, running your errands, working, and folding laundry. He's with you in your entire day.

In everything you do and everywhere you go, God's presence never leaves you. Sometimes God can feel far away. We think we need to find Him. He seems distant. But even then, He's there. Perhaps He feels distant because we're pushing Him away. Sitting down to spend time with Him can sometimes feel hard; it's tricky to find the time to quiet our hearts before Him. But He patiently waits. Anytime you want to be with the Lord, He's there waiting. But He knows you have to go about your day, too, and He stays by your side. Know today that God's presence truly never leaves you. Have faith that He is with you in your day and check in with Him throughout your day. His presence will give you peace and joy as you remember that He never leaves you.

Lord, help me to remember that Your Spirit never leaves me.
Help me to tune into Your presence today as I go about my day.
Thank You for Your faithful presence in my life.

There's nowhere you can go that God isn't with you!

REVIVE YOUR SOUL

The fear of the Lord is the beginning of knowledge.

Proverbs 1:7

When spending time in God's Word feels hard, take a moment to remember that all the knowledge and wisdom you need for life is found in its pages. God is your heavenly Daddy, and He is inviting you, His little girl, to discover true wisdom for life and to find the path of abundant life through His Word.

Sometimes approaching God's Word feels like work. Our Bible looks daunting. We're not sure where to start. We feel guilty for how our Bible is collecting dust on our night-stand. But if we just keep opening it, we will discover that God's Word really does refresh our hearts like nothing else. The hardest part sometimes is simply opening our Bible.

Let the psalmist's word sink in:

The law of the Lord is perfect, reviving the soul;
The testimony of the Lord is sure, making wise the simple;
The precepts of the Lord are right, rejoicing the heart;
The commandment of the Lord is pure, enlightening the eyes;
The fear of the Lord is clean, enduring forever;
The rules of the Lord are true, and righteous altogether.
More to be desired are they than gold, even much fine gold;
Sweeter also than honey and drippings of the honeycomb. (Psalm 19:7-10)

God wants to revive your soul, give you wisdom for life, enlighten your eyes, and give you a sweet feast of joy and delight as you soak in His beautiful Word. Keep returning to His Word a little bit each day, and you will find that it refreshes your heart like nothing else.

**Lord, oftentimes it feels so hard to open my Bible.
Revive my love for Your Word today.**

*Don't be intimated by God's Word. It is God's gift to you.
Open it page by page and let God speak to your heart.*

CHOOSE HIM

Blessed be the God and Father of our Lord Jesus Christ, Who has blessed us in Christ with every spiritual blessing in the heavenly places, even as He chose us in Him before the foundation of the world, that we should be holy and blameless before Him.

Ephesians 1:3-4

When you long to connect with God in a deeper way, choose Him. Choose to spend time with Him. Choose to check in with Him before doing other things. Choose to pray. Choose to listen for His gentle voice on your back porch. Choose to take a walk around the block and tune your heart to His. Choose to seek Him.

God chose you before the foundation of the world. Before He laid the foundations of the earth, He had you in mind. He chose you to be His daughter. He has blessed you with every spiritual blessing in Christ, and you will forever be His daughter.

The Lord is passionate about cultivating His relationship with you. Don't miss that part! Jesus is your Savior, but He's also your Friend and Counselor. He's your High Priest and your Mighty God. He's not a distant God—you have access to Him every day and every moment! Your relationship with God is where the sweetness is. That's where you will find the treasure of knowing Him.

Set distractions aside today and choose God. Choose Him in the little moments of the day and in how you spend your time. Choose to set your mind on Him, to think of Him, to sing songs in your heart to Him. You are forever chosen by God to be His daughter. Choose Him today, and you will connect with Him in a deeper way.

Lord, thank You for choosing me. Help me to choose You today.

You will find God in your day when you choose Him.

THE GREATEST COMFORT

*So the church throughout all Judea and Galilee and Samaria
had peace and was being built up. And walking in the fear of
the Lord and in the comfort of the Holy Spirit, it multiplied.*

Acts 9:31

As you walk with the Lord, you will experience the comfort of the Holy Spirit. I tend to think of the Holy Spirit mostly as a guide and counselor. And He absolutely is our Guide and Counselor, but He's so much more—He's our Comforter.

What brings you comfort? Is it a warm blanket and slippers? A hot cup of tea on your back porch? Having your loved ones close? Sitting by the fire with a good book? A hug from your husband? A cozy sweatshirt? When I tuck my boys into bed at night, two out of three of them have a thing for blankets. Every night, I layer them in blankets—not one, not two, not three, but most nights, four blankets. They want their beds to be as cozy as possible, so I tuck them in like I am making a burrito. A weighted blanket further adds to the coziness.

God wants to wrap you in a blanket of comfort by the presence of His Spirit in your life. He wants to layer you with warmth for your heart by the fellowship of His Spirit in your heart. That is the greatest comfort in life.

I feel kind of bad for the people of the Old Testament, who lived when God's presence was more distant and less accessible. But God knew what He was doing all along. Jesus came. When Jesus died on the cross, the people must have been devastated. They couldn't fathom what was to come. Yet that is how God made a way for the Holy Spirit. And now we get to have the Spirit with us at all times. We get to have the greatest comfort with us every moment.

**Lord, thank You for being my Comforter.
Help me to always look to You for the comfort I need.**

The Holy Spirit is your Comforter.

KEEP HIS WORD CLOSE

But I am like a green olive tree in the house of God.
I trust in the steadfast love of God forever and ever.

Psalm 52:8

As you look to God for strength, direction, comfort, and wisdom, He will establish you like a strong and sturdy tree. As you trust in His steadfast love, He will cause you to flourish and thrive. You are blossoming into a woman after God's heart. He is so pleased and delighted by You. You make Him smile and laugh. You are one of His masterpieces, and He has a purpose for your life. You will do amazing things with His strength in you. Your life will bear fruit as you keep your eyes and heart on Him.

Keep God's Word close. It is your fuel and your food, your nourishment and your guide. Keep it close and you will thrive. God is working in your heart to make your heart more and more like His. And He's always drawing you closer and closer to Himself. He loves your company. He loves spending time with you. He loves helping you through your day and being there when you need encouragement. Remember that He's on the back porch, but He's also in the kitchen. He's at your place of work and in the laundry room. He's everywhere you are. Tune into His whispers and trust Him with everything.

**Lord, help me to keep Your Word before me. Grow me
into the woman You created me to be. And most of all,
help me to focus on cultivating my relationship with You.**

*Let God's Word be your go-to source
for encouragement, wisdom, and strength.*

HE WILL RESCUE YOU

Rescue the weak and the needy.

Psalm 82:4

Maybe it's hard to see God's fingerprints over your life. Perhaps it's been the most difficult year of your life and your circumstances have overwhelmed you and drained the joy right out of your heart. It's okay to feel like you can't see God's work in your life. It's okay to struggle to see the good. It's okay to be in a place of loneliness, grief, or sadness.

Sometimes there are no words that seem to comfort. We can quote all the right Bible verses, but our pain is too deep for them to make a difference. We are in a season of hardship, and the Lord feels far off. Dear sister, it's okay to feel weak. It's okay to feel needy and desperate for God's intervention. Know that God will rescue you. He will rescue you from this season of hurt and pain. He will lift you up again. His timing is good and His ways are good. You will feel joy again. You will feel the delight of God's company again. You will feel the pleasure of God's Word again. And you will come out stronger from this hard season.

Today's verse is one I underlined in my Bible. I scribbled down a date next to it, and when I look back at that date, I can remember the feeling I had in my heart. It was a feeling of desperately needing rescue. I felt like I was floating in the deep waters of the ocean, treading water, and I was running out of air. My circumstances felt dark. My prayers felt like they were hitting the ceiling. I wasn't sure what to do, but I knew where to turn. Years of practice helped my faith muscles keep turning to God even though I couldn't see how He would come to my rescue. Even though I felt discouraged and even though my circumstances felt impossible. I can look back now, and with full confidence say that God did indeed rescue me from those circumstances. He came through in greater ways than I could have fathomed or prayed for. He rescued me from the deep waters of stress and worry, anxiety and fear.

And He will rescue you. He will come through in greater ways than you can fathom or pray for. He will rescue you from the deep waters of your stress, worry, anxiety, and fear. Keep turning to Him, even though it's hard. Keep pulling your heart up to Scripture even though the words on the page can be hard to believe in your current circumstances. Rescue is coming.

Lord, when I need a rescue, help me to keep turning to You.

God will come through for you.

RUN TO GOD
FOR SATISFACTION

For He satisfies the longing soul,
and the hungry soul He fills with good things.

Psalm 107:9

When your soul feels restless, but you can't quite put your finger on why, remember that the Lord will satisfy your longing and hungry soul. God created us to crave His presence. We have a longing in us for Him. But it's so subtle at times that we push that longing away like it's a bad desire. Or we attempt to fill the void with things that don't satisfy.

When we choose to run to God for satisfaction, our longing is met. We find Him, and there's no greater peace than when we let Him fill the empty places in our soul. But in the moment, it's hard to choose Him. Instead, we choose to flip on the television, check our phones, check our email, wash the dishes, search the internet, buy something new—we attempt to stuff the longing of our souls with things that simply don't satisfy.

When we let God fill the longing of our soul, He fills the empty places in our souls perfectly. So today, when you feel that restless feeling that something is missing or you're craving more but you're not sure more of what—when something feels off in your soul—try something different:

- Head to the back porch with a cup of coffee and listen for God's voice.
- Grab a cozy blanket, find a cozy chair, and open your Bible to the Psalms.
- Take a journal to a quiet place outside and talk to God through your pen.
- Set aside the phone and pray in the quiet of your car.
- Write down a Bible verse that speaks to your heart.
- Pray a simple prayer asking God to fill the longing in your soul.

You will be amazed by the satisfaction, joy, and peace you will feel as you turn to God in those moments when your soul is restless.

Lord, help me to run to You when my soul is longing for something.
Help me to recognize my thirst and hunger as a desire for You.
Help me to turn to You throughout my day.

Small choices to run to God for satisfaction will
make a huge difference in your day and in your soul.

FREE FROM FALSE GUILT

*Godly sorrow brings repentance that leads to salvation
and leaves no regret, but worldly sorry brings death.*

2 Corinthians 7:10, NIV

Guilt can cause an emotional battle in your soul. Is your guilt a kind and tender emotion that convicts and corrects your heart, eventually transforming your character? Or does your guilt feel more condemning in nature, causing you to feel shame? It's helpful to note that there are two kinds of guilt.

True guilt can be your friend, guiding you to reflect Jesus in your ways. True guilt redirects you toward repentance and leads you back to God's grace. But false guilt is suffocating. It's harsh and irrational. It's unkind and relentless. And false guilt is straight from the enemy.

While the Holy Spirit will allow us to feel guilt in order to redirect us, His ways are gentle and kind. Godly sorrow brings life to your heart because it redirects you back to God. But the enemy loves to condemn. He loves to stir up shame in your heart and make you feel unlovable.

The next time you feel guilt in your heart, check in with the Lord. Ask Him if this guilt is of God, steering you to follow Him more closely, or if it is false guilt from the enemy, steering you toward shame and condemnation. Romans 8:1 says, "There is therefore now no condemnation for those who are in Christ Jesus." False guilt needs to go!

**Lord, thank You that You gently redirect me without shame
and condemnation. Help me to be aware of the enemy's schemes
to shame my heart. Help me to recognize and let go of false guilt.**

*False guilt is tormenting your soul. Recognize
the enemy's schemes, resist him, and don't let
false guilt make itself at home in your heart.*

DON'T DISCOUNT YOUR EMOTIONS

*O Lord, all my longing is before You;
my sighing is not hidden from You.*

Psalm 38:9

Too often we discount our emotions. When they bubble up inside our hearts, we typically want to suppress them. But God formed us with emotions. He truly cares about the state of your heart and how you feel. Acknowledging how you feel isn't a sign of weakness. Rather, acknowledging your emotions is a step forward in your spiritual growth. That's because your emotions keep you dependent on the Lord. They cause you to live from your heart, in tune to your passions, which in turn helps you identify your purpose in life. Emotions also allow you to feel, which is a beautiful thing.

The Lord knows the depth of your emotions. He knows what's behind them and He knows what's causing them. As we bring our emotions to God instead of stuffing them, we learn more about God and more about ourselves. Our emotions help us evaluate our lives to determine how we're really doing at a heart level.

God wants to help you sort through your emotions. Your honesty about your emotions cultivates a deeper intimacy with the Lord. So be honest with Him. Bring Him your emotions. Tell Him what's really on your heart. And watch and see how He sorts your heart out and brings you back to a peaceful sense of well-being.

**Lord, help me to bring my emotions to You.
Thank You that my emotions draw me closer to You.**

Your heart was made to be dependent on the Lord.

December

CHRISTMAS FOR YOUR HEART

Glory to God in the highest.
Luke 2:14

The Christmas bustle feels like a divine sprinkle of joy and grace hanging over our homes and streets and cities. It's like there's a bit of magic in the air—hope, the sweet reminder that something deeper and bigger holds us and watches over us.

I felt that first hint of Christmas spirit recently when I made a quick trip to our local hardware store. My plan was to be in and out so I could get back home where the boxes of Christmas decorations waited for me. I walked into what felt like a Christmas winter wonderland. There was soft Christmas music playing (or was it in my head?) and the place was filled from left to right, top to bottom, with Christmas trees and sparkling decor. Be still my Christmas heart! I smiled as I walked past two grandpas discussing which tree they liked best. My heart melted when I saw dads and kiddos picking out lights for their mom. I scooted through the Christmas wonderland and headed to the gardening section of the store, grabbed what I needed, and headed back through the wonderland to check out. I got totally distracted and may have found some Christmas pillows and a doormat to go along with my purchases. I think I heard jingle bells, too.

As I drove home from my Christmas wonderland excursion, it struck me that perhaps this gift of Christmas is a touch of the divine. Perhaps the joy we feel at Christmas, even if it's just a tiny spark, is the touch of God reminding us that He is real and He truly is with us. He really is the God of miracles.

Lord, may the Christmas season be a reminder of You.

God is in your midst. He sent His Son in swaddling clothes as a baby for you. Jesus is the reason for Christmas.

THE ONE THING WE NEED THIS CHRISTMAS

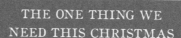

One thing is needed.
Luke 10:42

This December, in all the busyness of the season, may we hold on to the one thing that we need the most: time with our Savior. May our time with Him rise to the very top of our priority list—not to check it off our list, not to prove anything to God, not to get on God's good list. No, just to hang out with Him, because hanging out with Jesus is the most important thing that can prepare us to handle the daily stresses of life. That time looks different for each of us, but the important thing is that we make it happen.

Time with Jesus is where you will gain everything you need for life. He invites us to spend time with Him and get to know Him in order that He may reveal His heart to us, love on us, and transform us.

Dear one, maybe you just need to hear this today: God has a special design and purpose for *your* life. He created you with incredibly special plans in mind. His plan for your life is better than anything you could possibly imagine. And He's calling out to you and inviting you to spend time with Him so that He may lead you through this dance of life. He wants you to find the life He created you for. He doesn't want you to miss it, or miss Him.

Will you stay busy like Martha of the Bible—trying to keep moving, making things happen, and striving in your own strength? Or will you choose to be like Mary—will you choose the *one thing* that will prepare you best for this dance of life? Will you choose Him?

Lord, thank You for taking hold of my heart this Christmas. Thank You for showing me that Christmas is for me personally—that You sent Your Son to equip me, prepare me, and help me through this dance of life.

In all the busyness of the season, take some time to just be with your Savior. He delights in your company, and He will refresh your soul as you turn to Him.

THE GIFT OF BEING YOURSELF

Do not be afraid, Mary, for you have found favor with God.
Luke 1:30

God intentionally purposed Mary of the Bible with a mighty calling to carry the Son of God in her womb. He had this perfect plan for Mary's life, a holy design made just for her.

Today, I want to encourage you that God sees you, He knows you, and He wants you to just be yourself. You may feel like nothing special. You may wonder what you could possibly be good at or how God could possibly use you for His kingdom purposes. But know this: trying to be someone else is putting an obstacle between you and who God designed you to be. Today, you can let go of trying to be like someone else. Just be you. God wants you to embrace the gift of you. He picked *you* out. He intentionally purposed *you* with a mighty calling—to carry His presence into a hurting world. He has a perfect plan and a holy design for your life.

The gift of Christmas is the Baby wrapped in swaddling clothes, born in a manger. Because of Him you can be yourself. You carry the very presence of God within you because you know Jesus. You can be yourself because you have God in you. And He wants to do some amazing things through you. Will you let Him take over in your heart? When you let Christ take over, you start becoming who He designed you to be, sweet one. You, like Mary, are highly favored! The Lord is with you!

**Lord, this Christmas, may I unwrap the gift of
becoming myself as I let You take over in my heart.**

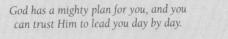

*God has a mighty plan for you, and you
can trust Him to lead you day by day.*

SAVOR THE SEASON

*And Mary said, "My soul glorifies the Lord, and my spirit rejoices in
God my Savior, for He has looked on the humble estate of His servant."*

Luke 1:46-47, NIV

Savor the season by taking a pause from the hustle and bustle and soaking in the
beauty of Christmas. Let the glowing lights of the season remind you of the One
whose light shines bright in your heart and whose love keeps your heart dancing.
Because of Him, we always have hope. We always have a way out of worry and stress.
We always have a Helper. No matter what the situation, we have His light in every
situation.

Christ's light in us never goes out. Sometimes it can feel like it's a bit dim, or like
it's fading even, but sweet one, Christ's light in you will never leave you. Sometimes it
just needs some fuel to keep it shining. And as we slow down, savor, ponder, and soak
in the reality of God's light we hold in our hearts, we begin to feel the warmth of His
light in a new way. And His light in us shines brighter to those around us as we reflect
on the beauty and gift of God in us and with us.

Know today that just like God was mindful of Mary, God is mindful of you. He
has done great things for you and continues to do so every day. He lifts you up and
fills your soul. He brought you salvation through His precious Son and wants to help
you through life. Unwrap the gift of Christmas this season. Savor the beauty of being a
daughter of God through Jesus. His light shines bright over your life and in your heart.
Ponder the wonder of it all as you soak in the beauty of your own dance with the Lord.

Lord, help me to savor the true meaning of Christmas. Help me tune into You,
reflect on the incredible gift of salvation that you provided through Your Son,
and sense Your presence and light in my life in a fresh way this season.

*May you allow the beauty of the Christmas season to
remind you that God knows you and is always with you.*

REST ON EVERY SIDE

And the LORD gave them rest on every side.
Joshua 21:44

Rest on every side. Take a deep breath today as you settle onto your back porch. God wants to give you rest on every side. In all the things that are wearing you down, causing you stress, or dampening your spirit, He wants to give you rest. When was the last time you felt truly rested—not just physically, but emotionally and spiritually? When was the last time you felt God's deep peace invade your soul?

One December, I felt the urge to read a good Christmas novel. You know, the feel-good kind. I wanted all the snowy log cabins, the twinkly Christmas lights, and the Christmas wreaths hanging on the front door. I found just the right book and settled onto my couch with a blanket, a heating pad on my back and soft Christmas music playing in the background. It was an intentional pause, a break from the busyness that I desperately needed. It was a rest from the pull of distractions and the news of the world. I needed to quiet my heart, and I needed to rest from the constant doing.

That December, I found myself always looking forward to those quiet pauses to read. It sounds so simplistic, but life had gotten so busy and so fast-paced that I had forgotten how to sit down and rest. Looking back, I couldn't tell you what my Christmas novel was about, although I do know that it was a story that touched my heart in all the ways good Christmas stories do. But what I do remember is the incredible sense of rest that I felt, the kind of rest where your shoulders relax and all the tension you've been holding dissipates. It was the kind of rest where you're so in the moment that you're not stressing about the future or worrying about the details of life. It was the kind of rest where you feel peaceful and content.

I think God wants to give us rest on all sides—physical, emotional, mental, and spiritual. He wants us to feel His deep peace in tangible ways. He wants to give us reprieve from our busyness so that we don't overdo it. He wants to give us rest from our daily routines so that we stay healthy. Dear friend, in what ways do you need rest today? Jesus wants to provide the rest you need. Whether you need to sit by the fireplace and soak in a good Christmas novel or you need a nap, God wants you to rest and take care of yourself. Find some moments this week to take a good rest. You can rest awhile; God will keep the world running.

**Lord, sometimes I don't feel like I have time to take a good
rest and reprieve from the busyness. Help me rest today.**

*Rest will revitalize your spirit, rekindle your passion,
and restore your energy. Jesus wants to give you rest on every side.*

SAVORING CHRISTMAS

My soul glorifies the Lord, and my spirit rejoices in God my Savior,
for He has looked on the humble estate of His servant.
Luke 1:46-48

One morning before the sun came up, I found my way to the family room to let out our very loved pup, Shaka. I opened the crate, and he immediately curled up on the couch right there in the middle of all the Christmas pillows. I grabbed a blanket and curled up next to him, hoping to catch a few more minutes of sleep before the day began. Just then I heard little footsteps coming down the stairs. I watched with one eye open as my little seven-year-old snuck in right next to Shaka. Colt has always been my early bird. I must have fallen asleep for a few more minutes, because I woke up to a shuffling sound around the Christmas tree. Like a little Christmas ninja, Colt found his way to the Christmas light switch, and with delight, turned on the lights of the tree and the mantel. In one quick ninja move, he darted back to the couch and snuggled in close to Shaka again.

It made me smile to see Colt's absolute delight in turning the lights of the Christmas tree and mantel on. He was so excited to see the glow and magic of the colored lights. It got me thinking. I want to see Christmas with childlike eyes. And I want to be similarly excited about the light of Jesus that I get to have in my heart every day and that I get to hold out to the world around me.

Today, ponder a bit over the wonder of Christmas. Let yourself soak in the gift of a Savior born for you. Look at the Christmas season through the lens of a child, and may a fresh perspective spur on a childlike faith in your heart.

Lord, stir up my delight for You, the true Light of Christmas.

Ponder the wonder of Christmas today as you soak
in the beauty of your own dance with the Lord.

WHEN YOU NEED TO KNOW GOD IS IN YOUR LIFE

*Thus there were fourteen generations in all from
Abraham to David, fourteen from David to the exile
to Babylon, and fourteen from the exile to the Messiah.*

Matthew 1:17, NIV

Genealogies in Scripture remind us that God is in the details. He is not only aware of the details of the lives of His people, but He uses the details for His purposes. God is incredibly intentional about placing His people in specific places, at specific times, and on specific missions. He is precise and particular in His plans. This shows us that God cares deeply for His people. One generation to the next, God's timing is perfect. The way God lines things up and moves through His people and circumstances is maybe something we cannot fully grasp this side of heaven, but when we walk through the genealogy of Jesus, we see that God's timing is perfection. Before Jesus was born, He knew who needed to meet whom and when, as well as all the in-between details. And He navigated each person—even fancy Amminadab and Shealtiel—to be a part of the Savior's line.

God sees each person as a part of His story. Each person in Jesus' genealogy had a story. Each one had eyelashes and toes and hands and ideas and creativity and purpose. Each person had storms and joys all their own. God saw each and every person as an individual and knew them intimately. He specially formed Abraham and Ruth and Jehoshaphat and Amon and Zerubbabel in the womb. And He knew that each one of them was a part of His greater story. They were going to bring Christmas to our hearts forever through Jesus.

God is in the details of your life too. He is in tune to every specific, and He is using all of them for His purposes. He is precise and particular and intentional in your life. You are not just a blob of cells to God, you are a specific person with specific qualities and character. You were made on purpose by a God who loves you. You can trust that His timing in your life is perfect. He is navigating your life. Won't you let Him lead the way?

**Jesus, help me to grasp the wonder of Your careful
attention to details, both in Your purposes in Your story
of bringing salvation to all and personally in my life.**

*May your Christmas joy bubble up today as you look to
the One Who knows you, sees you, and cares deeply for you.*

WHEN YOU NEED TO KNOW GOD STILL DOES MIRACLES

She was found to be with child from the Holy Spirit.

Matthew 1:18

Young Mary was engaged to Joseph. I imagine she was so excited to marry the man God had brought into her life. One tiny hiccup, though—an angel comes and tells her that she is going to have a baby, and this baby will be the Son of God. How could this be? Scripture tells us Mary was a virgin. She must have felt confused and overwhelmed. And I'm sure the conversation with Joseph where she tried to explain how she became pregnant was a little tricky. Can you imagine the look on his face? Joseph planned to quietly divorce Mary so he could escape the reality of their situation. But there's a phrase in today's verse that speaks of something divine, something holy, something good, something special, something miraculous.

She was found to be with child *through the Holy Spirit.*

God was writing a miraculous story, and He chose Mary as a conduit. This Christmas season and always, God wants to do something divine, holy, good, special, and miraculous in your life. He wants to amaze you with His majesty and bring wonder to your heart. Just like the Holy Spirit came over Mary and produced a miracle in her, the Spirit of God is hovering over your life and wants to produce miracles in and through you. Maybe Mary wondered why in the world God chose her. And maybe, like Mary, you're feeling a bit ordinary today. Maybe you're feeling small and unseen. Maybe you wonder how in the world God could use you.

Let Mary's miracle encourage you today that you're not ordinary to God. You're seen. You're loved. And God wants to come into your heart and life and use you in extraordinary ways. He wants to be miraculous in your life. As you savor the Christmas season today, remember that God began His journey on earth as a miracle. And He's still doing miracles today.

**Help me to see You as the miraculous God—the One Who
sees me and loves me and wants to be miraculous in my life.
Help me to believe You for the miracles I need today.**

*May you believe today that God
wants to be miraculous in your life.*

WHEN YOU LONG TO LET GO OF YOUR FEARS

An angel of the Lord appeared to him in a dream, saying,
"Joseph son of David, do not fear to take Mary as your wife,
for that which is conceived in her is from the Holy Spirit."

Matthew 1:20

Step into the shoes of Joseph for a moment today.

He is considering what his next right move is—to journey on with Mary through an uncertain future and a confusing circumstance, or to quietly step away from her. I imagine his sleep was restless as he debated back and forth between what his heart was urging him to do and what his head was telling him to do. Marrying a gal who was miraculously with child—on one hand, it sounded like a God thing that he wanted to know more about, and on the other hand, fear told him to run as far away as possible. But then an angel of the Lord stepped in and broke through Joseph's confusion.

God sent a messenger, an angel, to speak to Joseph. God's message to Joseph, "do not be afraid," is a message we hear over and over again in Scripture. The phrase "do not be afraid" appears over seventy times in the Bible. According to scholars, it is the most frequent command in the Bible. So God's message to Joseph is His message to us. God was assuring Joseph that all was well. He was reminding Joseph that this gift conceived in Mary was a gift from the Holy Spirit. God rescued Joseph from his fears and convinced him to stay with God through this journey—to trust God and step into the adventure with Him.

I don't know how fear may have a hold on your heart right now. I don't know what circumstances leave you feeling a bit uncertain about the future or seem a bit confusing. I don't know what may be causing your heart to feel restless as you debate back in forth between what your heart is urging you to do and what your head is telling you to do. But just like God could foresee Joseph's future, God can foresee your future, and it's good. Just like God saw Jesus—his life, his ministry, his resurrection, and how He would ultimately be a Savior to all who believe—God sees your whole life. And He doesn't want you to be afraid.

Lord, help me to stay with You through my journey,
trusting You each step of the way. Bring Christmas—true hope and
light and the reality of Christ—to my heart today in a tangible way.

Stay with God through your journey.
Trust Him enough to step into the adventure with Him.

WHEN YOU NEED TO KNOW YOUR PURPOSE

She will bear a son, and you shall call His name Jesus,
for He will save His people from their sins.

Matthew 1:21

The angel of the Lord lets Joseph know not only that his baby will be a son, but also who this baby will be—His name and His purpose. A son. Jesus. He will save His people from their sins. Perhaps many of us wish our birth certificates included not just our gender and our name, but our clearly defined purpose. Maybe, like me, you've spent a great deal of time searching for your purpose in life. Maybe you've tried something, only to realize it's not your thing. Maybe you've jumped around from one thing to the next, trying on different purposes for size. Maybe you think you found your purpose, but the doors to walk in it are all tightly shut. Or maybe you were walking in your purpose and then you got totally burned out. Maybe you've given up trying to find your purpose because it feels too complicated. Maybe you feel like you don't have a purpose. Maybe it feels easier to not think about it.

God knows your purpose. Before you were conceived, He knew you, your name, and your purpose. And Jesus' purpose—to save His people from their sins—covers your life, including your purpose. Instead of feeling discouraged and frustrated about what your purpose is, how to find it, or how to walk in it, you can trust the One Who knows all the details of how He wants to use you in purposeful ways for His purposes. Daughter of Christ, wanting to know your purpose is a God-given desire of your beautiful heart. How wonderful that you *want* to walk in God's purposes for you. How precious that you desire to be who God created you to be.

We don't have to feel tied up in knots about our purpose. As we live one day at a time, with our Savior as our guide, purpose will happen. As we walk with Jesus, purpose will happen. As we listen for His whispers, trust His heart for us, pray and ask God to guide us, and follow Him day by day, He will guide us in living out the purposes He had in mind when He made us.

You have a purpose—many, in fact. God will use you in all kinds of ways this side of heaven and in every season of your life.

Thank You for sending Your Son to save me from my sins,
to give me purpose, and to fill my life with everyday hope.
You know the questions I have about my specific purposes. Help me to
rest in You, trusting You day by day to fulfill the plans You have for me.

You will find true purpose as you seek to know Jesus.

WHEN YOU NEED TO KNOW
GOD IS ALWAYS WITH YOU

Behold, the virgin shall conceive and bear a son, and they
shall call His name Immanuel (which means, "God with us").

Matthew 1:23

We don't just have God in heaven. We don't just have God on earth. We don't just have God around us. We don't just have God looking over us. We have God *with* us. Immanuel. With us and in us, always. The miracle of Christmas is that God came to be with us. He chose to get as close as possible to us. He chose to dwell with us. And He chose to live in our hearts. Right before today's verse, it says, "All this took place to fulfill what the Lord had spoken through the prophet." And if we look back in Isaiah 7:14, the prophet Isaiah proclaimed, "Therefore the Lord himself will give you a sign. Behold, the virgin shall conceive and bear a son, and shall call his name Immanuel."

This Christmas child was a prophecy fulfilled. I love how God fills Scripture with prophecies proclaimed and then fulfilled because prophecies give us assurance and hope that He will ultimately fulfill His promise to return again: "Surely I am coming soon" (Revelation 22:20). Prophecies fulfilled show God's faithfulness over and over and over again throughout Scripture.

As you go about your day, doing what you do—maybe you're working or studying, dancing or teaching, Christmas shopping or writing Christmas cards— may you remember that God is with you and in you. Always. God is faithful. Always. And as you look to His promises and rehearse His truth, your desire to walk with Him and alongside Him will grow. You won't have to manufacture a deeper trust in God; He will grow your faith and trust in Him as you see His faithfulness over the course of history through Scripture.

Lord, thank You that You came to be with us and in us.
Thank You that You never leave us. Help me to sense
Your presence in a more tangible way today. Help me to believe
You are always with me. Bring the joy of Christmas to my heart today.

May your joy overflow and your heart feel a deeper sense of
peace as you look to the One Who brings Christmas to your soul
every single day through His living presence right in your heart.

December 12

WHEN YOU NEED TO KNOW GOD IS LEADING YOUR LIFE

*Where is He who has been born King of the Jews? For we
saw His star when it rose and have come to worship Him.*

Matthew 2:2

The Christmas baby, Jesus, was born in Bethlehem. God, wrapped up in baby skin and baby toes and baby eyelashes, entered our world. And the wise men came looking for Him. God led the wise men to Jesus with a star—no ordinary star, I imagine. They saw His star in the east and followed it step by step so they could worship Jesus. In the Old Testament, God guided His people with a pillar of cloud by day and a pillar of fire by night. He supernaturally guided His beloved people. And here again, in the New Testament, we see that God used His supernatural ways to guide the wise men to Jesus.

Here's a little Christmas hope for you to keep close to your heart today:

God is supernaturally guiding you. He's probably not going to use a pillar of cloud or fire. You're probably not going to see a fancy star in the east as you head out the door tomorrow. But that doesn't mean God doesn't do supernatural things anymore. That doesn't mean He doesn't still lead His people. Remember, we have the Holy Spirit, God Himself, dwelling in our hearts. And as we tune into Him, He will supernaturally guide us. Sometimes I know I can get so comfortable and used to the idea of God living inside me and guiding me that I forget that God leading me is supernatural.

The way He gently nudges, steers, guides, and leads our hearts is something only God can do. The way He gets our attention, draws us closer, or puts an impression on our hearts is something only He can do. The way He brings Scripture to mind, redirects our thoughts, and sorts out our hearts is something only He can do. When you need to know that God is leading you, remember that you have His Spirit in you and that the leading He does in your heart is supernatural. Perhaps this Christmas season you can occasionally pose a question similar to the one the wise men asked: *God, where are You? Because I want to know You more, I want to follow You, and I want You to lead me.*

Lord, thank You that You stepped into human form to bring the greatest hope, peace, and deliverance to Your people. Thank You that You dwell in me, lead me, and steer my life. Help me to remember that Your work in me is supernatural.

May Christmas remind you that God's leading is supernatural.

WHEN YOU DON'T WANT TO MISS CHRISTMAS

On coming to the house, they saw the Child with His mother Mary,
and they bowed down and worshiped Him. Then they opened their
treasures and presented Him with gifts of gold, frankincense and myrrh.

Matthew 2:11, NIV

Gift-giving and gift-receiving are the sweetest parts of Christmas. Every child dreams of their Christmas morning surprises, and every gal hopes for a little bit of Christmas joy under the Christmas tree. For a lot of us, shopping for all the gifts can be a source of stress. We strive to make everybody's Christmas wishes come true, and we do our best to make Christmas magical for our loved ones. Often I see the weariness in women's eyes as we talk through our Christmas to-do lists.

Your gift-gifting and gift-receiving is a beautiful picture of the gospel. Your gifts point to the ultimate gift of Christ. Every gift you give can be a celebration of all that you've been given in Christ. So when the shopping lines at the mall are long, when you're struggling to come up with the perfect gift for that special person, when you're weary from the busyness of your calendar, when your Christmas to-do list feels overwhelming, take a moment to let your soul breathe. Take a moment to remember why we give. Take a moment to remember that you don't have to do Christmas perfectly. Take a moment to let the joy of Christmas return to your heart as you savor the Gift-Giver.

The hustle and bustle of Christmas is good, but don't let it wear out your soul. Don't let the jingle bells and busyness overwhelm you. There's plenty of time. Don't miss Christmas by rushing through your lists in a hurry. Savor every moment: the shopping, the wrapping, the decorating, the gatherings, the cooking, your family, and the giving. Keep the gift of Christmas front and center, and remember that you're blessing others with your time and gifts. Let all your Christmas doing be your worship, your gift, to the Gift-Giver.

Lord, help me to keep You front and center this Christmas season.
Help me to lean on You as I go about the busy Christmas season.
Help me to slow down and savor You and remember that all the gifts point
to You. Help me to be a blessing to others with my time, energy, and giving.
Thank You for the gift of Christmas. Give me grace and joy for the season.

We savor Christmas to savor God. This Christmas, may you slow
your steps, soak it all in, and enjoy the season of Christmas.

GOD-SIZED ASSIGNMENT

Do not be afraid, Mary, for you have found favor with God.
Luke 1:30

Mary was just a teenager when God intersected her life. She was just starting to think about who she was and how to be a wife. Can you imagine the uncertainty she must have felt when God gave her that God-sized assignment?

Maybe she thought, *This is too big. This is too crazy. There are too many unknowns. This sounds too hard. Who am I? Why me? God, could You fill me in a little bit more? How in the world am I going to do this?*

God chose a seemingly ordinary gal for a God-sized assignment. But God knew that Mary was the perfect one for the job. God didn't expect her to know all the answers or perfectly execute His plan on her own. All He needed was her willingness to be open to God and His plans for her.

You knew I was going to turn this around to you, right? Sweet one, I know sometimes the uncertainty of what God is calling you to do feels heavy. Maybe, like Mary, you think, *This is too big. (or too small.) This is too crazy. There are too many unknowns. This sounds too hard. Who am I? Why me? God, could You fill me in a little bit more? How in the world am I going to do this?*

I have a feeling that throughout our whole lives, we are going to feel uncertain about our God-given assignments. But today, remember what the angel told Mary: "Do not be afraid … you have found favor with God."

God wants you to know today that you don't have to be afraid and that you have found favor with Him. He has chosen you for some God-sized assignments, and He knows you're the perfect gal for the job. He doesn't expect you to know all the answers or to perfectly execute His plan on your own. All He needs is your willingness to be open to Him and His good plans for you.

God, thank You for giving me specific, God-given assignments.
When I'm unsure, uncertain, or full of doubt, restore my
confidence that You are with me and guiding me always.
Help me to be willing and open to You and Your good plans for me.

The favor of God rests on your precious life.
He is with you in every step.

WHEN YOU NEED GOOD NEWS

But the angel said to them, "Do not be afraid. I bring you good news that will cause great joy for all people. Today in the town of David a Savior has been born to you; He is the Messiah, the Lord.

Luke 2:10-11, NIV

For some, Christmas is more of a difficult season than a joyful one. Maybe you've lost a loved one or are dealing with difficult circumstances. We are human gals with human emotions, and to acknowledge any pain inside us is to be authentic. But just in case you need some good news today, in case you need a reminder because your heart just isn't feeling the joy, in case you need to rehearse the truth again so that your heart can come up for air.

A Savior has been born. He's *your* Savior. He was born for *you*. And this good news of the gospel is for all people—including *you*. I know that doesn't make everything better. I know that doesn't make your problems go away. I know that doesn't erase your pain. But I want you to know and remember that because Jesus came, you don't have to do life by yourself. You don't have to walk through hard circumstances alone. You don't have to grieve or fear or be sad alone. You don't have to ever be alone. I know that you know that, but I hope you let the healing balm of the good news of Jesus minister to your soul for a bit today. Let the good news bring your heart the light it craves.

Lord, You know my heart, and You know my circumstances. When I can't seem to find my joy, restore me. When my circumstances feel too hard, give me strength. When disappointment haunts me, pursue me with Your love. When loneliness overwhelms me, help me to feel Your presence. When I need the joy of the good news of my Savior, restore to me the joy of my salvation.

 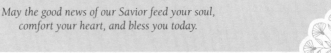

May the good news of our Savior feed your soul, comfort your heart, and bless you today.

PONDER IT ALL
IN YOUR HEART

But Mary treasured up all these things,
pondering them in her heart.

Luke 2:19

Mary pondered it all. She soaked in the miraculous and divine work of God in her life. She treasured every moment. She treasured God's faithfulness and nearness in her life. She treasured His power and His miracles. She treasured God Himself. And she tenderly kept it all in her sweet heart. I wish I could have heard her thoughts.

God wanted us to know about Mary's pondering. It must have been important to God that, like Mary, we take time to ponder. In our busy world and busy lives, pondering feels a bit old-fashioned. We have gadgets and devices and images and information at our fingertips, ready to fill every quiet moment. We have schedules to keep, calendars to fill, places to go, and people to see. Most days, we feel like we are racing through our days rather than savoring them. This Christmas, begin the life-giving practice of pondering in your life. Ponder, think deeply, meditate on truth. Take some moments throughout this Christmas season to treasure up all the goodness of God in your heart and quietly meditate on God.

When we take time to ponder God and His goodness in our lives, we will reap the rewards of joy, gratitude, peace, and contentment. And I believe our pondering will build our faith, because when we're pondering God, what we're really doing is meditating on His faithfulness and goodness.

Jesus, help me to treasure and ponder You and Your good gifts in my life.
Help me to take a few quiet moments here and there throughout the
Christmas season to think on You. Thank You for the gift of Your Son.

May this Christmas be a season of treasuring up all the
goodness of God in your heart and simply pondering Him.
May your pondering fill your heart with joy, gratitude,
peace, and contentment, and may it build your faith.

LITTLE-GIRL DREAMS

He lifted me out of the slimy pit, out of the mud and mire;
He set my feet on a rock and gave me a firm place to stand.

Psalm 40:2, NIV

As a little girl, I clearly remember dreaming of finding my first pair of pointe shoes under the Christmas tree. Until I received my first pair, I flitted around our house in my mom's old pair that she kept as a keepsake. They were broken in, well-loved, and seemed to fit me just right. After making sure no one was watching, I would sneak into our front living room, pretending in my heart that I was entering the very living room that Clara from the Nutcracker would have entered with its grand staircase, elegant grandfather clock, and magical Christmas tree. I pretended the guests had all left, and it was just me, my imaginary Nutcracker doll, and my pointe shoes. Deep in my imagination I dreamed that I glided across the stage in my pointe shoes, caught up in the fairy tale of The Nutcracker. But what is so vivid to me is that in that moment I wasn't performing. I actually believed that I was IN the story. I was Clara, not Sarah pretending to be Clara.

Those sweet memories of gliding through my living room remind me of the joy of childlike dreaming and childlike faith. And they remind me that God intends for us to live above a negative outlook, above a bad mood, and above the ho-hum routine of the daily grind. He invites us to abundant life, and the older I get, the more I realize that I think I have only tasted it in bits and pieces. The taste of it makes me want all of it—every realm and depth and height of God's presence—to know and believe that He gives me grace to live in a place of deeper joy than I have ever experienced.

We can grow comfortable with a negative outlook, a grumpiness, a "life is hard" mentality. We grow so comfortable with it that we do not even realize we don't have to live that way. Jesus invites us to fully enjoy and embrace the dance of life and to let go of the worry, the stress, and the fretting. He wants us to fully dive into the roles and the moments and the gifts that He has blessed us with. I want all the wonder, the awe, the joy, the peace, and the freedom that Christ came to give me. I want the wonder of Christmas in my heart all year long.

Lord, show me how to live with the wonder
of Christmas in my heart every moment.

Childlike faith infuses our walk with Jesus with joy.

GRACE UPON GRACE

And the Word became flesh and dwelt among us,
and we have seen His glory, glory as of the only
Son from the Father, full of grace and truth.

John 1:14

Think of the wonder of God becoming a human for us. He came down so that He could make a way for us to be in relationship with Him. The moment Jesus' feet appeared on earth, grace entered the world. Jesus shattered the law and gave us grace.

John 1:16-17 says, "For from his fullness we have all received, grace upon grace. For the law was given through Moses; grace and truth came through Jesus Christ."

We have been given grace upon grace. No longer do we have to follow the law perfectly. No longer do we have to sacrifice animals and perform rituals. No longer do we have to be distant from our Maker. Jesus came and grace entered. Jesus came and truth entered. Jesus came and made a way for us to be close to Him. God didn't stop at offering you the free gift of salvation, He went even further to offer you a relationship with Him.

Take a moment to snuggle up on your back porch with a hot cup of cocoa and a blanket, and soak in His grace upon grace.

Lord, thank You for Your beautiful grace.

God has showered you with grace
upon grace. Rest in His amazing grace.

LIGHT IN THE DARKNESS

The people who walked in darkness have seen a great light;
those who dwelt in a land of deep darkness, on them has light shone.

Isaiah 9:2

Jesus was the Messiah that the people of Israel were waiting for. They wondered for so long how and when He would come to their rescue. I imagine they grew discouraged in the waiting and wondered if He would ever show up.

You may be in a season of waiting too. Maybe you are wondering when God will come to your rescue. Maybe you've felt the weight of discouragement, and you're wondering if He will ever show up.

Just like Jesus showed up for His people when He came to earth, He will show up for you in your life too. God sent His son as a great light to illuminate the darkness of the world. He's here now. He's with you. He will brighten your darkness and shine His love and light in your circumstances. Trust Him to come through.

Lord, thank You for shining light into our darkness.
Help me to trust You to radiate Your light into my circumstances.

Jesus came to give you eternity with Him,
but He also came to light up your darkness today.

WOVEN TOGETHER

*There shall come forth a shoot from the stump of Jesse, and a branch
from his roots shall bear fruit. And the Spirit of the L*ORD *shall rest
upon Him, the Spirit of wisdom and understanding, the Spirit of
counsel and might, the Spirit of knowledge and the fear of the L*ORD.

Isaiah 11:1-2

We have a tiny Christmas tree in our front living room that looks a whole lot like a Charlie Brown tree. It's scraggly and old and looks a little sadder each year when I bring it down from the attic. But for me, it's a sentimental tree. It's not the prettiest tree, but it's special. This tree holds handmade ornaments that each represent stories from the Bible leading up to the birth of Jesus. Each year I pull the ornaments out of a red Christmas box and marvel at how God wove together His perfect story of redemption.

God deliberately orchestrated lives, people, families, and marriages to bring His son, Jesus, into the world. And in the same way, I am reminded that He is weaving our lives together for His kingdom purposes.

Maybe your life this past year has felt a little insignificant. Maybe it feels hard to see God at work, and you're wondering what He's doing, how He is orchestrating it, and how He is weaving things in your life together for good. Remember today that none of your life is haphazard and random. Just like God wove together Jesus' lineage, He's working in your life to weave together more than you can fathom. Trust the One Who is full of wisdom and understanding, counsel and might. Trust Him to weave your life into something beautiful for His kingdom.

**Lord, thank You for the reminder of Your sovereignty today.
Help me to trust You to weave my life into something
beautiful and good for Your kingdom purposes.**

*You were woven together in the womb, and God
is weaving together your life as you walk with Him.*

YOUR GREATEST
SOURCE OF PEACE

And He shall stand and shepherd His flock in the strength of the Lord, in the majesty of the name of the Lord his God. And they shall dwell secure, for now He shall be great to the ends of the earth. And He shall be their peace.

Micah 5:4-5

If there's anything I hope you've gained this year from these back-porch moments, I pray you've felt God's peace in a deeper way. The Lord is your Shepherd and your strength. And as you turn to Him each day, you will dwell secure. You dwell secure eternally through Jesus, but you can also dwell secure each day as He becomes your truest source of peace.

There will still be storms and trials. There will still be mountains and valleys. But you know whom you belong to. You know who is shepherding your life. And you know that He will never leave you to do life on your own. Stress and worries will still pull at your heart, but you know that you can bring them to God at any time. You can return to your back porch again and again and fill back up with His peace.

This Christmas, ponder the Prince of Peace. He wants you to experience the peace that only He can offer.

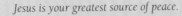

Lord, thank You that You are my Shepherd, my strength, my security, and my peace. Help me to turn to You again and again for the peace I crave.

Jesus is your greatest source of peace.

HOW WILL THIS BE?

And Mary said to the angel, "How will this be … ?"
Luke 1:34

As you wrap Christmas presents and bake Christmas cookies, I know there are some lingering prayer requests that still sit unanswered. Perhaps you have been faithfully praying through your requests, and some of them you just can't imagine how or when or if they will be answered.

We can take comfort in Mary's reaction to the angel, Gabriel, when he lets her know, "Behold, you will conceive in your womb and bear a son, and you shall call his name Jesus" (Luke 1:31). I love her sweet and gentle reaction: "How will this be, since I am a virgin?" (Luke 1:34).

You can trust God to work out your prayer requests even though you may be asking yourself, *How can this be, Lord? How will You work this out? This is impossible. I don't see any way around this obstacle. How will You come through?*

Mary couldn't fathom what God would do! And you cannot fathom what God will do when you pray. Ask Him those questions. Don't be afraid to ask Him how He will answer. He loves your questions. He loves your tender faith. He knows it's challenging to believe Him. But after all the questioning, you can trust Him to do far and beyond what you can think.

Lord, I have prayer requests that seem impossible.
But I will keep praying in faith, trusting You to work in ways that
I cannot fathom. Help me to keep believing You and trusting You.

Christmas is a great time to believe in miracles.

NOTHING WILL BE IMPOSSIBLE

For nothing will be impossible with God.
Luke 1:37

As Christmas approaches and a New Year sits just around the corner, what are the impossible things that you want to believe God for? My mom gave me a little white cross, lettered in purple with the words of Luke 1:37 and edged with flowers. It sits on my bookshelf in my small office space, reminding me to believe for impossible things. To believe that God is more powerful than I can imagine, more capable than I can fathom, and more sovereign than I can see. Sometimes when something feels impossible, we stop praying and stop believing God for the miracle we need. But when we choose to believe that truly nothing is impossible with Him, we can rest from worry. We can trust that His ways are good and His timing is perfect.

The words "for nothing will be impossible with God" were spoken by the angel Gabriel. He told Mary, "The Holy Spirit will come upon you, and the power of the Most High will overshadow you; therefore the child to be born will be called holy— the Son of God. And behold, your relative Elizabeth in her old age has also conceived a son, and this is the sixth month with her who was called barren. For nothing will be impossible with God" (Luke 1:35-37).

The angel was full of surprises, and I imagine Mary was overwhelmed by the news. God is full of surprises, and He wants to delight you as you trust in Him for impossible things in the year ahead!

Lord, help me to believe that nothing is impossible with You.

Believe God for impossible things.

THE FREE GIFT OF GOD

*But now that you have been set free from sin and have become slaves of God,
the fruit you get leads to sanctification and its end, eternal life. For the wages
of sin is death, but the free gift of God is eternal life in Christ Jesus our Lord.*

Romans 6:22-23

I imagine it's cold out on your back porch this Christmas Eve. I hope you are snuggled up in a blanket and have a steaming mug of coffee or cocoa in your hand. I hope you're enjoying a few quiet moments with God before the festivities of the season today and tomorrow.

Just know today that you are loved. God sent Jesus to offer you the free gift of God—eternal life. And this life will be a journey of sanctification as you walk with Him day by day. Your life will bear fruit as you look to Jesus. And God will use you to help others find the free gift of God too. Keep coming out to the back porch to fill up with God's peace. Now off you go! Enjoy this Christmas Eve as you ponder the wonder of God's free gift of salvation, wrapped especially for you.

Lord, thank You that You have set me free from sin and that with Your sanctifying help, my life will bear fruit in Christ. Thank You for the free gift of eternal life in Christ. Help me to ponder the gift of God every day of the year.

You don't have to earn your salvation; it's a free gift from God.

THE GIFT OF GOD'S PRESENCE

To the King of the ages, immortal, invisible, the only God,
be honor and glory forever and ever. Amen.

1 Timothy 1:17

On this Christmas Day, may you feel the peace of God in a fresh way as you ponder the gift of your salvation in Christ. He is your King, immortal, invisible, the only God!

Today may you feel the Lord's presence as you enjoy a quiet moment on the porch. May the sparkle and joy of the season fill you to overflowing. May you enjoy the company of loved ones and receive God's comfort as you draw close to His heart. He has gifts and blessings for you for this day and for the year ahead!

And remember that day by day, you can unwrap the gift of His presence right here on the porch. You can meet with Him anytime, any day, and any moment. Keep pouring out your prayers to Him, keep meeting Him in the quiet moments of your day, and keep listening for His still, small voice in your life. You have full access to the King!

Lord, thank You for this Christmas day; to You be all the glory!

Unwrap the gift of God's presence every day.

THE KINDNESS OF GOD

But when the goodness and loving-kindness of God our Savior appeared,
He saved us, not because of works done by us in righteousness, but according
to His own mercy, by the washing of regeneration and renewal of the Holy Spirit,
Whom He poured out on us richly through Jesus Christ our Savior, so that being
justified by His grace we might become heirs according to the hope of eternal life.

Titus 3:4-7

Jesus saved us out of His goodness and loving-kindness. He did not save us because of our works or because we somehow earned His favor. He saved us by His mercy and grace. And if that wasn't enough, He gave us His Holy Spirit to guide us, lead us, renew us, and comfort us. You, dear sister, are an heir to the King. You are justified by His grace, and you are granted eternal life.

You don't have to prove yourself to God. You don't have to justify your worth. You don't have to serve enough, do enough, or be enough. God's gift of salvation is free. And His love for you is not dependent on what you do or don't do. You can rest in His saving grace, knowing that You are dearly loved and eternally saved.

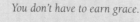

Lord, thank You for Your goodness and loving-kindness.
Thank You that You love me in my imperfect state. Thank You that
I don't have to earn Your grace or Your love. Help me to release striving,
performing, and proving myself, and to rest in Your beautiful grace.

JUST BREATHE

Let not your hearts be troubled. Believe in God; believe also in Me.
John 14:1

Sometimes the smallest things can get under our skin and cause our stress to sky-rocket. It's the little things in life that oftentimes throw us off balance and kick our peace to the curb. Jesus reminds us, *Let not your hearts be troubled.* But what should you do when your heart is troubled and you just can't shake it?

Breathe. Just breathe. Take a moment. Head to the back porch if you need to. And express your trouble to the Lord. Tell Him how it ruffled your spirit. Tell Him how it caused anxiety in your heart. And breathe again. Just breathe. Your Savior and Counselor is here. Imagine taking that troublesome burden and handing it over to Him.

Lord, this is causing my heart to be troubled.
I need You to take over.
I release control of this situation to You.
I trust You to calm my heart.
I believe You will help me.
I believe You will bring my heart back to peace.

So much of our stress is connected to control. When things feel out of our control, we get anxious! When we don't get our way, we feel frustrated. When we're trying so hard to glorify God in everything, and yet we bump into trouble, we feel defeated.

There will be trouble. There will be stress. But you can always just breathe, take a moment, and express your trouble to the Lord. He will help you. He will deliver you from your stress. He will meet you in your moments of anguish. He loves to help His people.

Lord, You know the troubles of my heart. Help me not to let my heart be troubled, but instead, help me to believe that You will help me and guide me.

Let your troubles point you to a quiet
moment to regroup with the Lord.

DATE WITH GOD

For Christ also suffered once for sins, the righteous
for the unrighteous, that He might bring us to God.

1 Peter 3:18

Jesus brought us to God. He made a way when there was no way. He carved a path when there was no path. He made a stream in the desert. He made a pool in the wilderness. He made a way for you to find God.

Now you can climb up into God's lap, like a daughter in her daddy's lap. He's got a hold of you, and He will never let you go. He will never let you stray too far away. He will always draw you back to Him.

Take some quiet moments on the porch today to dream with God about the year ahead. Give Him your prayer requests. Talk to Him about the dreams of your heart. Listen for His quiet, guiding voice. Ask Him the questions of your heart. What needs to change for you in the year ahead? How can you make more time and space for quiet moments with God? He has so much peace, joy, and love to give you. He wants to delight you and surprise you as you trust in Him.

Lord, thank You for making a way to You. Help me to make my time
with You my greatest priority this upcoming year. Thank You for all
You have done in my life, and thank You for leading me day by day.

Keep your date with God on the back porch going all year long.

TAKE TIME TO CELEBRATE

He will keep your life.
Psalm 121:7

Take some time to celebrate the ways God has answered your prayers and showed up in your life. Take a look back at this year.

- How have you seen God answer a specific prayer request?
- What did you learn about God?
- Whom did God use in your life to encourage you?
- In what ways did God comfort you?
- How have you grown closer to God?

It's so good for our souls to take time to celebrate God's work in our lives. It's so good to take a pause and to see what He had done! When we do, our faith grows more and more, and our love for God deepens.

God will continue to answer your specific prayer requests. He loves hearing about the details of your life. He loves the sound of your voice. He loves that you trust Him with the desires of your heart. And God wants to show you new things about Himself in this upcoming year. He wants to reveal Himself to you as you seek Him. You can trust that God will continue to put people in your life to encourage you. He strategically places people in your life, and you will be amazed by the words of encouragement and comfort you will hear through His people. God will continue to comfort you day by day as you look to Him. He will always be there for you. And God will continue to draw you closer and closer to His heart. You are so dear to Him.

Take time to celebrate what God has done in your life this year, and let it stir your faith for what is to come!

Lord, thank You for all You are doing in my life. Help me to take some time to look back and see Your fingerprints all over my life.

God is more present than you can fathom, more loving than you can comprehend, and more real than you imagine. He's with you, dear sister. See His handiwork all over your life.

YOU'RE ENOUGH

I was … intricately woven.
Psalm 139:15

I sat down in the office for a doctor's appointment, and I noticed two little signs on the wall. They read,

> *You're enough.*
> *Be still.*

I realized in that moment—as my shoulders relaxed a bit and the tension I didn't even know I was holding melted off my shoulders—that I really needed to hear those words. Maybe you do too.

Dear sister in Christ, you're enough because you were intricately woven together by God. You can stop striving. You can stop trying hard to be more, because you're already enough. God has your life. You can be still and let Him work. Let Him guide you. Take your hands off the steering wheel of your life and let Him take control. God is in your corner. He's not out to get you, and you don't have to be more than you already are this moment. You've been through so much; you're weary and need a rest. Be still. He is God, and He is in control of your life.

Lord, thank You for Your love toward me. Thank You that You intricately wove me together in the womb. Help me to embrace who You made me to be and to know that I am enough just as I am.

Give yourself grace. Show yourself compassion.
You are God's daughter, and you are enough.

BACK-PORCH MOMENTS

But my eyes are toward You, O God, my Lord.
Psalm 141:8

Hopefully your quiet moments with God on the back porch have inspired you to return to the porch again and again. Look over this past year and celebrate all God has done in your heart and in your life. Take a quiet moment to ponder the year, to notice the ways God has encouraged your heart and answered your prayers.

As this year closes and a new one unfolds, keep your eyes toward the Lord. Let Him be your guiding light as you walk through each day of the new year. Trust Him like you've never trusted Him before. Let His Word be your foundation. Let His company be your sweetest delight. Keep coming back to the porch, rain or sunshine, and keep meeting Him in the quiet of your heart.

Don't let the distractions of life keep you from pulling in close to God's heart. Consider your back porch to be holy ground—the place you hear God's whispers, the place you encounter His presence. You can return to Him again and again, and you will never overstay your welcome. You're always welcome in His company.

Let the back porch be your haven and fortress. Let it be your sanctuary and your refuge. Let its holy ground point you to Jesus again and again. He will always be waiting to meet you. He will always be ready to pour His peace into your heart as you unload your cares onto Him. Let the porch be your strengthening place and your place to recharge.

God is with you, and He loves you. Keep your eyes toward Him. He loves you dearly, and He wants to be the One you run to for all that you need.

Lord, help me to keep my eyes toward You on this journey of faith.
Thank You for being my constant companion.

God will always be waiting for you on the back porch.